© Carson-Dellosa

W9-AXW-356

The 21st Century Mentor's Handbook

Creating a Culture for Learning

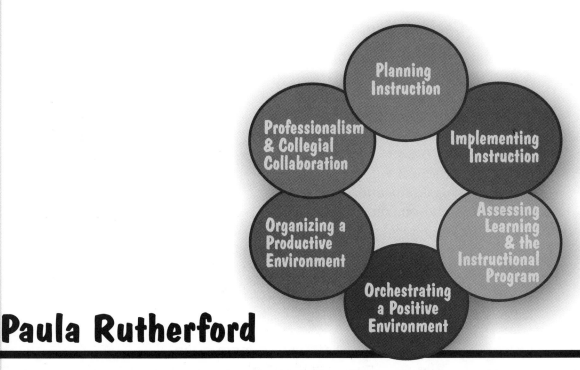

Planning Instruction

Professionalism & Collegial Collaboration

Implementing Instruction

Organizing a Productive Environment

Assessing Learning & the Instructional Program

Orchestrating a Positive Environment

Paula Rutherford

Just ASK Publications, Attitudes, Skills, & Knowledge (ASK), Inc.

About the author

Paula Rutherford is president of **Attitudes, Skills, and Knowledge (ASK), Inc**. **Just ASK Publications** and **ASK Group** are divisions of ASK, Inc.

She is an **educational consultant** specializing in instruction, educational leadership, induction, and supervision and evaluation. Much of her time is spent in multifaceted work with school districts where leadership and staff are committed to educating all students and are willing to engage in the hard work necessary to make educational excellence a reality for all. In addition to her extensive work as a consultant and trainer, her experience base includes work in regular education K-12 as a teacher of high school history and social sciences, physical education, Spanish, and kindergarten, and as a special education teacher, coordinator of special education programs, school administration at the middle school and high school levels, and as a central office staff development specialist.

Paula is also the author of **Why Didn't I Learn This in College?**, **Instruction for All Students**, and **Leading the Learning**.

She may be contacted directly at paula@askeducation.com for training, consulting, or facilitating services.

See the last page for **Just ASK Publications** ordering information.

Contact ASK, Inc. at info@askeducation.com for information about **ASK Group** consulting services. Visit **www.askeducation.com** for an overview of the Group's consulting services.

The 21st Century Mentor's Handbook

Published by Just ASK Publications

A division of Attitudes, Skills, and Knowledge, (ASK), Inc.
2214 King Street
Alexandria, Virginia 22301
TOLL FREE 800-940-5434
VOICE 703-535-5434
FAX 703-535-8502
email: info@askeducation.com
www.askeducation.com

Printed in the United States of America
ISBN-13: 978-0-9663336-6-4
ISBN-10: 0-9663336-6-7
Library of Congress Control Number 2005900289

Table of Contents
The 21st Century Mentor's Handbook

Acknowledgements
Introduction

Acknowledgements

Throughout this book there are **Through the Voice Of...** reflections on and accounts of induction and mentoring practices in action. These words of wisdom were gathered during workshops and interviews or written at my request. These pieces are important because they translate research into day-to-day practice. The authors of the pieces are noted on the pages where their work appears.

Three school districts in particular serve as induction and mentoring learning labs for me. Those districts are St. Vrain Valley School District, Longmont, Colorado; Alexandria City Public Schools, Alexandria, Virginia; and Greece Central School District, Greece, New York. The Directors of Professional Development in those districts, Brenda Kaylor in St. Vrain, Roger Rudy in Alexandria, and Ann Mitchell in Greece Central, are committed to quality induction programs and do whatever it takes to obtain the resources needed for the programs and to ensure alignment of the induction program with all the other processes in their districts. Each of them has spent countless hours with me thinking through how to implement research-based best practices in their school districts.

In the spring of 2002, I met with the induction coaches and clinical professors in St. Vrain Valley School District, Colorado, to design the essential questions of a workshop series for teachers new to that district. That meeting, which focused my thinking on induction and mentoring, led not only to the workshop series **Why Didn't I Learn This in College?** but also the book by the same title and now the **The 21st Century Mentors Handbook**. St. Vrain coaches and clinical professors who contributed so much to my thinking include Crista Keppler, Ellen Gury, Dorthea Ekx, Jon Larson, Donna Begley, Pat White, Cindy Payne, Nancy Wesorick, Linda Neill, Glendora Shaffer, and Marsha Hansard.

Over the past two years, Lead Mentors have taken a stronger and stronger lead in the induction and mentoring of teachers new to Alexandria City Public Schools (ACPS), Virginia. They have literally invented their jobs and in the process, have developed strong voices for new teachers and for mentors. During training sessions and planning meetings throughout the years, these educators have also shaped my thinking about how to best provide support to new teachers while continuing to work full-time in their own classrooms. ACPS Lead Mentors include Mike DiSalvo, Kim-Scott Miller, Jennifer Nobriga, Ed Slavinskas, Chris Gutierrez, Pat Gomez, Rubye Harper, Roxy Chitlik, Elisabeth Casey, Michelle Ross, Donna Murphy, Becky Harris, Louisa Porzel, Jackie Swift, Sue Ditmore, Karen Westcott, Donna Bucchiere, Joan Wheeler-Kump, Jennifer Fisher, Susan Polk, Elizabeth Hagood, Beth Cronin, Whitney Greisinger, and Nancy Pasfield.

What new teachers need to know when, who will provide the information and support, and what format the communication and interactions should take are important variables that must be determined in any induction and mentoring program. In Greece Central School District, New York, Ann Mitchell, the Director of Professional Development, uses feedback from new teachers, input from building and district administrators, and strong collaboration with Marguerite Dimgba, the Director of the Teaching and Learning Center, to answer those questions and implement the necessary processes and practices. The development of the multifaceted and multi-year induction program in Greece Central, which provides differentiated support for new teachers by offering both school-based and district-based support sessions, has been a rich source of learning for me as I have interacted with the program designers, the standards area leaders and mentors, and the new teachers.

Special accolades go to the special educators who contributed so much wisdom in helping put together the **Especially for Special Educators** sections of the **Mentoring Calendar**. Mary Sires, Director of Student Services in St. Vrain Valley School District, Longmont, Colorado; Ed Slavinskas, Lead Mentor at Lyles-Crouch Traditional Academy, Alexandria City Public Schools, Virginia; and Sue Flood, Director of Student Services, West Irondequoit Central School District, Rochester, New York, responded to my plea for refinement and additions with invaluable suggestions.

Reaching back in history, important learning for me came from my work with Terry Wildman and Jerry Niles, College of Education, Virginia Polytechnic Institute and State University, in their work with the Office of Staff Development (OSDT) in Fairfax County Public Schools, Fairfax, Virginia in the 1980s. They provided much guidance and support as we implemented the Colleague Teacher Program in support of the Virginia Beginning Teacher Assistance Program (BTAP).

A special thanks to Heidi Pappas who typed and formatted, retyped and reformatted, and then retyped and reformatted yet again.

Introduction

In the 1980's Ann Michnowicz and I led the Colleague Teacher Program in Fairfax County Public Schools (FCPS), Virginia. The program was designed to support the 700 new teachers who were participating in the Virginia Department of Education's Beginning Teacher Assistance Program (BTAP), which was a forerunner of today's comprehensive mentoring programs.

The Colleague Teacher Program included
- training for colleague teachers/mentors
- training for novice teachers
- clear expectations about the support that mentors/colleague teachers would provide
- clearly articulated competencies and criteria
- up to three observations by impartial trained observers whose task was to "establish, through observations, that the teacher possessed the professional knowledge needed to perform satisfactorily."
- coaching sessions on each of the competencies. All new teachers were invited to attend the coaching sessions and those not yet demonstrating a particular competency were strongly encouraged to attend the session focused on the unmet competency.

A unique characteristic of the FCPS Colleague Teacher Program was the collaboration with higher education. Terry Wildman and Jerry Niles from the College of Education, Virginia Polytechnic Institute and State University, were partners in the design of the program. This partnership provided a treasured opportunity to combine the research base on induction and our passions for the process in the design and implementation of the FCPS Colleague Teacher Program.

Wildman in the ***Colleague Teacher's Supplement to The Beginning Teacher's Handbook*** quoted Frank McDonald's 1980 ***Study of Induction Programs for Beginning Teachers***:

> "It is a truism among teachers and especially teacher educators that within the first six months of the first experience of teaching, the teacher will have adopted his or her basic teaching style. Experience indicates that once a teacher's basic teaching style has stabilized, it remains in that form until some other event causes a change, and at the present time, there are not many such events producing change. If the style adapted is a highly effective one and is the source of

stimulation to continuous growth, there would be no problem. But if teachers abandon their ideals and become cynical, see management at any price as essential, constrict the range of instruction alternatives they will try or use; if they become mediocre teachers or minimally competent, then the effect of the transition period on this is a major concern and a problem that needs direct attention."

This excerpt from McDonald's study has had a major impact on my work for the last 25 years. It created for me a sense of responsibility to pay particular attention to teachers entering the profession and to focus my work with them not only around classroom practice but on instilling in them an acted-upon belief that collegial collaboration is an integral part of their professional lives.

The purpose of this book is to provide guidelines and tools for mentors to use in their mentoring work with novice and experienced teachers new to the district or school. The first chapter presents an overview of the roles and responsibilities of all educators in the induction process. Given that mentoring must be seen as only one component of a well-designed induction program, it was tempting to elaborate at length on the multifaceted induction programs with which I have been involved. In the end, I limited this text to its focus on the mentoring process.

The purposes which guided the writing of *Instruction for All Students* serve well here. The focus of mentor practice should be to lead new teachers to engage in their professional practice with:
- A sense of self-efficacy
- A focus on clearly articulated standards of learning
- An ever growing repertoire of skills for teaching and assessing diverse learners
- A passion for engaging all students in the learning process
- The use of data to make and assess instructional decisions
- A mission to promote high standards and expectations for students and educators
- A commitment to collaborate with colleagues and parents.

Above all, it is my hope that mentors work with new teachers to ensure that they do not get caught up in management issues and that they do not see their goal as well-managed students but rather well-educated students. If new teachers can learn that the best management program is a good instructional program they will be both more satisfied and more highly qualified as teachers. Mentors must help new teachers keep their eye on the goal of student learning and constantly remind them to make their decisions through that lens. One-on-one collegial support is essential for new teachers as they learn to plan great lessons and establish productive organizational systems for themselves. What an awesome responsibility and honor it is to be a mentor!

Roles and Responsibilities in Induction Programs

Chapter I

Creating A Culture for Learning

The essential question for our work is, **"What do schools look like when they are organized around a commitment to the achievement of high standards by all students?"** This question has many different answers but there are some constants that hold true. In such a school, learning is not a goal just for students; it is also a goal for all staff members. In such a school, all educators are committed not only to the achievement of high standards by all students but to the achievement of high standards by all educators. In such a school, the answer to a query of what are we going to do to make that happen is, **"Whatever it takes."**

In such a school, all staff members say **"It's my job!"** to actively ensure the success of new staff members. In such a school, induction is not an event; it is a way of life. The induction process is not defined by a new teacher orientation in the late summer and the assignment of a mentor whose appointment absolves the rest of the staff from any responsibility for the success of new staff members. In fact, in such a school, it is the norm for all to mentor and all to seek a mentor.

In such a school, **student success is a criterion for measuring the success of teachers collectively and individually.** It is the norm for all to examine student work and use what is learned from that examination to make decisions about instruction. In such a school, **teacher success and administrative success are criteria for measuring the success of everyone else.** That is, it is the collective goal of staff to have a fully qualified and satisfied teacher in each classroom so that more students can be successful more of the time. In such a school, general education teachers, special education teachers, and administrators study and learn together.

In such a school, **there is little turnover of staff.** Richard Ingersoll writes of teacher attrition and teacher migration as major contributing causes for the need for over two million new teachers in the next decade. He notes that while teacher retirement creates many job openings, it is the "revolving door" that significantly increases the number of new teachers needed. Among the causes given by teachers who leave are lack of administrative support, conflict and strife within the organization, and lack of input into organizational decisions. If we want to ensure that there is a fully qualified and satisfied teacher in each classroom we need to expand our efforts toward creating an inclusive culture for learning in ways that include the new professionals. Given the diversity of backgrounds and life experiences 21st century new teachers bring to the workplace, we need to capitalize on their knowledge and skills and help them apply what they know in this new environment. Therefore, in such a school, **value is placed on shared leadership, responsibility, and decision making in recognition of individual and collective commitment to student learning**.

Creating A Culture for Learning

In such a school, there would be **clearly articulated, commonly held, and acted upon beliefs**. Those beliefs would value student learning and professional growth of staff in the interest of that student learning. Acting on those beliefs means that in such a school, **teachers seek to be mentors and actively pursue the learning of knowledge and the acquisition of skills identified as critical for successful mentors**. They are analytical and reflective about the impact of their actions on the professional growth of the novice teachers with whom they are working and use that analysis and reflection to make adjustments to their mentoring practices. Those selected as mentors are recognized as role models and are supported by colleagues and organizational policies and practices.

When these conditions are in place, there is a culture for learning in the school that will support and contribute to the success of trained and highly skillful mentors as they take leadership roles in the induction process. In the absence of these conditions, we will continue to see the revolving door described by Ingersoll. Our students would continue to miss out on opportunities to be taught by strongly supported novice teachers or teachers who have moved successfully through their induction period, achieved competency, and are now able to mentor the next class of novice teachers. Since we are committed to providing every opportunity for student learning, let's make sure that we have created a culture for learning.

Collective Commitment To Creating A Culture for Learning

We will...
- teach the essential learning of the course and provide evidence of the extent of each student's proficiency
- be positive contributing members of our team as we work together interdependently to achieve common goals
- provide timely feedback to students, parents, and designated staff regarding student achievement
- continually look for ways to help each other help all students achieve success

The staff of Thoreau Middle School, Fairfax County Public Schools, Fairfax, VA

We Are All on the Same Team!
Roles & Responsibilities in Induction Programs

In a well established multi-year induction program, all district personnel have multiple roles to play in ensuring that there is a fully qualified and satisfied teacher in each classroom. Induction programs should include orientations, professional development, personal and professional support, opportunities for new teachers to observe best practice in teaching and learning, and receive feedback on their work in light of student achievement data and district performance criteria. Clearly, a well-trained and caring mentor plays a pivotal role in induction programs but mentoring occurs in the context of the culture of the school and school district. It is, therefore, essential that all members of the educational community know and execute their own responsibilities in supporting new teachers. The following list describes roles and responsibilities as well as some specific actions by various team members that have proven productive in multifaceted induction programs.

All Members of the School District Staff

- Ensure a strong start to the school year by providing time, resources, and support to new teachers. The school board, superintendent, district office staff, and school-based staff to include the administration, the teaching staff, the clerical staff, and the custodial staff should all play a role.
- Provide information and support. Do not ask, "Do you need anything?" Instead identify what new staff members are most likely to need in:
  - ➤ Instructional support
  - ➤ Professional support
  - ➤ Personal support
  - ➤ Logistical support

  ... and provide it!

The District Office Staff
Includes the superintendent, curriculum and instruction office, professional development office, and human resources

- Inform new hires of district expectations not only around contractual obligations, but around teaching practices and professional interactions
- Develop a document or collection of documents that communicate the essential-to-know information about the school district. This document can be presented in hard copy, on a CD, or on the district website. Provide it to new teachers as soon as they are hired.

We Are All on the Same Team!
Roles & Responsibilities continued...

- Conduct a new teacher orientation program before the opening of school and repeat it in September or October for late hires.
- Include an overview of the mentoring program in the new teacher handbook and in the new teacher orientation program.
- Provide copies of new teacher resources like *Why Didn't I Learn This in College?*
- Provide differentiated professional development opportunities designed to meet the needs of novice teachers and those new to the district.
- Clearly communicate expectations for peer observations, frequency and focus of interactions, and reflection and goal setting by both new teachers and mentors.
- Set up processes for shadowing and peer observations.
- Provide opportunities for teachers new to the district to network with one another.
- Establish mentor selection criteria and selection process.
- Identify key roles and responsibilities of mentors.
- Communicate the rationale for and the components of the induction and mentoring program to all staff members especially building principals and mentor candidates.
- Provide mentor training program and follow-up support sessions.
- Organize opportunities for mentors and new teachers to celebrate successes, plan their own next steps and provide guidance for future mentors and new teachers.
- Use surveys, questionnaires, logs, interviews and focus groups to evaluate the effectiveness of the mentoring program.
- Organize an end of the school year celebration for new teachers and their mentors.

We Are All on the Same Team!
Roles & Responsibilities continued...

The Principal

- Create a culture for learning so that mentoring is a natural outgrowth of professional practice.
- Convey to new teachers your philosophy of how students learn, the school history, the special traditions and accomplishments, as well as the essence of the school improvement or strategic plan and how they can play a role in the implementation of that plan.
- Provide working conditions for the new teacher that facilitate success: minimize special programs, moving from room to room, multiple preparations.
- Inform staff of rationale for and the components of the mentoring program.
- Clearly articulate to the staff that all have a responsibility for informal mentoring of new teachers.
- Organize the school environment so that collaboration is more easily accomplished, meeting time is focused on instruction, where instructional decision making and student work is made public,
- Include mentoring as a component of the school improvement plan with indicators for individuals, departments, grade levels, or team.
- Identify mentors or facilitate the identifying of mentors using criteria established by the district.
- Facilitate interaction between mentors and new teachers by providing release time for them to plan, reflect, and observe together. Hire a substitute teacher one or two days a month to create time for this interaction.
- Reduce as much as possible additional responsibilities of mentors and new teachers so that they can have maximum time to work together.
- Check in frequently with mentors to see how the work is going and offer assistance in any way.
- Observe with the mentors to ensure that you are all aligned around best practice in teaching and learning.
- Let new teachers know the best mode of communication and the best time to contact you.
- Interact with each new teacher face-to-face at least once a week the first semester. Have lunch with them once a month or organize an after school social for new teachers.
- Either build on the district document or create a school document that provides new teachers the essential-to-know information about the school and the district and provide it to new teachers as soon as they are hired.
- Provide recognition of the extensive work done by mentors.

We Are All on the Same Team!
Roles & Responsibilities in Induction Programs

School Staff
- Connect the names with the faces of the new staff members and greet them by name as often as possible.
- Department chairs and/or team leaders share unit and lesson plans, as well as unwritten customs and norms of behavior, and provide "big picture" of how the department or team functions.
- All staff members make resources readily available and work to articulate rationales for actions, directions, or requests.
- Be mindful of internal jargon and references to "the way we have always done it" and explain what that means.
- Front office staff and custodial staff explicitly offer assistance in obtaining and/or adjusting resources both at the beginning of school and throughout the year.

Lead Mentors
- Coordinate the work of multiple mentors in the building.
- Keep the principal informed about the mentoring initiatives in the building and coordinate the acquisition of resources such as time and materials.
- Help identify and train new mentors.
- Organize building level support sessions for new teachers and mentors.
- Serve as liaison with district office personnel responsible for the mentoring program.
- Share with other lead mentors the strategies that are working well in your building.
- Engage in problem solving with other lead mentors.
- Facilitate the professional development of mentors and new teachers as requested by the district and school.
- Coordinate various aspects of the mentoring program such as on-line mentoring or a monthly newsletter, or the mentoring of career switchers, special educators, or other sub-groups.

We Are All on the Same Team!
Roles & Responsibilities continued...

Mentors
- Lead by example
- Serve as an advocate
- Serve as a resource
- Maintain a confidential relationship with the new teacher
- Provide a variety of perspectives rather than only own perspective
- Serve as the "go-to" person
- Model analytical and reflective practice
- Implement guidelines established by district and school
- Serve as member of mentoring team if a teaming approach is used in your school or district
- Keep colleagues informed about mentoring initiatives
- Engage colleagues in welcoming, supporting, and collaborating with new staff members

Novice Teachers
- Seek out help
- Observe other teachers teaching, planning, reflecting, and conferencing
- Ask why things are done the way they are
- Self-assess and self-adjust as data dictates
- Set quarterly professional goals and reflect on and analyze the accomplishment of those goals
- Participate in professional development opportunities
- Demonstrate a willingness to watch, listen, and learn
- Share own expertise gained from recent university and student experiences
- Take the initiative in getting to know principal
- Get to know the front office staff
- Avoid negativity
- Join and actively participate in support groups

We Are All on the Same Team!
Roles & Responsibilities continued...

Experienced Teachers New to District, School, Team, or Department
- Seek out help
- Demonstrate a willingness to watch, listen, and learn
- Observe other teachers teaching, planning, reflecting, and conferencing
- Ask why things are done the way they are
- Diplomatically share past experiences that can help inform practice in this new setting
- Participate in professional development opportunities
- Agree to serve on committees and task forces in areas of professional interest and/or school focus

Through the Voice of the Principal...
Beginning the Mentoring Process

The mentoring program at Thoreau Middle School, Fairfax County Public Schools, Fairfax, Virginia, begins in the spring preceding the new school year. As vacancies occur, and as the hiring of new teachers begins, I keep a running list of the "new faces" that will be part of the next school year's faculty. I meet periodically with the Mentor Lead Teacher as new personnel are hired, and we begin conferring on the best matches for mentors and new staff members.

Matching new teachers with veteran teachers is not always a simple and straightforward process. The mentor must be knowledgeable, have a positive attitude, and be a good role model. Sometimes making the match isn't easy. It is, of course, preferable to match a new teacher with a teacher who teaches at the same grade level or who teaches the same subject. Where this is not possible or practical, I identify other variables that the two individuals may have in common such as being new parents, being from the same part of the country, having similar backgrounds, or living in close proximity to one another.

The matching process continues throughout the spring and summer months as teaching vacancies are filled. It is the responsibility of the Lead Mentor Teacher to contact veteran staff members and ask them to serve as a mentor for teachers new to the staff. When these matches have been made, the Lead Mentor Teacher makes sure to give mentors the phone numbers of the new teachers so that the veteran can make a phone call during the summer officially welcoming the new teacher to the school.

In the late summer, our administrative staff holds a three-hour orientation session for the new staff members. It is at this setting that the new teachers are introduced to the "nuts and bolts" of the school. This orientation is held in the library in a very informal setting. Following introductions, the new staff members are provided with a faculty handbook as well as a welcoming gift, a pin with an eagle, the official school symbol. We explain everything from the school's discipline policy to how to obtain a substitute to who's who on the staff. A highlight of this orientation is a small handout that contains the pictures and names of existing staff members. The pictures are reproduced from the yearbook from the previous school year. We have found this to be especially valuable as the new teachers begin matching names and faces. We leave time at the end of the session to answer questions that may be on the minds of the new teachers.

The next step in welcoming the new teachers to the school is a meeting with their mentors. As these two groups come together the Lead Mentor Teacher orchestrates introductions. It is a long standing tradition at Thoreau that the mentors and new teachers go as a group to have lunch in the sumptuous cafeteria

Through the Voice of the Principal...
Beginning the Mentoring Process continued...

of Thoreau's school/business partner. This "getting to know you" opportunity in a warm and inviting setting helps the new teacher feel like a true professional and makes them know that some thought has been given to welcoming them to their new work setting.

After the luncheon, mentors and new teachers typically return to Thoreau where the discussions continue, usually in the new teacher's room. In this setting, the veteran can assist the new teacher with preparing his/her room, obtaining instructional supplies and appropriate books, and generally make the new teacher feel welcome. I go around the building in the afternoon of this orientation day to engage in informal conversations.

The first agenda item at the year's first faculty meeting is the introduction of the new teachers to the staff by their mentor. These introductions are always light-hearted and usually include interesting stories about the new teachers that will make them feel special and help them make attachments to other staff members.

The feedback from the new teachers about the orientation procedures we have followed has always been very positive. But we all know that this is only the beginning. The Lead Mentor Teacher continues to check in with both mentors and new teachers to make sure that things are going well as the school year begins. The administrative staff also keeps in close contact with the newest staff members to make sure that their start is the best that it possibly can be.

Bruce Oliver, former Principal of Thoreau Middle School, Fairfax County Public Schools, VA

Through the Voice of the Director of Professional Development...
Creating a Standards-Based Mentor Program

Over the past few years, we have developed a three-year new teacher induction program based on research-based best practices. Our program has evolved from a few teachers released from their teaching duties and some informal school-based mentor support in 1999 to our current program, where every newly hired teacher is aligned with a mentor in his/her own standards area.

Most of the 25 mentors in Greece are released full-time from their classroom responsibilities to provide support to new and experienced teachers. Mentors provide classroom support by coaching and collaborating and often participate in a shadowing opportunity when new teachers spend a day visiting a more experienced teacher's classroom. Mentors also play a significant leadership role in designing and delivering professional development. In addition, many of our schools have established a mentor-new teacher buddy system in the school for on-site, more "in the moment" support.

The mentor-new teacher relationship begins in the summer for approximately 150 teachers during our August three-day New Teacher Induction Program. The mentors participate along with the new teachers. The afternoon of day three is scheduled in each school and planned by the school-site leadership team, with mentors often assisting.

Over the course of year one, new teachers participate in monthly **Teachers First** seminars, which alternate between school-based and district-based programs that focus on the essential knowledge and skills required of new teachers. Topics include literacy integration, support of inclusive education students, assessment, grading, and record-keeping in a standards-based environment. **Teachers First** culminates with a celebration of success held each May. In subsequent years, teachers attend **Teachers Two** and **Teachers Three**, intended to continue the conversation and support required for new teachers to become satisfied and successful members of the Greece School Community.

This three-year induction model is a collaborative venture between the Office of Professional Development and the Greece Teaching and Learning Center. A planning committee comprised of many school and community stakeholder groups meets several times a year to continually assess the effectiveness of the new teacher program and to make refinements for the subsequent year. We solicit feedback through e-mail correspondence after each program to obtain information from individual teachers about their induction experience. Our long-term goal for each new teacher hired in Greece Central is for them to be a satisfied and successful employee. We see mentoring as a component of our new teacher induction efforts contributing significantly to this outcome.

Ann Mitchell, Director of Professional Development, Greece Central School District, Greece, NY

Through the Voice of a Lead Mentor...
Getting Started Our Second Year

Our mentor program for this school year actually started last spring. A great deal of time was spent selecting the mentors for this year. Our selection criteria included professional qualities, subject, grade, and location. A cadre of 22 mentors was recruited based on projected needs. Most of this group were experienced mentors. It was decided that Hammond would have a more comprehensive staff development program for our new staff during the week of the new teacher orientation sessions.

All mentor pairings were given out at the mentor training the week before the new teachers reported. As the Lead Mentor, I contacted all the new teachers by phone and most of the mentors did likewise.

During **New Teacher Orientation** week, our new teachers attended the district level meeting in the mornings and we crafted the following activities for them at school in the afternoons.

Day One
- New staff were introduced to the mentor group.
- A general orientation took place.
- Mentors gave the new staff a tour of the building.
- New staff received the keys to their rooms.

Day Two
- New teachers met in curriculum groups to go over curriculum and classroom materials with mentors.
- Pacing guides and teacher's editions were made available.

Day Three
- New teachers received their laptops and spent the afternoon with the Technology Resource Teachers (TRTs) in training.

Day Four
- New staff had the day to work in their classrooms.

Mentor meetings were held weekly throughout September and bi-weekly throughout October. Many topics were discussed at these meetings but the main topic was setting up a peer observation program that would particularly benefit our eight first-year teachers. We used a district Professional Evaluation Program (PEP) Specialist to help us develop an observation tool that we could easily use to create a profile of the classroom needs of our new staff. In late September we explained the observation process in which they would participate to the new

Through the Voice of a Lead Mentor...
Getting Started Our Second Year continued...

teachers. Each was asked to team up with a partner and do two observations of either their mentors or other faculty. The observed faculty member was asked to create a detailed lesson plan so the new teachers would know what they were observing. The mentors were also required to observe their new teachers and use the observation tool we designed. The response by everyone was very positive.

The mentor group met in November to go over observed areas of strengths and areas in need of growth. Lists were compiled and are being used to plan mini-courses for new staff.

Our mentors have worked very hard to get their new teachers started well. From finding staplers to helping with lesson plans, a great deal of time has been put in. Everyone has participated in the observation process, and I have high hopes that we will reap great benefits from the observations that have been done and that are ongoing.

Mike DiSalvo, Lead Mentor, Francis C. Hammond Middle School, Alexandria City Public Schools, VA

Through the Voice of an Induction Coach...
Learning for New Teachers and Their Mentors

Why wasn't such support available when I began teaching? Those of us who coach novice teachers ask that question frequently. When we look back on those initial years of classroom experience, we wonder how we were ever able to maintain a sense of equilibrium. How does a new teacher balance instruction theory, management systems, state and district standards, and have the resources to provide meaningful instruction for all students? Is there residual physical and mental energy to have a life outside the job?

My school district, St. Vrain Valley School District, in Longmont, Colorado, provides new teachers with mentors who can share, enlighten, reflect with, and nurture them in the field. Induction coaches, who are released for two years from classroom responsibilities, spend two or more hours each week working collaboratively with each novice teacher assigned to us. We work on defining essential components of a specific content area, planning and designing assessments and lessons, and observing research-based instructional strategies in action. Release time is also provided for the novices to observe exemplary teachers in other schools. These interactions yield intense discussions on how specific techniques and materials can be adapted or modified. The new teachers consistently report that this field experience has an incredible impact on their teaching.

As a professional development coach and clinical professor, I quickly realized the impact and power these interactions had on my own practice. While accompanying these novice teachers to the classrooms of master teachers, I realized how easily one can spread the seeds of knowledge and pedagogy to others in the field. Countless hours are spent mapping out the year, the units, and the lessons; these efforts not only aid the individual teacher and his/her students, but also are shared with colleagues throughout the district.

The ultimate application of my experience has been the opportunity as a clinical professor at Colorado University to sift through the most essential ingredients of teaching and then demonstrate them to pre-service teachers. What a gift it is to leave student teaching, with a genuine understanding of professional expectations and quality tools that can be used for implementation. Tying together my learning gained from observing master teachers, the information provided on standards-based instruction and data analysis during district professional development seminars, and opportunities to collaboratively examine research on practices that enhance academic growth arms me with the practical information necessary to thoughtfully guide those who are beginning their careers in education.

Donna Begley, Induction Coach and Clinical Professor, St. Vrain Valley School District, Longmont, CO

Through the Voice of New Teachers...
Messages for New Teachers

If I could say one thing to next year's new teachers that would help make their year a success, I would say...

- You are a teacher. Now, remember what it was like to be young and trying to learn hard, new things every day, and you will be a good teacher. Patience, a smile, and sense of humor go a long way.
- Don't be shy about asking for help.
- You've got the whole year ahead of you, pace yourself. If you don't ask, the answer is "no."
- Don't be afraid to ask questions if you are unclear about something. Also, don't be afraid to exhibit your own individual teaching styles and techniques. We should always be able to learn from each other.
- Talk to other teachers. Get to know teachers on your hallway. Finally, remember you are not alone when you have a problem in class or with a student.
- Relax. Take things as they come. Find out what needs to be done first and get that done. Laugh!
- Organize a filing system and pick one day a week to file and organize all your papers.
- Be open to suggestions.
- Communicate with fellow teachers, administration, parents and departments often. Ask questions to clarify expectations and follow through on information given.
- It is going to be tough, but you can do it! When in doubt, ask lots of questions and don't give up. Have fun with your students and staff.
- Grade a couple of assignments daily. Papers can pile up before your eyes.
- Sit down with your mentor at the beginning of each quarter to look at the school calendar. Then prioritize and schedule all of your duties and tasks. Enjoy the year!
- Ask questions! Ask questions! Ask questions!
- Stay on top of paperwork. It can get away from you. Ask questions of your mentor. That's what they are there for.
- Develop a relationship with someone who is positive and willing to offer advice, someone who has a few years' experience and can give insight.
- Make one day out of your weekend a "school-free" day. Work expands to fill the space allowed.
- Make sure that you make the most of official and unofficial mentors. There are many people in this organization who are willing to assist you. All you have to do is ask.

Through the Voice of New Teachers...
Messages for New Teachers continued...

- Take one day at a time! Believe in yourself! Take time for yourself!
- Make sure to ask your mentors questions if you have them. There is so much new information thrown at you, it is hard to sort it all out at first. Everyone was very willing to help. You just have to ask.
- Be proactive and don't be afraid to ask questions and/or raise concerns.
- Find someone in your grade who can share ideas, resources, advice, etc. with you.
- Learn your needs: instructional, environmental, administrators' expectations, etc. Take the steps necessary to meet these needs and don't be afraid to ask. Many people are here to help. Help them help by asking.
- Don't be afraid to ask your mentor for help. That's what they are there for!
- Learn from your mistakes! Use all of your resources! Plan, plan, plan! Don't hesitate to ask for help!
- Ask, don't hesitate! The best resources are your fellow colleagues! Take notes. Use your agenda binder. There's too much information to remember.
- Don't be afraid to ask for help. Once you ask, then everyone will help.
- Set up a time to meet with your mentor each week. At the beginning of the year, go over the expectations for you and your mentor so that you know what to expect. They are getting PAID to help you!
- Use your mentor as a sounding board for your concerns, questions and even successes. They are there to help, listen and support you. Make the effort even if they don't.
- Don't be afraid to ask questions and ask for help when you need it.
- Tell everyone "Hi" with a smile. Making a positive first impression on even teachers/administrators you do not work with helps people remember your face!
- Listen and learn from experienced teachers.
- Make sure you understand what happens when you escalate a behavioral issue. Where does the referral go? How is the assistant principal responding? What is the next step or expected outcome?
- Take advantage of your mentor or another veteran teacher who is near your classroom.

Through the Voice of a Novice Bilingual Teacher... Professional Development in an Induction Program

I am grateful that I took the course, **Why Didn't I Learn This in College?** in June preceding my first year of classroom teaching. I was able to use many of the ideas in my summer of planning. With all the responsibilities and planning week to week, there is little time for big picture planning once school begins. I am teaching second grade bilingual, so the pressures of teaching in my second language, learning the curriculum in both languages, and of course, assuring that the students are learning has been a huge challenge. I am glad that I had **set up the systems** I had preplanned. The opportunity for collaboration with other teachers of all grades and disciplines was invaluable because during the school year, there is just not enough time to meet with other teachers as much as I would like.

The guiding principle for my teaching is **the best management program is a strong instruction program**. Before the course, I thought that I needed a lot of tricks for classroom management, and was nervous that I didn't have that in place. Instead, I now have a very strong instructional plan, based on standards in all of my subjects, and that is the basis of my classroom management. I work every week on being prepared to work on the attitudes, skills, and knowledge of my students. I am constantly working on my repertoire of resources as I learn more and more about how to reach all students. I am personally learning more from the students every day.

Using **the standards-based planning process**, I design the summative assessments in advance, so that I know what the students will be able to do. I have tried to integrate the same themes into all parts of the day, in order to enrich learning. This has involved planning ahead for resources in both Spanish and English literacy, including reading, writing, and oral language development, in addition to integrating math curriculum whenever possible. I have found that spiral planning involves constant reflection and re-evaluation. As I try to plan ahead, I am working to figure out pacing, what to revisit and for how long. My overarching question is how to develop student skills, confidence, and enthusiasm for the basics of reading, writing and math.

Why Didn't I Learn This in College? helped me collect and learn to use tools that I need to become a reflective classroom teacher. The questions that we pondered, the techniques presented, and the collaboration offered by the group setting were invaluable in my learning process.

Karen Mygatt, Second Grade Bilingual Teacher, St. Vrain Valley School District, Longmont, CO

Through the Voice of a Novice Teacher...
Reflections on Planning and a Plea for Help

I am a first-year teacher so I have been planning week by week. I know what I have to do but I haven't had the time to lay it all out in front of me to plan with the end in mind. When I plan my lessons, I always try to meet the needs of all my learners.

As a result of attending **Why Didn't I Learn This in College?** my thinking about planning and pacing has evolved because I see how crucial it is to plan with the end in mind. I knew that before, but now I understand that it will help reduce the amount of stress and frustration I am having by planning week by week.

I did not have time after I was hired last summer to plan because I was out of state finishing my masters. When I finished graduate school in August, I had to spend the remaining time cleaning and setting up my class and attending new teacher orientation.

I need to have time to sit with my team and plan out the year. Unfortunately, I have not had a productive mentoring relationship because my mentor is not a member of my team and we have had very little interaction since the first day of school. I have adopted one of my teammates as my mentor even though she has only been teaching for two years.

I need to feel supported by my team so that I can see how they plan for the year and what they have for instructional materials. I feel very isolated at times because the veteran teachers on the team do not seek me out to see how things are going or offer any guidance or support. I have to take the time to step back, breathe, and realize that I am new and can't do everything. And, that's okay.

I need to get all of my benchmarks and standards together and organize them. This will help me see what students need to learn and go from there. My looming problem is, when do I get the time? Where do I find the time?

I need assistance from my fellow teachers. I need all of the resources from subject areas: benchmarks, standards, teaching manuals. My class was "swept clean" by the previous teacher who either threw out or took all of the district documents and the teaching materials. I have to borrow the teacher's manual for our math book which limits when I can use it to plan! How can I plan well without having the appropriate materials at all times?

Through the Voice of a Career Switcher...
What I Expect from My Mentor

A career switcher is caught between two realities. In one reality, a career switcher is a person with rich life and career experiences outside the world of education. We come from diverse backgrounds that vary from former lawyers and doctors to former administrative assistants and interior designers. A career switcher can be 26 years old. A career switcher can also be 56 years old, or anything in between and beyond! For example, after returning from World War II, my grandfather took evening classes to earn his BA in English, all while maintaining a busy family farm in Illinois. He later became an English teacher at age 50 and then continued to work as a substitute teacher well into his seventies!

The other reality is that despite our varied degrees of age, wisdom and experience, we are starting over in an entirely new career. This means learning a new vocabulary, learning new systems for thinking, and learning about the intricacies of daily life and survival within the social and educational settings of a school district. Imagine hearing phrases such as "IEPs," "Pacing Guides," or "Virginia SOLs" for the first time and this challenge becomes more understandable.

In my opinion, the key to melding and making the most of these two realities is having a skilled mentor. As I look forward to my first year of teaching, I have many expectations for my mentor. I expect my mentor to inspire me, to be available to me, to anticipate my successes and my slumps, to laugh with me, to be a resource, and to be my teacher and my guide.

I also expect my mentor to remember that I am an adult learner and that using feedback, validation, humor, and choice to guide my learning experiences will help ensure a successful transition in the classroom and the profession. I anticipate my mentor facilitating great goal setting opportunities as well as wisdom and advice. I look forward to my mentor providing me with "back door" information such as a custodian's birthday, the best copy machine in the building, or a co-worker's favorite football team, so that eventually I won't simply be working "at" a school, but instead I'll be working with and alongside my fellow professionals.

Finally, I look forward to the day when my mentor is tired, or frustrated, or needing advice. I look forward to that day because not only will my mentor be an asset to me, but like all career switchers, with my experiences, knowledge, and fresh perspective, I will be an asset to them.

Heidi Pappas, Career Switcher, Regent University, Alexandria, VA

New Teachers as Colleagues and Learners

Chapter II

An Awesome Array of New Teachers

There seems to be general agreement that there will over two million new teachers in the next decade. **Who are they and how will they change the face of public education?** What do we need to know about them in order to ensure that there is a fully qualified and fully satisfied teacher in each classroom?

According to a January 2000 Issue Brief published by the National Governors' Association (NGA) Center for Best Practices, that year 55 percent of the candidates entering teacher preparation programs at the graduate level and 11 percent at the undergraduate level entered teaching from career fields other than education. When asked to describe her colleagues in the Regent University Career Switcher program in Alexandria, Virginia, Heidi Pappas described them as a 50-something owner of architect contracting business, a 40-something retired military officer, 30-somethings who were a dietician, a journalist, and a current member of the armed services as well as a 60-something former attorney and judge. The ages, ethnicity, and backgrounds of those entering the field is incredibly varied. Mentors may share the same grade level or content area class but there is more to the mentor-new teacher match than that. We have to realize that our new teachers are in many ways just as diverse as the students in our classrooms.

Almost a third of "new" teachers are former teachers returning to the profession. As current teachers know, the standards movement, Individuals With Disabilities Act (IDEA), No Child Left Behind (NCLB), and changing demographics have caused a great deal of change in teaching and learning expectations. Depending on how long these teachers have been out of the teaching field, there could be real re-entry shock. A well-informed and skilled mentor is essential for these colleagues returning to work.

Just as our students learn in many varied ways, adults exhibit different learning preferences. Mentors have to not only be knowledgeable about adult learning theory, they need to be aware of and use information about information processing styles, and understand and accept the generational differences that are present in a work force; the four generations have very different life experiences and those experiences greatly impact their professional practices. For example, the technology savvy of teachers in their twenties and thirties sets them apart from most of those in their fifties. It is our responsibility to recognize and maximize their knowledge and skills while at the same time support them in the challenges they face in their classroom as young teachers.

This chapter provides guidance in the use of adult learning theory, information processing styles, generational differences, and good communication skills in our mentoring practice.

New Teachers as Adult Learners

Because adults...

- **need to be validated for what they already know and do, we need to recognize and build on their experience.**

  Each teacher new to the school has a lifetime of experience as a learner, teacher, follower, leader, colleague, and friend. They have even known some children, from near or afar. 21st century new teachers come from a wide range of backgrounds so their life experiences may be quite different from those of their mentors; it is, therefore, essential that mentors and all other staff members get to know each new teacher so they know the life experiences each new teacher brings to the organization and capitalize on those experiences. There is little chance that one size fits all induction program and mentoring relationship will work.

- **experience a dip in their sense of self-efficacy when new initiatives with new skills and language are introduced, we need to provide encouragement and recognition of effort.**

  A golf lesson or the purchase of a new car requires us to learn a new way of approaching a familiar task. Try implementing the new ways while at the same time using new clubs or driving in a new location and the process becomes even more difficult. The more changes or the bigger the change the new teacher is making, the more their sense of self-efficacy dips. Without thinking about it, educators can use educational terms, or terms and acronyms unique to the local school district and cause new teachers to be completely confused, and perhaps even frustrated, with their incapacity to understand what is happening.

- **are social beings and as K-12 teachers spend much of their time in a confined space with children, they need opportunities to make personal adult connections and have congenial interactions with colleagues.**

  While time is precious for all of us, it is essential that we find the time to ensure that collegial mentoring relationships are accompanied by congenial personal relationships. This is not to be interpreted as a requirement that the new teachers are to become the mentors' new best friends. It does mean, however, that care should be taken to connect the new teachers with others on the staff who have similar interests and backgrounds. It is hard to take risks with people we do not know well. Glasser identifies a sense of belonging, power, freedom, and fun as the four most desired human interactions. A sense of belonging and the opportunity to have fun are of particular importance here.

New Teachers as Adult Learners

Because adults...

- **value choice, freedom, and power, we should offer choice in how they learn as long as what they are learning is based on the mission and vision of the organization and is in the interest of student learning.**

  Life-long learning is not multiple choice. The format of the learning should be. Mentors should make it clear that there will be a structured learning process during the multi-year induction program and clearly explain the options for learning. Peer observations, planning sessions, dialogue journals, analysis of student work and student achievement data, conference attendance, leading professional development sessions, and a combination of all of these should be laid out as an array of choices. Each district may require a minimum number of peer observations or require dialogue journals and that baseline expectation should be met by all new teachers. It may be that the new teachers want to refine and enhance their learning by doing more observations and journal entries or they may want to advance their own professional growth and the learning of their students by other means. Mentors need to have on-going discussions about the options for learning, the effectiveness of the learning, and the next steps in the learning process.

- **internalize and use strategies that they experience far better than they internalize strategies that they only hear or read about, we need to structure our interactions to provide new teachers opportunities to experience proven teaching/learning strategies.**

  If faculty, team, grade level, and department meetings are structured so that best practice in teaching and learning is modeled during those interactions, this adult learning variable is more easily addressed. In any case, mentors can orchestrate opportunities through peer observations or small group meetings of mentors and new teachers for new teachers to experience the strategies we want them to implement in their classrooms.

- **engage when they are asked what they would like to know about the topic, we need a repertoire of ways to gather, analyze, and use data about their concerns, goals, and needs.**

  This adult learning variable calls for the use of informal conversations, structured interviews, and self-assessments as tools for gathering data about what new teachers think they need to know. Just as skillful classroom teachers ask the right questions to move students to the level of thinking we want them to have, skilled mentors ask the questions in one format or the other to engage the new teachers in identifying their own next steps of professional growth.

New Teachers as Adult Learners

Because adults...

- **need to see and hear examples from classrooms similar to the ones in which they work, we need to be sure that they have ample opportunity to study students and teachers who are working in settings similar to their own.**
  We can provide written exemplars, do peer observations such as walk-throughs/learning walks within the school, do model teaching in their classrooms, and watch and analyze videotaped teaching and learning episodes together.

- **want to know why and how the mentor is qualified to lead their learning and whether or not the leader has "walked the talk," we need to be storytellers...but not braggarts.**
  Storytelling is a powerful teaching tool. Be clear about your purpose for telling a given story. Check for understanding and meaning making to ensure that the new teachers heard the key points to be gleaned from the story. When sharing a story, always include the self-doubts, the alternatives considered, the rationale for the actions taken, and a focus on lessons learned from the experience. When the story features no false starts and no self-doubt but rather absolute brilliance in instructional decision-making, be sure that the person who is so brilliant is someone else.

- **respond to humor, we need to be able to enjoy the moment and, as appropriate, build in humorous stories.**
  A well selected cartoon or a humorous quote from the numerous books published about teaching and schooling can be the perfect antidote for a discouraging day or week.

- **expect feedback on work they do, we need to provide them appropriate feedback and we need to teach them strategies and protocols for asking for and giving each other feedback.**
  Mentors need to develop strong skills for providing appropriate feedback in ways that keep lines of communication open and promote professional growth in new teachers. Finding the balance between consulting, collaborating, and coaching is a complex task and one for which mentors need training and support. Additionally, systems for helping new teachers learn to ask for and provide one another data-driven feedback need to be a strong component of any mentoring program.

Information Processing Styles

Our own personal experiences combined with our natural tendencies to process information in certain ways makes influencing or guiding our thinking a complex endeavor. We should never underestimate the power of understanding how others view the world and the lens through which they process events, information, and authority. If we can predict or at least consider why people react and respond the way they do to us, to new initiatives, to new directions, to conflicting information, to financial and political realities, and to data, we can better plan our mentoring interactions.

No way of processing information is better than any other way. The mentoring dilemma is the need to step out of our own comfort zones in order to establish cognitive empathy, to think like the other person is thinking. Use the list below to assess your own tendencies and then read through it again trying to see the world the way you think those you are mentoring do. Once you identify the potential differences, you can plan how to accommodate them. You may want to discuss these information processing variables with the new teachers with whom you are working. The information can be valuable to them in their interactions with colleagues, students, and parents.

Do You Hear What I Say? Do I Hear What You Say?

introverted or extroverted: Do you prefer to respond to new information immediately doing your thinking out loud or do you prefer information in advance so that you have time to think about the issues before you have to respond?

global or analytical: Do you tend to see the big picture and like to have scaffolding on which to hang details or do you prefer to see the bits and pieces and then put them into the whole?

random or sequential: Do you prefer to work through steps in sequence or are you more inclined to jump around and deal with ones that interest you in the moment?

concrete or abstract: Do you want to see the real thing rather than hear about the theory or the possibilities?

sensing or feeling: Do you prefer to deal with what you can see, hear, and touch or do you prefer to go with gut instincts?

in the moment or in the past or in the future: Is what happened in the past, what is happening right now, or what the future will bring that matters most?

decisive or open ended: Do you tend to make quick decisions and stand by them or do you prefer to continue to gather information and have several options?

Information Processing Styles

Do You Hear What I Say? Do I Hear What You Say?

head or heart: Do you lead primarily with your head or your heart? Do you say "I think" or "I feel?"

why or how: Which question is the first to come to your mind when someone presents information, "Why is that a good idea?" or "How would that look?"

observer or hands-on active learner: Do you learn best by observing from a distance or do you need to get into the action and mess around with new ideas and processes?

research or personal practice experience: Do you tend to seek out and cite research or do you prefer to rely on past experience?

plan ahead or wait until last minute: Do you finish projects well in advance and put them away until needed or are you inclined to fill all available time no matter when you start?

internal attributions or external attributions: Do you tend to question the effectiveness of your own efforts or attribute success or failure to the variables that are beyond your control?

negative or positive: Do you view the world through a rose-colored lens or are you more likely to see problems just around the corner?

logical or intuitive: Do you prefer to measure and quantify things or are you comfortable knowing without knowing how you know?

systems thinker or focused personal view: Do you think more about how actions and information impact the complex organization around you or do you focus on the world right around you?

position power or personal power: Do you define authority primarily by the titles people hold or from the respect they have earned?

After you have assessed your own view of the world and made your best predictions about the person or persons with whom you are working, it is important that you not think that you have the correct view and they have the wrong one. It is a waste of energy to try to convince them to see the world through your lens. The reality of the information or data that you want to share does not change so there is no need to back off from doing it. **The way you present the information or data is the variable that can be adjusted in order to promote acceptance, understanding, and action.**

Generational Differences

Generational differences, as well as age differences, need to be considered in communicating with, and establishing mentor relationships with, novice teachers in their twenties, novice teachers who are career switchers, and those entering or re-entering the work place later in life. Some of our values and actions are transitory and, therefore, change as we age. It is important to note that not all people of the same age have the same outlook though there are patterns and trends that are often associated with those in their twenties, thirties, forties, and so on. Values and actions are also shaped by personal and world events that occurred at a given point in our lives.

In the 1970's, Dr. Morris Massey was featured in a video entitled "What You Are Is Where You Were When." In this video, he put forth the theory that values are established or programmed around the age of ten. Ask people to discuss what was going on in their lives when they were ten to fifteen years old, and you quickly see how events, heroes, movies, and music have a lasting impact on who they are. It is through this lens that the histories and values of four generational groups are presented as variables to consider in planning how to interact with, mentor, and learn from members of each group.

These generational differences influence thinking about family life, selection of jobs or careers, balance of work and family, gender roles, organizations, politics, culture, lifestyle, and outlook about the future. We need to study these differences and their impact on the lives of colleagues so that we have an awareness, develop an understanding, accept the differences and then interact in appropriate and productive ways.

Impact on work environments
- When one of the four generations is much larger in number than the other three, the environment is greatly influenced and perhaps even controlled by that generation.
- Given that people are working longer and often move on to new jobs after their retirement from another, there is a strong possibility that an educator from an older generation can be mentored and/or supervised by someone quite a bit younger.
- Four areas related to mentoring practice that may be impacted by generational differences:
  - feedback
  - professional development
  - supervision
  - appreciation and recognition

Traditionalists
Born 1920-1942, Age 10 in 1930-1952

Events, Trends, and Technology That Shaped Their Lives
- The Great Depression
- WWII
- Pearl Harbor
- Atomic Bomb
- Korean War
- Stay-at-home moms
- Listened to the radio as youth
- Remember when "high tech" was a slide rule and a blackberry was only a fruit.
- Remember when PDA meant public display of affection not personal digital assistant

Values and Characteristics
- Privacy
- Hard work
- Trust
- Formality
- Respect authority
- Loyal to institutions
- Believe in law and order
- Follow the rules
- Material possessions

Building on Their Strengths and Life Experiences
- Acknowledge and ask about their experiences.
- Be explicit about the ways they have made a difference.
- Let them know that they are the historians of the changes in education.
- Use retired teachers as mentors who will share their institutional history and their belief that hard work is the right thing to do.
- May expect "perks" given their age so provide them when possible and explain rationale for alternative decisions.

Baby Boomers
Born 1942-1960, Age 10 in 1952-1970

Events, Trends, and Technology That Shaped Their Lives
- Viet Nam
- Civil Rights movement
- The Cuban Missile Crisis
- The assassination of President Kennedy
- Man walked on the moon
- Woodstock
- Kent State
- Watergate
- Sexual Revolution
- Grew up in a time of economic growth
- Many moms stayed home
- Touch tone phones
- Three TV channels
- Calculators

Values and Characteristics
- Competition
- Change
- Hard work
- Success
- Personal gratification
- Teamwork
- Inclusion
- Involvement
- Health and wellness
- Optimism
- Independence

Building on Their Strengths and Life Experiences
- They are often looking for chances to move up the "career ladder" so offer them opportunities to be involved in school life beyond the classroom while watching for overcommitment and burn-out. They can be "workaholics."
- They are process-oriented so may need guidance to keep eye on desired results.

Gen Xers
Born 1960-1980, Age 10 in 1970-1990

Events, Trends, and Technology That Shaped Their Lives

- Challenger disaster
- Fall of the Berlin Wall
- Operation Desert Storm
- LA riots
- Latch-key kids
- Sesame Street
- Grew up with the Internet
- Hundreds of TV channels
- Computer games
- Silicon Valley
- Watergate
- Energy crisis
- AIDS
- VCRs
- Cell phones
- PDAs
- AOL
- TIVO

Values and Characteristics

- Entrepreneurial spirit
- Global thinking
- Independence
- Self-Reliance
- Informality
- Creativity
- Fun
- Feedback
- Quality of work life
- Diversity
- Balance of personal and professional lives

Building on Their Strengths and Life Experiences

- Gen X'ers prefer action to talk so have them "do" rather than listen and watch. Honor that preference but monitor the work because often their focus is on getting the task done rather than thinking through alternatives, considering pros and cons, cause and effect, and then identifying the best course of action.
- Use their technology skills to enhance the work of the organization.
- Because they value relationships over organizations, earn their respect with personal power rather than with position power.
- Use their creative energy to help the organization "think outside of the box."
- Let them know that they are on the right track and give them space to work as independently as possible.
- Given that they value patience and trust, do not try to micro-manage them.
- Recognize their productivity and results.

Millennials
Born 1980-2005, Age 10 in 1990-2015

Events, Trends, and Technology That Shaped Their Lives*
- 9/11
- Oklahoma City bombing
- Gulf War
- Operation Desert Storm
- Israeli/Palestinian conflict
- Columbine
- Downsizing of corporations
- Dot Com crash
- The Internet
- DVDs
- Play Station
- PDAs
- IPOD
- Mp3s
- Ctrl+Alt+Del
- Yahoo
- Google

Values and Characteristics
- Time with family
- Autonomy
- Confidence
- Positive outlook
- Diversity
- Optimism
- Money
- Technology

Building on Their Strengths and Life Experiences
- Use cutting-edge technology whenever possible
- Use email to communicate
- Make the work environment a fun place
- Use humor
- Understand that they can multi-task
- Let them know that they are the future, that you believe in them, and that they will be mentored
- Millennials want feedback and may view silence as disapproval

* For an eye-opening list of the life experiences of Millennials, do a Google search for "Beloit College Mindset List." Each year professors at the Beloit College, Beloit, Wisconsin, publish a list explaining how the entering freshmen have experienced the world. The purpose of the list is to help professors use references, analogies, and examples with which their current students can make connections. These lists can serve mentors well in relating to teachers in their twenties.

New Teachers as Colleagues and Learners
Communication Skills in Review

All of us have participated in several communication skills workshops. It never hurts, however, to review the basics. Use the following reminders as needed. When mentoring relationships are not working as well as they might or when conversations and conferences are not being productive no matter what approach you select, consider these communication practices as other variables to adjust in your mentoring practice.

- Make eye contact.
- Stop talking and listen.
- Concentrate. Do not be planning your response while the other person is still talking or you will miss part of what is said.
- Do not interrupt.
- React to the ideas being expressed, not to the person who is speaking.
- Listen to what is not said.
- Listen to how something is said. Use your knowledge of information processing styles.
- Listen for external and internal attributions and use attribution retraining to help reframe external attributions. See page 18 in *Why Didn't I Learn This in College?* for a brief description of this process.
- Try to identify the underlying cause of any concerns and then match your response to your best guess as to the cause of the concern.
- Monitor your own filters and do not jump to conclusions or judgements. Be sure that generational differences or language choice does not cause you to react in an unproductive way.
- Put away all papers that might be a distraction.
- Nod affirmatively and make minimal encouraging responses like "I see", "Hmmm," and "Interesting."
- Paraphrase what is said.
- Ask clarifying questions.
- In conference situations, be prepared with notes analyzed, connections to past experiences clarified, and questions and discussion points ready.
- Avoid communication stoppers like
  - "If I were you, I would have tried...,"
  - "Based on my experience, I feel that the best thing to do is...,"
  - "I told you that wouldn't work."
  - "Eveyone knows that..."
  - "Wouldn't you agree...?"
  - "Where did you get that idea?"
  - "Everyone ought to..."
  - "People should..."

New Colleagues as Teachers and Learners
Communication Skills continued...

If You Want to Signal That You Want to Work Collaboratively...

Do all of the above and...

- Sit beside the new teacher rather than on the other side of a table or desk.
- Explicitly teach the six-step problem-solving process and follow the steps in working together.
- Provide the new teacher copies of any notes you took during an observation prior to the conference.
- Prepare copies of any materials you are going to refer to during the conference.
- Share copies of units, lessons, assessments, rubrics, newsletters and other parent communication artifacts. Ask new teachers to share what they create with you and others.

If You Want to Signal...

- That the professional conversation is over... digress to personal topics, look at your watch, begin to check your calendar, let others interrupt your conversation, stand up, and head toward the door.
- That you are just going through the paces... follow only your own script and do not respond to the teacher's silences, emotions, questions, and concerns; take phone calls, leave your cell phone on, have difficulty finding your notes from the last meeting or other necessary papers.
- That you are taking a position of authority and/or superiority... sit behind a desk and control the flow of the conversation
- That you have better things to do... flip through your calendar, make notes about unrelated issues. Remember all teachers are really good at reading upside down and knowing when students are writing notes!
- That you do not believe the mentoring process provides a valuable opportunity for professional dialogue... cancel appointments, be late for meetings, always be in a hurry, or forget to bring materials you promised to bring.

Mentor-New Teacher Interactions

Chapter III

Mentor-New Teacher Interactions
The Bottom Line

So, exactly what is a mentor supposed to do? The short answer is, whatever it takes to help ensure that there is a fully qualified and satisfied teacher in every classroom. This chapter provides dozens of possible discussion points and interactions for mentor-new teacher work. In addition to words of wisdom from new teachers and mentors, suggested support systems for potential challenges and concerns of new teachers are provided. The support systems in this chapter are organized in categories adapted from Camp and Heath-Camp's Teacher Proximity Continuum for beginning career and technical educators. Let's begin with some basic information about the logistics of mentor-new teacher interactions.

Communication Possibilities
- Face-to-face interactions including conversations, meetings, conferences, co-teaching, and socialization
- Peer observations
- Telephone/email conversations with novice teacher
- Peer observations
- Written communication including notes and dialogue journals
- Professional development and networking opportunities
- On-line mentoring

Frequency of Interaction
- The frequency of interaction depends on the needs of the new teachers and district requirements and expectations.
- Guidelines for frequency of interaction with novice teachers are
  - As much as possible before school starts
  - Once a day during the first month of school
  - Two to three times a week throughout the first semester
  - At least once a week throughout the second semester
- Guidelines for frequency of interaction with experienced teachers new to the district, as well as second and third year teachers are
  - As much as possible before school starts
  - Once a day during the first week of school
  - Once a week throughout the rest of the school year
  - More as needed

Mentor-New Teacher Interactions
The Bottom Line

District Documents to Structure Mentoring Work
- State and district standards, benchmarks, and indicators
- Curriculum guides
- School Improvement Plans
- Professional development catalog
- Teacher Evaluation Performance Criteria
- School and district handbooks and policy manuals
- Staff and student directories
- School district calendar
- New Teacher Handbook
- Standardized test results

When to Do What

Chapter VI: Mentoring Calendar provides month by month guidance matched to the developmental stages of new teachers, typical school calendars, and the realities of school life.
- For each month, the suggested mentoring actions are categorized by personal, professional, curriculum and instruction, organizational systems, students, colleagues, school and school system, and parents and community areas of support.
- There is a special section in each month entitled **Especially for Special Educators.**
- The list of possible mentoring actions for August and September is quite extensive so mentors will want to enlist the support of the entire school community in implementing appropriate actions.

Experienced teachers new to the district, grade level, department or team need mentors too. Use the above recommendations or create your own using only the headings. No matter how many years military or foreign service personnel have accumulated in their careers they are assigned a "sponsor" when they arrive at a new post overseas. The sponsor is responsible for making them feel welcome, introducing them to their friends and others they need to know, providing them what they need to live until their own goods arrive, and explaining the "way things are done around here." We in education should do no less!

Through the Voice of New Teachers...
Messages for Mentors

If I could say one thing to next year's mentors about supporting new teachers, I would say...

- Be available for your new teacher. The first year of teaching is extremely overwhelming.
- Help your new teacher prioritize and schedule duties and tasks each quarter.
- Definitely make time to observe your new teacher or have your new teacher observe you. Even if you think you are bothering your new teacher, you're really helping.
- Have special events in the morning to facilitate communication, check-in, or to brainstorm ideas teachers could use that day (i.e., small breakfast, etc.).
- As a mentor, your "teachings" and support have a far-reaching and profoundly important effect because they touch every student that this new teacher will ever instruct. Thank you for being there.
- Be "there" without being too pushy.
- Tell new teachers to always have a back-up plan in mind in case students just don't get the lesson.
- Stay in contact daily with your new teacher for the first two weeks of school.
- Set your calendars for regularly scheduled meetings.
- You're going to learn about as much as you teach. If you want to keep what you've got, you've got to give it away.
- All mentors need to help new teachers with testing procedures and test administration.
- Let new teachers know they can come to you with any questions or concerns.
- Be patient, open, welcoming, and be available.
- Don't wait on new teachers to come to you with concerns; be proactive and check with them frequently.
- Help new teachers set up their classrooms. This is most helpful because there is so much to be done and so many meetings to attend that first week.
- Make sure you're willing to answer lots of questions. There is so much information thrown at new teachers, it is very difficult for them to keep it all straight. Many times they won't realize they have questions until they're in the middle of it.
- Get organized before you start.
- Meet with your new teacher weekly even if it's just for lunch or a quick chat. Try not to play the role of an evaluator as you help your new teacher. You should be their peer.
- As a mentor, you become their seeing-eye dog. You guide them through all the expected and unexpected ups and downs of the school year– personally and professionally.

Through the Voice of New Teachers...
Messages for Mentors

- Interaction is the key. Keep an open-door policy complemented with daily communication.
- Remember that we have not been here, so anytime someone says, "Just like last year," your new teacher has no clue what to do!
- Please make sure you check on your new teacher periodically. It really makes us feel like someone cares about how our year is going.
- Spend time with your new teacher. Set aside a weekly time to just talk, not always at school. Also, plan lessons together. Be sure s/he observes other disciplines.
- Do not assume too much. Make an effort to have at least several weekly contacts with the new teacher.
- Make sure your new teacher knows you from the beginning. It's a very tough transition to school from the outside world and they need help!
- Definitely assist your new teachers in any way possible. At the same time, however, allow them to work towards their own individual teaching style and approach.
- Have a cup of coffee with your new teacher so they know that your interactions are more than being under a microscope.
- Just be there and listen.
- Let your new teacher know that you are available for help or, if you don't know the answer to a question, help him/her find the answer.
- Be there to support your new teacher's questions, concerns and successes. They need someone to talk to and share what happens in and out of the classroom. Make the effort and take the time to get to know your new teacher.
- Be more pro-active with your new teachers. Ask them what specific help they need and then follow through!
- Often both parties don't know exactly what is needed. That can be more easily found by building a close professional relationship.
- Continue to support new teachers throughout the year, not just at the beginning.
- Reinforce the breath of fresh air newcomers bring to the profession. Listen to their ideas for new projects to try.
- During your 'formal' meeting once a week, have your new teacher plan what you will talk about one week and the mentor plan the next week.
- Make sure your new teacher has a reasonable course-pacing guide and feed him/her an occasional worksheet.
- Let the new teacher know that you will probably learn as much from him/her as he/she will from you!

Responses to Potential New Teacher
Challenges and Concerns
Personal

A quick review of Maslow's Hierarchy of Needs reminds us that our physiological needs, safety needs, and need for love and belonging must be met before we can turn our energy to developing competency and maximizing our potential. Mentors can play an important role in minimizing new teachers' concerns in this area and create the conditions under which new teachers can more quickly focus on competency and potential. See the **Personal** section for each month in **Chapter V, Mentoring Calendar.**

Suggestions for supporting new teachers on a personal level:
- Spend time getting to know each other as human beings. Take notes and then introduce them to others on the staff who have the same interests and hobbies or come from the same part of the country.
- When new teachers are moving into the area, offer tips on finding a place to live, the most convenient super market, library, post office, gym, and best restaurants. In over 70 cities you can point them to *www.craigslist.org* as an incredible source of information about housing and other local issues.
- Have everyone (staff, students, custodians, etc.) in the school wear name tags for the first two weeks of school so that everyone gets to know everyone.
- Celebrate birthdays...theirs, yours, George Washington's, or Eleanor Roosevelt's.
- Set a fixed time for getting together each week such as meeting for coffee on Tuesdays or a cup of tea after work on Thursdays.
- Be a professional role model.
- Escort them to faculty, team, department, or committee meetings and sit with them at the meetings until they establish their own network of collegial friends.
- Use humor.
- Be available just to listen; keep an open door.
- Send a note, a flower, a muffin, or a candy bar to commemorate special days like the 100th day, supervisory observations, first day of quarter or trimester, pi day, Cinco de Mayo, the start of Daylight Savings Time, or for no reason at all.
- Give the new teacher your home phone or cell phone number.
- Note, encourage, and validate efforts in the interest of student learning.
- Bolster their confidence and provide moral support, especially on bad days.
- Let them know that everyone feels overwhelmed at one time or another.
- Do not stifle fresh idealistic attitudes.
- Do not gossip.
- Check on a daily basis to see how they are doing.
- Show them where to park.

Responses to Potential New Teacher
Challenges and Concerns

- Help them navigate whatever bureaucratic roadblocks they encounter.
- Take them to lunch before school opens or on a workday.
- Have the PTA send new teachers a rose after the first day of school with a note saying something like, "You made it!"
- Have the PTA send a plant after the first week with a note welcoming them to the school community.
- Keep a folder or notebook of the new teacher's work and/or student work. Use a digital camera to capture images of the classroom, the teacher, and the students at work. This collection makes a great end-of-the-year celebration of the accomplishments of the new teacher's first year at the school.

Responses to Potential New Teacher
Challenges and Concerns

Professional

These professional issues are beyond-the-classroom issues that have to do with human resource functions like certification, payroll, benefits, sick leave, contracting, and with issues of professional growth and collegial collaboration. These topics are generally not addressed in teacher preparation programs so some novice teachers may not even know that they should be concerned about these issues. Even very experienced teachers coming into the district from another location need assistance with these human resource issues. In some districts, the human resource department may make a presentation about conditions of employment, benefits, and evaluation procedures; if that is the case, mentors still need to check in with new teachers to ensure that they understood the information and know what to do in their own situation. See pages 195-206 in *Why Didn't I Learn This in College?* and the **Professional** section for each month in **Chapter V, Mentoring Calendar.**

Suggestions for supporting new teachers with professional issues:
- Ensure that the new teachers have complete information on investment opportunities and benefit packages; as appropriate, help them make decisions about medical, dental, life, and disability insurance and investments. New teachers in their twenties may never have dealt with these decisions so this is of particular importance to them.
- Go over the certification and tenure requirements for your district and state and help the new teachers identify the actions they need to take and the timeline they need to follow to ensure compliance.
- Explain the induction program, including the role and responsibilities of mentors, new teachers, and all other educators in the district. Clearly articulate the role that peer observations, self-assessment, goal setting, and reflection play in the process.
- Provide information about and explain the teacher performance evaluation system used by the school district. Throughout the year, provide information, exemplars, and coaching with the evaluation process.
- If portfolios are a component of the teacher performance evaluation system, assist the new teachers in the selection of artifacts to include in their portfolios and help them articulate why these artifacts best represent the expected decisions and actions and how they represent professional growth.
- Assist the new teachers with the professional goal setting process used in your school district.

Responses to Potential New Teacher
Challenges and Concerns

- Let new teachers know about the local, regional, state, and national professional organizations available to them and advise them as to which ones you and others have found particularly valuable.
- Keep them informed of professional development opportunities provided by the district and professional organizations. Attend a workshop together.
- Explain the priority the district places on using student achievement data and student work samples to inform instructional and organizational decisions.

Responses to Potential New Teacher
Challenges and Concerns

Curriculum, Instruction, and Assessment

The issues addressed in this section focus on what is to be taught and best practice in instruction and assessment. This area is often neglected by mentors who serve as "buddy mentors" and provide primarily nuts and bolts information rather than supporting the development of instructional capacity in new teachers. Because novice teachers may wrongly assume that they need to spend their time and energy time creating complex discipline systems and fancy bulletin boards, mentors need to ensure that the focus of their efforts is on designing strong instructional programs. New teachers, whether novice or experienced, can spend hours and hours outside of school developing lessons and units. Strong mentor support can greatly reduce the number of hours new teachers have to work to develop appropriate learning experiences. The mentor's responsibility is to ensure that the lessons are aligned with district standards, are effective in meeting students' needs, and that data is used to make informed decisions. District documents, successfully used standards-based units of study, components of learning centers, and useful supplemental materials provided by mentors and other staff members can make a huge difference in the success and sanity of new staff members. See the **Curriculum, Instruction and Assessment** section for each month in **Chapter V, Mentoring Calendar.**

Suggestions for supporting new teachers with curriculum and instruction:
- Provide all the instructional materials and ready-made copies of student materials for one standards-based lesson.
- Co-develop a lesson plan for use in your classroom and the beginning teacher's classroom.
- If you teach the same grade or subject, always make extra copies of everything. Put the extra copies in the new teachers' mailboxes or a designated place in their classrooms.
- Brainstorm possible ways for the new teacher to introduce a curriculum unit.
- Suggest a cooperative learning strategy for reviewing literature.
- Identify the strong points in a lesson design.
- Discuss the use of data and pre/post assessment results in making instructional decisions.
- Coach them with the development of rubrics, performance task lists, and checklists.
- Model how to teach writing strategies, group students, access prior knowledge, or check for understanding. Model, model, model!
- Meet weekly for planning sessions.
- Suggest activities and materials pertinent to each unit.

Responses to Potential New Teacher
Challenges and Concerns

- Explain how to integrate literacy.
- Set up observations for them with outstanding teachers who use a variety of research-based instruction strategies.
- Provide an overview of any basal programs and the supplemental reading materials. Even if the district provides a three-hour session on the materials, new teachers need to process what they heard and how the materials will really work in their classrooms.
- Share projects that you have used successfully with students in this school. Include book reports, social studies and science projects. Provide student directions, exemplars of student work, and assessment criteria. It is possible that the novice teachers did their student teaching in another grade level or another course within the content area and that new experienced teachers have in the past taught a different grade or course.
- Preview common assessments.
- Lend new teachers pre-made centers.
- Discuss ways of assessing student learning without using pencil and paper.
- Ask questions that help the new teacher prioritize issues/concerns related to instruction.
- Ask for advice from beginner about "new" approaches to lessons.
- Review the short-and long-term instructional goals.
- Assist in adapting instruction to meet individual needs.
- Do a demonstration of teaching techniques in their class.
- Help them with curriculum mapping.
- Help the new teachers organize lessons so that different learning styles are addressed.
- Help organize subject matter so that the new teachers do not fall into the trap of trying to cover the book.
- If you teach a different grade level or course, become familiar with the curricula with which the new teachers are working. Identify materials and resources that could be useful to them.
- Investigate state, district and on-line curricular and instructional resources available to new teachers and make them aware of them as appropriate. See pages 359-362 for **Web Sites for New Teachers.**

Responses to Potential New Teacher
Challenges and Concerns

Organizational Systems

The literature is replete with information about classroom management and strongly suggests that this is the most important task of new teachers. Given that **we want well-educated rather than well-managed students**, concentration on establishing effective and efficient classroom organizational systems in the interest of student learning is a better goal for new teachers. This can be a challenge for mentors if they have been in the habit of working for control and compliance of students rather than thinking that any classroom management or organizational system should have student learning as its primary goal. Mentors have to be ever mindful of the language they use when discussing setting up the procedures and routines for the classroom. Mentors can not only provide invaluable assistance in the moment but also increase the probability that new teachers will think about organizational systems in the interest of student learning throughout their careers. We will know that we have been successful in helping new teachers establish productive organizational systems when we hear them saying, "My organizational systems are working (or not working)" rather than, "My students will not do what I tell them to do." When the focus is internal, the new teachers have control of the situation because they can change the systems. See the **Organizational Systems** section for each month in **Chapter V, Mentoring Calendar.**

Suggestions for assisting new teachers with organizational systems:

- Provide the new teachers with a set of files with printed labels for the main categories of paper they need to file. See page 209 in *Why Didn't I Learn This in College?*
- Help them set up their classrooms. Some school districts may schedule time for mentors to return to school early to set up their own classrooms. This practice allows them to be available to help new teachers set up their classrooms and also provides demonstration classrooms for new teachers to visit and analyze. See pages 237-240 in *Why Didn't I Learn This in College?*
- Prepare a list of supplies the new teachers need for their classrooms and show them how to obtain them. See page 212 in *Why Didn't I Learn This in College?*
- Provide a check-list on how to plan and organize for field trips for the year. This may be available in the staff handbook.
- When they appear to be overwhelmed or behind, offer to duplicate copies of materials for them.
- Show them how to order supplies and to reserve videos and films.
- Provide guidance in how to access materials and resources from the media center and the professional library.

Responses to Potential New Teacher
Challenges and Concerns

- Share your record-keeping strategies.
- Volunteer to do a bulletin board for new teachers so they have more time to look through cumulative folders and read teacher's manuals. This is a great opportunity to model how bulletin boards can relate to curriculum and feature student work.
- Be mindful of the problems experienced by new teachers who are assigned multiple preparations or to teach in multiple classrooms. See page 235 in **Why Didn't I Learn This in College?** for ideas on how teachers can move instructional materials from classroom to classroom or even building to building.

Responses to Potential New Teacher
Challenges and Concerns

Students

Learning about and working with the personalities, learning profiles, and achievement levels of students may be the biggest challenge new teachers face. The students with whom novice teachers worked during their student teaching experience, or observed as a part of their career switcher programs, are not the ones who walk through the door the first day of school. For the experienced new teacher, the challenge may be that they are working with a demographic profile quite different from what they have encountered before and that can present its own set of challenges. Novice teachers have to appear to have their professional acts together from the first moment; all of us know that is not the case. As mentors we can provide much wisdom and a strong shoulder to lean on as our new colleagues figure out how to take the young bodies and minds that appear at their classroom doors and shape them individually into high performing learners and collectively into communities of learners. See the **Students** section for each month in **Chapter V, Mentoring Calendar**.

Suggestions for learning about student interests and needs, examining their work, building relationships, and creating a learning community:

- Suggest strategies for building a learning community and for sending the message that they believe in the capacity of all students to learn at a high level.
- Help them design a process for establishing classroom rules.
- Share strategies for starting the school year.
- Have student government officers go to the classrooms and welcome new teachers.
- Suggest that they learn about the extracurricular activities in which their students engage as well as the interests and hobbies they pursue outside of school. Further suggest that they attend some of their students' performances, exhibits, and athletic events.
- Examine examples of student work together.
- Brainstorm strategies to use with resistant or reluctant learners.
- Before giving advice on responses to unmet expectations, ask what they have already tried or what they have considered trying.
- Suggest various options for dealing with difficult students rather than saying use this tactic and it will work. When only one way is provided by the mentor and it does not work in this situation, the new teacher feels inadequate rather than considering that the approach was not the right one for this situation.
- Work with the new teacher to identify the cause of any disruptive or resistant behavior and to plan the intervention based on the identified cause.
- Teach new teachers to use the six-step problem-solving process with individual students and with groups.

Responses to Potential New Teacher
Challenges and Concerns

- Share your own strategies for the flexible grouping of students. Discuss the variables you consider in putting groups together and the learning experiences that are best matched to group work.
- Stress the power of calmness and patience when problems occur.
- Encourage them to seek guidance or assistance early rather than trying to go it alone.
- Help them learn how to solve behavior problems on their own.
- Discuss referral procedures for special needs students.
- Advise them to document behavior problems, responses, and interventions that the teacher has implemented to alleviate the problem.

Responses to Potential New Teacher
Challenges and Concerns

Colleagues

Many researchers, including those at The Project on the Next Generation of Teachers at Harvard, cite a sense of isolation and the absence of a collegial culture in the school as primary reasons new teachers leave the profession. This problem is one mentors and other staff members can fix any time we want to do so. While we cannot ensure that all the students will show up ready to learn, that the parents will be appropriately supportive, or that all policy decisions are in the best interest of student learning, we can control our own behavior. Yet we do not often act purposefully and collectively to support new teachers. In fact, there appears at times to be a hazing mentality in effect. New teachers are often assigned the least desirable classrooms, provided left over materials, set up with mismatched furniture, given multiple preparations, and asked to do time consuming extra duties. What are we thinking? See the **Colleagues** section for each month in **Chapter V, Mentoring Calendar**.

Suggestions for supporting the new teachers in building congenial and collegial relationships with the other educators in the school and school system:

- Take the lead in making sure that all staff members understand the purposes and structure of the induction and mentoring program and that they are well aware of the important role they play in the induction process.
- Serve as a liaison between administration, colleagues, and new teacher.
- Ask a secretary and a custodian to be the "go-to" person for the questions and needs of new teachers.
- Identify the building personnel who are responsible for specific academic and logistical tasks. Explain the job responsibilities of each and introduce the new teachers to each of them.
- Encourage the new teachers to share successful lessons at grade-level meetings.
- Reflect together on the mentoring process and set goals for future work together.
- Encourage discussion of the pros, cons, and implications associated with any concern or problem.
- Watch out that too much is not piled on the new teacher.
- Protect them from the sole responsibility of club sponsorship or coaching. If they want to be involved with extra-curricular activities, strongly recommend that they co-sponsor a club or serve as an assistant coach during their first year in the school.
- Suggest to novice teachers that they join just one committee their first year.
- Work with the new teachers to ensure that the general education and special education teachers learn to work collaboratively as equal partners.

Responses to Potential New Teacher
Challenges and Concerns

- Give tips on how to work with instructional assistants and aids.
- Assign grade level buddies on a monthly basis; that way new teachers will have nine informal mentors, a new one each month.
- Accompany them to school social functions.
- Introduce them to other faculty members.
- Sit with them at meetings.
- Include them in conversations at faculty meetings. Ask them to contribute their opinions and ideas.
- Suggest that they team up with other teachers for field trips.
- Write a brief note of thanks when new teachers make suggestions or provide instructional ideas.
- Co-observe and conference together afterwards.
- Anticipate or solicit questions about teaching; make things happen.
- Schedule monthly or quarterly meetings of all new teachers and mentors to help them build a network of colleagues to whom they can go for assistance.
- Suggest avenues of assistance should problems arise. Keep in contact with the specialist, coordinator, or director of the content or grade level that the teacher(s) are teaching.

Responses to Potential New Teacher
Challenges and Concerns

School and School System

New teachers are always surprised at the sheer volume of paperwork that comes across their desk and the number of e-mails they receive each day. They often have no idea what needs to be kept, what can be thrown away, or how to organize the papers they keep. The earlier section on **Organizational Systems** provides suggestions about filing systems for those documents. This section focuses on how mentors can assist new teachers in understanding, using, and responding to the content of those documents. See the **School and School System** section for each month in **Chapter V, Mentoring Calendar**.

Suggestions for supporting new teachers in navigating the policies and the procedures of the school and school system:

- Be sure that the new teacher knows how to access school and district policy and regulation manuals. Forecast what they need to know when and interpret school policies and regulations as they are needed throughout the year.
- If available, review staff handbook. See pages 199-203 in *Why Didn't I Learn This in College?* for suggestions about topics that need to be discussed.
- At the beginning of the school year, assist new teachers in filling out administrative paperwork and be alert for potential uncertainty about paperwork throughout the year.
- Put reminders of important administrative tasks on their desk a day or two before they are due.
- Explain acronyms and jargon.
- Discuss school protocol and traditions with new teachers.
- Give a new teacher a guided tour of district office and facilities.
- Provide copies of documents that communicate the rights and responsibilities of students and staff.
- Explain procedures and guidelines for using telephone, fax, and email for professional and personal communication.
- Discuss "unwritten" school policies.
- Show them around school and how to use school equipment. Be sure to show them the supply room and any secret closets.
- Take them to the school division's professional library and media center.
- Make them aware of the administrative philosophy of the school.
- Explain the school year, semester, quarter, weekly, and daily schedule for the school. Point out particularly busy or challenging times as well as any unique or significant events.
- Explain county grading policies.

Responses to Potential New Teacher
Challenges and Concerns

- Explain school procedure regarding field trips.
- Help them locate student records and discuss regulations and procedures for accessing, amending, duplicating, and replacing these records.
- Go over all nitty-gritty details associated with attendance procedures, monitoring halls between classes, administrator's expectations, referral procedures, fire drills, etc.

Responses to Potential New Teacher
Challenges and Concerns

Parents

Novice teachers often do not fully understand the necessity of setting up positive partnerships with parents until there is a problem for which they need parental support or until a parent wants teacher support. New experienced teachers may encounter a set of parent expectations quite different from those of the parents of students in previous schools. This may manifest itself in parents who want to be overly involved or in parents who are unaware of how to work productively with the school. It is the responsibility of mentors to ensure that new teachers are aware of and address the responsibility of working with parents early in the year so that these relationships do not become huge challenges and concerns later in the year. See the **Parents** section for each month in **Chapter V, Mentoring Calendar.**

Suggestions for supporting new teachers in building their relationships with and working with parents as partners:

- Take the new teachers on a tour of the neighborhood to help them gain perspective on attendance area demographics.
- Provide examples of introductory letters to parents.
- Provide models, either your own or a collection from other teachers, of newsletters and letters home to parents designed to convey on-going information about classroom learning and school events.
- Suggest that parents be invited in as guest speakers or volunteers.
- Recommend positive telephone calls home.
- Assist in writing comments for report cards.
- Discuss individual parent problems as they occur.
- Share ideas on objectives and agendas for Open House or Back-to-School Night.
- Talk about unique features of parent conferences with special needs students.
- Show beginners how to document a problem situation before bringing it to the attention of a parent.
- Sit in on initial or difficult parent conferences.
- Invite beginner to sit in on one of your parent conferences.
- Conduct a mock parent conference after the first month of school to provide practice. Switch playing roles of both the teacher and the parent.
- Use student agendas for communication.
- Discuss the home visit process.

See pages 253-266 in *Why Didn't I Learn This in College?* for tips on creating positive and productive relationships with parents.

Through the Voice of Mentors...
What Do You Do When Your New Teacher

Does not have the same planning period?
- Use e-mail
- Use phone calls
- Use work days
- Use before and/or after school meetings
- Talk over lunch
- Treat him/her to a cup of coffee or drink after work

Does not want to meet or routinely cancels appointments?
- Let the new teacher set the next meeting time/date
- Meet informally, outside of school
- Get to the reason; ask what the issues are
- Provide food at the meetings

Does not seem to feel a need for your assistance?
- Continue to make new teacher aware of time line issues (e.g., grade meetings, policies, procedures, etc.)
- Schedule weekly or bi-weekly meeting times
- Don't use e-mail to correspond; go to their location to talk face-to-face
- Make yourself available during hectic times (e.g., report card preparation time, the days before parent conferences, etc.)
- Perhaps the new teacher's years of experience result in his/her not needing as much assistance
- Observe the new teacher informally
- Schedule an observation to provide topics for discussion/reflection
- Have the new teacher draft the quarterly summary report
- Explain that being part of a mentor-new teacher team is part of being a professional
- Emphasize the differences between policies and practices from division to division and the importance of understanding policies and practices
- Be direct: "You do need to have a mentor."
- Note the importance of knowing who's who in the division and how to use diplomacy to "work the system."
- Get together informally in casual settings
- Share/swap lesson plans and resources
- Build trust by honoring confidentiality
- Use open-ended questions: pose scenarios (e.g., "How would you handle...?")
- Suggest joint work sessions on tasks (e.g., report card preparation, etc.)
- Propose swapping portfolios as a way of idea-sharing

Through the Voice of Mentors...
What Do You Do When Your New Teacher

Does not teach the same grade level?
- Hook up with the appropriate grade level/subject area person
- Use peer coaching techniques
- Make arrangements to observe a class together
- Join your two classes by having the students pair up as "book buddies."
- Schedule before-or-after-school time together
- Use e-mail to communicate (but not exclusively)
- Focus professional conversations on general teaching practices applicable across grade levels/subject areas (e.g., management, differentiation, portfolio-keeping, etc.)

Is special education and you are general education?
- Employ the same strategies as used when grade levels differ (see above)
- Some inclusion issues are shared by both; the special education person could help the general education person

Is very stressed?
- Go on an outing away from school
- Introduce him/her to others who can help
- Offer problem-solving suggestions
- Use food as a special treat
- Adjust expectations
- Share a joke, hug

Is having difficulty establishing relationships with other members of the department or grade level team?
- Establish norms for behavior/communication; remind new teacher of the nature of professional relationships
- Brainstorm situations and solutions
- Work on developing/improving "people skills"
- Go directly to the person(s)
- Remind teacher of any "chain of command" that exists
- Establishing relationships takes time and professional/emotional maturity, just be patient
- Encourage the new teacher to stand up for him/herself
- Encourage participation in/establishment of "happy hour" event(s)
- Encourage contributions to/participation in assignments that the group must complete or respond to cooperatively
- Share your experiences in getting to know new colleagues

Through the Voice of Mentors...
What Do You Do When Your New Teacher

- Find and emphasize common interests within the group
- Make time for team-building
- Consider whether "backing off" the problem is the best response

Is having difficulty with organizational and management issues?
- Offer room organization suggestions, emphasizing student-friendly arrangements
- Label basic expectations
- Have new teacher visit other classrooms
- Video tape the new teacher's instruction and reflect on the tape jointly
- Teach the use of binders, folders, and other organizational tools

Has one or more really difficult students and does not have the skills or support needed to work with them effectively?
- Model work with such students
- Arrange observations of other classes
- Put the new teacher in touch with team members
- Remind new teacher of the "chain of command"
- Review differentiation strategies
- Suggest ways to involve the parent(s)
- Suggest ways to communicate one-on-one with the student(s) after class
- Explain use of "proximity" as a management tool
- Be sure expectations and consequences are clear and consistent

Is saying, "Everything is fine," and you don't know what to do?
- Set an agenda for meetings with the new teacher
- Be prepared with conversation-starting questions for the new teacher and use follow-up questions
- Have meetings in a casual setting (e.g., over lunch or after-school "happy hour")
- Offer to observe the new teacher's instruction
- Ask the new teacher to share something that is working and something that is not working
- Describe the challenges/obstacles you face in the job of teaching
- Share ideas and/or resource materials
- Don't ask, "Is everything okay?" Ask more open-ended questions that invite professional conversations/reflection

Through the Voice of Mentors...
What Do You Do When Your New Teacher

Has not been able to schedule/engage in the peer observation process?
- Set a deadline by which observations must have been done
- Help the new teacher prepare substitute plans

Is not dressing or acting professionally?
- Give the new teacher a "heads up" about the problem
- Lay it on the line (be direct)

Is having problems communicating with parents?
- Model how to communicate with parents
- Establish a format to follow when communicating with parents
- Alert the new teacher to situations to look out for
- Suggest that you or another appropriate teacher/staff member join the new teacher for conferences with parents
- Encourage the new teacher to document parent communications carefully

Is talking about leaving the teaching profession?
- Have a heart-to-heart talk with the new teacher about his/her thinking
- Determine the reason(s) for this thinking
- Suggest resources to help with frustrations
- Consider that this decision may be appropriate for this person

Needs help saying "No" to requests to take on additional responsibilities?
- Help the new teacher understand that it's okay to say "No"
- Encourage his/her use of, "Let me think about it" as a response

Responses to the stem "What Do You Do When..." provided by Alexandria City Schools, VA, mentors.

Focus on Novice Teachers

Chapter IV

Stages of Development

As Terry Wildman and Jerry Niles point out, novice teachers are simultaneously teaching and learning to teach. That is so because while they may well be knowledgeable about their content and, in most cases, knowledgeable about learning theory, it is when they need to apply their knowledge that they can run into difficulties. There are stages that novice teachers move through as part of the learning and change process; mentors can, however, minimize the lows that novice teachers often feel when they discover that their passion for learning and for the content they are teaching is not enough to make them into successful teachers whose students all achieve at high levels. Mentors can maximize their mentoring time and energy by refining their own knowledge about those stages and their own skillfulness in identifying the underlying causes of novice teacher attitudes and behaviors.

There are multiple approaches to identifying the stages through which novices in any field move as they are learning to be competent in their work. The ASK Construct developed by this author and The Stages of First-Year Teaching developed by Ellen Moir at The University of Santa Cruz, California can guide mentors in identifying the stages or phases of development through which novice teachers move during their first years of teaching.

ASK Construct

We make decisions about how to proceed in our personal and professional lives based on our **attitudes, skills, and knowledge (ASK)**. These three variables cause us to move forward with, procrastinate about, or even avoid certain tasks. What appears to be an attitude problem can in fact be a lack of knowledge or lack of skillfulness in using acquired knowledge. Mastering the content we are to teach, using learning theory, and building a repertoire of strategies for connecting students with the content are the areas in which teachers must attain knowledge and build skillfulness. Novice teachers may well be knowledgeable about the content they are to teach, about learning theory, and even know a repertoire of ways to connect content and learners. Knowledge is not enough. A lack of skillfulness in identifying key concepts and generalizations and then chunking the content in age appropriate ways, applying the learning theory to the students who make up the class, and/or selecting strategies that would be the best match for the content and the learners can cause either the appearance of an attitude problem or an actual attitude problem. A knowledgeable and skillful mentor must diagnose the behaviors of novice teachers to identify the root cause of any challenges, concerns, or problems and intervene accordingly. When knowledge is the issue, mentors need to provide it in appropriate ways. When skillfulness is the cause of the problem, mentors need to identify ways to demonstrate appropriate decision-making or actions, help novice teachers task analyze situations, and reflect on what worked or did not work and why.

Stages of Development

Phases of First-Year Teaching

This model developed by Ellen Moir at The New Teacher Center at Santa Cruz identifies the sequence and most likely timing for the attitudes novice teachers hold and exhibit as they move through their first year of teaching. The graphic below and the new teacher comments on the following pages provide clear guidance for mentors in tracking the attitudes of their novice teachers. Given the additional pressures of parent conferences, grades, and formal observations, it is no wonder that new teachers move into a survival mode and become disillusioned with teaching in October and November. The complexities of planning a strong instructional program, creating efficient organizational systems, and attending to these additional responsibilities challenge their knowledge and skillfulness. Mentors are tasked with supporting novice teachers during these low periods, helping them move as quickly as possible into the rejuvenation and reflection stages, and promoting and celebrating the return to the anticipation stage at the end of the year. That return is essential if we want to retain our novice teachers. For more information on Moir's model visit www.newteachercenter.org.

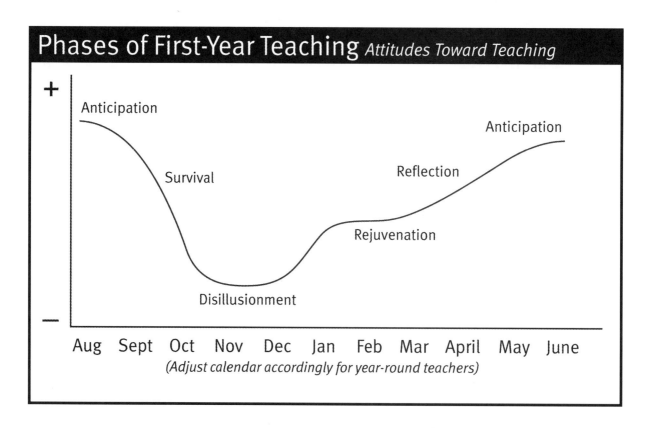

Phases of First-Year Teaching *Attitudes Toward Teaching*

Anticipation

Survival

Reflection

Anticipation

Rejuvenation

Disillusionment

Aug   Sept   Oct   Nov   Dec   Jan   Feb   Mar   April   May   June

(Adjust calendar accordingly for year-round teachers)

Through the Voice of New Teachers...
The Anticipation Stage

These exciting and optimistic statements are representative of new teachers' thinking as they approach the opening of the school year. We need to use the ideas and dreams reflected in these statements to help new teachers set realistic goals for the first quarter of school and identify action plans as well as mentor support systems that can help them move toward making their dreams a reality.

It may be useful to have the new teachers with whom you are working complete such a reflection and review the statements throughout the year whenever you need to refocus or whenever the new teachers need to be reminded of why they became teachers.

The following statements were written by teachers new to Greece Central School District, New York, during New Teacher Orientation. **The Tool for New Teachers entitled In Your Mind's Eye** found on page 239 was used to focus the thinking of those new teachers. These statements are in response to the prompts found in that tool.

> **Picture you, your students and the classroom learning environment next June.**
> **What would students know and be able to do as a result of having spent the school year with you?**
> **How will they be different? How will you be different?**
> **How would the classroom learning community be functioning?**
> **How will you measure your success?**

- My goal is to establish a cooperative learning environment where students work together to learn the basic building blocks of a second language. I want the students to be comfortable with experimentation and practice because the goal is to teach them communicative skills. I also hope to give them an appreciation of other cultures when many are at a point in their development when being different is perceived as undesirable.

- The students will know how to be responsible, interactive citizens in the community. They will leave my classroom with the tools needed to be successful outside of school. They will be different because they will be excited about graduating and moving on to life after high school. They will have the motivation to continue learning, whether in college or not. They will learn to be both independent and collaborative. They will respect each other with regards to individuality and character traits. I will be much different; each student will affect me in the class and I will learn from them everyday. I will be both happy and sad to see them go into the world. My success depends on if they can be confident leaving high school and if they have the tools to succeed. Their success will be measured by growth from start to finish.

Through the Voice of New Teachers...
The Anticipation Stage

- I would like to see a cohesive working environment that includes independent learning, making connections to the real world, successful group relationships, the ability to question their environment and see how they can make a difference, and leads to success on the Regents.

- In June, I envision a classroom with students enthusiastically helping other students to learn. I envision students feeling empowered by the skills they have mastered. I envision skilled learners who know how they learn best. I can see in my mind's eye a room with no student left behind, no student who fears reading or writing, and no student who fears stepping out in the learning environment. The students will respond to my cues and push themselves toward success. The students will be ready and eager to move on to 8th grade. A positive atmosphere will reign.

- I want my students to gain confidence in their activities to learn a second language. This will facilitate their actual learning and acquisition. I want them to gain appreciation for cultures outside of their own and at the same time learn how to step away from themselves and see themselves through the eyes of other cultures. I think this exposure to language and culture will give them a different perspective by the end of the year. I will be different as I was affected by each of my students. Through them I will learn how to improve my lessons and I will consider things from their perspectives. Beyond the required tests, I think success will be measured at the end if the students gain a more worldly outlook and satisfaction of learning how to speak another language.

- By June I see my students self-motivated, inquisitive, and applying skills taught throughout the year to answer questions they may have. I see student-run book talks that deal not only with the basics of a book (i.e. theme, character, and setting) but also the underlying, complex issues in novels. I hear them linking material from the book to their own lives. In science I see my 'thought box' full of questions from students concerning items related to the subject matter. In math I see them working in groups to solve concrete, real life math problems with a number of possible solutions. I also hear thoughtful discussions that show students listening to each other.

- The students and I will have created a positive learning environment in which we are all supported to take the risks necessary to grow as learners and individuals. Each student will have moved towards a positive identity formation for their life here as an English speaker, while continuing to develop and value the language and cultures they bring.

Through the Voice of New Teachers...
The Anticipation Stage

- I will be a teacher who is reflective and able to adapt to fit the needs of the learners, proud of the students and their emotional and educational development, confident in her ability to grow as a leader, and confident that she has made a difference in the lives of her students.

- In June, the children and I will have established a community in which everyone feels comfortable. They will work together and help one another to ensure the success of all of their classmates. They will have gained confidence in their abilities. They will have experienced and enjoyed hands-on learning. They will be able to tell what they have learned and why it is important they have learned that.

- I would hope the environment would be one of enthusiastic learners sharing in the responsibility of learning. Students would be teaching one another as well as me. I would like to have a better understanding through additional learning, reading, and training of how to provide an environment and lesson plans to encourage those attributes stated above. The assessment would hopefully be observing a classroom during a lesson and these attributes would be obvious.

- The classroom environment is orderly but relaxed. They are respectful of me and each other. They know each others' names. They work easily in groups and stay on-task even if I am not in their near vicinity. They know the day's objective and are used to the format of essential questions guiding classroom learning. They have a clear understanding of much of world history; it 'hangs together' for them, and is integrated by not only the overarching essential questions but also by the common thread of art and literature that people of all time periods have created. They are familiar with the state assessment and its format. They are confident they can pass, but also knowing it is not a complete assessment of what they have learned in my class.

- Come June, my goal is to be graduating a class of 22 kindergarten students who can read and write above grade level. The students will be cooperative and understand routines of the classroom. I will be a completely different person who will most likely be heartbroken my first class is moving on. My success in this first year will be measured through the reading of my students, as well as their writing ability. I see my classroom as a place with a safe environment for risk taking.

- At the end of the school year, I hope to be proud of my accomplishments as a first year teacher as well as my students being proud of me. This pride will come from the success of my students throughout the year in academics and their personal lives inside and outside of school. The difference in my students

Through the Voice of New Teachers...
The Anticipation Stage

and me in June will be our confidence in ourselves and one another. They will be confident in their understanding of the material because they have become confident in my teaching, and I will be confident in them and myself. I will measure my own and their success in June based on whether the learning environment is one that enables us all to succeed in the last few weeks of school in our Regents Math class.

- ESOL students will be comfortable in their classroom climate using reading, writing, listening, and speaking skills to participate in group activities, learn independently, explore and inquire and express in written language (pictorially or orthographically) ideas and concepts that are similar to their native speaking peers. I expect to accomplish this goal through collaboration with classroom teachers on creating individualized learning goals for ESOL students that complement and enhance content area objectives of the mainstream teacher. I will be different because I will have learned what works and doesn't work in facilitating second language acquisition and how to work effectively with others.

- Students will know that not all learning is free. Sometimes it comes at the cost of having to think and seek out answers on your own. Some of my students will have a new friend and someone who will always welcome them for guidance, collaboration and friendship. My classroom will be a place where students can feel comfortable learning in a variety of ways. The students will find that my classroom extends outside of the building to the environment around us. I want my students to work as a team, not as individuals. I want us to seek out answers together.

Through the Voice of New Teachers...
Survival and Disillusionment Stages

The statements and questions found on the next few pages reflect a huge change in perspective from the optimistic statements made by novice teachers before the beginning of the school year. They now realize that their enthusiasm for the content and for the learning process is not enough to do the complex work necessary for all students to learn well. The knowledge and the incredibly positive attitudes they brought into the classroom now need to be augmented by skillfulness in many areas. While many of the statements may sound like attitude problems, the reality is that lack of either knowledge or skills is causing most of the problems. Many of the statements and questions are, in fact, desperate pleas for help.

See **Chapter IV, Mentor-New Teacher Interactions** for supportive steps mentors can take as they work with new teachers before and as they move into these stages. Strong mentor support during August and September will not eliminate the sense of being overwhelmed that new teachers experience but it can minimize it. See also **Chapter VI, Mentoring Calendar**, for explicit recommendations about what actions to take during the months of October through December when new teachers are wondering why in the world they ever thought they wanted to be teachers.

If you are working with new teachers who insist everything is "fine," you can use these lists as a starting point for discussions. Sometimes new teachers are hesitant to admit that they are struggling, sometimes they simply believe that this is the way it is supposed to be, and other times they don't know how to articulate or categorize the struggles they are experiencing.

Personal
- New students always want to be recognized, so do new teachers. Communicate to teachers what we are doing right.
- I need to know if what I am doing is right. I know I need improvement in something, but I need a pat on the back also.
- I appreciate all of the advice and suggestions, but how about some feedback on what we do right?
- When will it get easier? I feel like I am going insane.
- Do you have tips for how to stay approachable, relaxed, positive, friendly with peers when you're really stressed, running, and distracted?

Through the Voice of New Teachers...
Survival and Disillusionment Stages

Curriculum and Instruction

- As a science teacher I have multiple preps which include accelerated students and lab. I have a rotating schedule so some days I have 4 preps. I need assistance with this.
- How do I learn or make the transition from planning day to day, to at least a few days?
- I need more information about mapping the curriculum across the year.
- How many days should I plan at a time?
- How do I get ahead in planning, grading, and copying?
- How do I plan for the upcoming weeks instead of day to day?
- I need help planning my schedule because I have two grade levels. It's a challenge learning both curriculums, trying to push-in, and finding time to meet with my entire caseload's teachers.
- How can you create planning time when there doesn't seem to be any?
- How do I set up independent reading projects?
- I need help dealing with multiple preparations.
- Where do you find materials needed to teach lessons? I find I need to spend tremendous amounts of time after school, evenings, and weekends finding the materials needed.
- I need help with the timing of lessons so that I can provide closure. We always run out of time; if we carry over to the next day, some of the impact is lost.
- How do I internalize all the material because there's so much?

Organizational Systems

- How can I be more organized especially in dealing with student absences?
- How do I deal with teaching in multiple classrooms that are far apart?
- I would love some suggestions about how to best handle teaching each class in a different room. How can I set up each room so that it has my personal touch in terms of appropriate decor/organizational systems, etc. How can I do this without creating a huge amount of work for me and without getting in the way of all other teachers using those rooms?
- What are some other ways I can organize materials so that students don't need to go back and forth to their cubbies, yet not keep a cluttered table?
- How can I organize my enormous number of e-mail messages?
- This was the first day I felt unprepared. I had continuous distractions and my planning time got swallowed up. Does this happen occasionally to everyone?
- Please help with grading procedures/systems? How many grades should I be giving? How often should I review grades with a student?
- When will I ever feel like I am organized?

Through the Voice of New Teachers...
Survival and Disillusionment Stages

- How do I manage my time to leave time to organize? My papers are currently exploding all over my desk.
- I need systems to make prep time be more efficient.
- I'm still working on organization. How can I catch up when I'm getting behind and have lots of piles to go through?
- I have systems I would like to use, but am still having a hard time finding the time to use them.
- Students forget to bring proper books and pencils to class. How can I fix that?
- How do you help keep kids organized?
- I need to work on my learning centers. How can I better organize my classroom set up so that my centers are evenly spaced in the room?
- How do you keep track of finished assignments so that you are not shuffling papers all the time?
- How do I organize my materials thematically and subject wise?
- How do I organize my district materials?
- I am still stumped by the amount of paperwork you are given. I do not know how many files to make and or when to get rid of stuff!
- How do I organize the room for community building?
- How do I organize the physical space for different grouping situations?
- I start out the year organized, but I can't seem to stay that way. How can I keep from getting "bogged down?"

Students

- What are some techniques to use on a kindergarten student who runs out of the room on a day-to-day basis?
- How do I get kids to work together when they don't get along?
- How can I effectively help students who are habitually absent?
- What can I do to motivate students who say over and over they do not care?
- What do you do with a child who, no matter what consequences you give him/her, the behavior doesn't change?
- How do I get my kids to settle down and stay quiet at the end of the day after recess? I am talking about the whole class, not just a few!
- How do you motivate the kids who tell you they don't want to learn, they don't care, and refuse to participate?
- How do you deal with teenagers who refuse to do any work or participate in any way?
- How do you deal with the "problem" student who doesn't respond to firm responses, detentions, and parent phone calls?
- I know you are supposed to focus on the 95% of students who are good, but how do you remove or ignore the other 5% when they are monopolizing the class?

Through the Voice of New Teachers...
Survival and Disillusionment Stages

- How can you instill patience and respect among students when trying to help them all?
- How do I get kids to take responsibility for their learning?
- How do you handle students who are in In-School Suspension? What work do you give them if you did group activities?
- How do I keep a class centered on learning when I have one student who is "melting down."
- Kids are not trying to learn. They are just going through the motions. There seems to be a lot of disorganization.
- I feel like I have some kids who are slipping through the cracks. I can't seem to keep on top of them. They are absent quite often and when in class, they are so far behind. They won't come in after school. I only have them for science for a 45-minute class period.
- I do not know how to deal with bullying, name-calling, teasing, and making fun of people. All of these are occurring in my classroom.
- What do I do with "blurt out kids?"
- How do I keep wandering students in one place?

Colleagues

- What is the best way to plan with teachers with whom you "push-in?"
- How do I go about having a chance to co-teach when the teachers I am working with have over 30 years of teaching in the school system and they don't seem to want to include me?
- I need time to plan with the teachers in my area. How do I find time? I feel like a fish out of water.
- Do I have a mentor?

School and Systems Issues

- Consider scheduling more time for teachers to plan and instruct and less time for meetings. I have a meeting after school every day this week and one before school. I feel overwhelmed!
- How do I get more reading materials to correctly implement guided reading in my room?
- How much of a budget am I allowed so that I can order books of interest pertaining to middle school students and their non-academic problems and social needs?
- How can I get more resources for my room without having to spend my own money all of the time?

Through the Voice of New Teachers...
Survival and Disillusionment Stages

- I would like more money for supplies, no questions asked.
- Could the district provide assistance with supplies and help with lessons for the first month? My room lacked many basic supplies at the beginning of the year.
- How do I get money for class supplies? Does it vary from building to building?
- How can I get supplies for a brand new classroom with no money? Requests have been made, but seem to be at the bottom of the list.
- The way supplies are purchased is very inconvenient. You have to make a list and then you receive them. Many of the items I need are related to my subject area and cannot be purchased at Staples. I've spent $100 out of my own pocket. There should be a budget per teacher.
- I am concerned that I ask four different people the same question and get four different answers. I wish there was more consistency.
- How can we improve the downward communication?
- When will the meetings end?

Parents and Community
- How do you get the parents to understand that you can only do so much, their child needs to be responsible for something?
- When I speak with parents, how do I convey how necessary it is that the students do work every night?
- Any suggestions for dealing with difficult parents?
- What are some best ways of handling confrontational parents who think their children are not at fault or responsible for the grade they received?
- How do you get the parents to understand that you can only do so much?
- I would like suggestions for managing parent contact. It seems to be taking a lot of time.

Through the Voices of New Teachers...
Reflection Stage
Lessons Learned

- Understanding the major concepts is more important than the memorization of details.
- Ask students to create daily goals when coming in for extra help. This helps us make good use of our time.
- I slowly, but surely, created file folders to organize my materials.
- The results of the in-depth responses to the reflection on their own work made me realize that students really appreciate opportunities to self-evaluate, and therefore, I gave them many more and varied forms of reflection on their academic growth.
- The stress of "re-inventing wheels" has taught me to collaborate more with other eighth grade teachers.
- Seeing the students begin to use reading strategies independently encouraged me to integrate strategies into every unit continuously rather than as exam prep or in problem areas only.
- The difficulties students have with elaboration has made me aware that I need to create more rigorous warm-ups that are more than just conceptual anticipatory sets, but also target this skill.
- Assess not only at the end of a unit, but daily throughout the unit.
- Be there for the students outside of the classroom, for example, during lunch, after school, sporting events and school functions.
- I ask students for their feedback after I try different teaching techniques.
- Instead of yelling or directing commands at students who are uncooperative, I say something on the order of, "John, you seem pretty angry right now. What happened?" The students will then de-escalate when they start to tell you why they are so upset or they will correct you and tell you the emotion they are feeling. By the end of the conversation, they don't see you as mean or demanding, but as a caring person who is interested in them.
- I gave students responsibility to "teach" each other as much as they can.
- I used students' interests to motivate learning.
- Immediate engagement at the beginning of the class.
- I learned to stagger project dates. Also assign sub-groups a certain day to turn in their journals.
- Use audio books to allow lower level students the opportunity to enjoy literature.
- Try to call parents when I see any major changes in their child.

Through the Voices of New Teachers...
Reflection Stage
Lessons Learned

- Use Clock Buddies for group work.
- I e-mailed parents about positive progress.
- Have students create charts, diagrams and matrix instead of generating my own.
- Recognize a class's hard work publicly and frequently.
- Offer personal connections and stories. Laugh aloud and laugh a lot. Enjoy the students.
- I changed my guidelines at semester break.
- I tried to listen more.
- I took advantage of the excellent learning/professional opportunities to better myself as an educator.
- I used a variety of graphic organizers.
- Take the time to build student-student, student-teacher, and parent-teacher relationships.
- Provide modification for one and provide all students the opportunity to use the same modification.
- I worked with test taking strategies when the data showed students were missing answers due to misreading for key ideas.
- I began working with individual students after low test scores.
- I realized I didn't have to know how to do everything.
- Typically when Special Education students are struggling, there is a good chance that several regular education students are also struggling.
- Regular parent communication is very helpful. E-mail is best.
- Document everything!
- The "bad students" need to be complimented and hear what they are doing that is right.
- Time spent with students in a non-instructional setting is often more educational.
- I have increased the use of peer evaluation on writing assignments.
- I have given students more choices for unit projects to accommodate a variety of learning styles and interest.
- I found better results when I focused less on multiple choice questions and more on written assessments.
- I have increased my awareness of male students' struggles.
- Technology has become a big part of my class.
- Students work better after being helped over a first hurdle, so I moved more quickly to help students encounter success during an exercise.

Through the Voices of New Teachers...
Reflection Stage
Lessons Learned

- I realize that bringing my life into the classroom is important for scaffolding for students who have not had experiences to build upon. This helps students when it comes to testing.
- By rearranging books, students thought they were new and would sign them out.
- You can learn what a student knows without giving them a test.
- Find a positive in everything.
- To increase student results, increase expectations.
- I gained parent influence and support by contacting them first.
- I relaxed more.
- Use a bar graph to measure homework completion. Have a class by class competition.
- I changed my homework policy from not accepting late work to accepting all late work as homework that was still worth doing.
- Have each student answer essential questions on paper rather than verbally.
- I am more comfortable, aware, and confident in dealing with parents.
- Learned to use as many visuals and models as possible.
- I contact team members more readily for help or advice.
- I take more risks and try new things.
- Reading responses are now in the form of a personal letter to me. Students who do not like to write do like to tell me about their books.
- Conversations about books make reading more fun for some struggling readers.
- Spelling lists now come from content units and student personal need.
- I created three centers for each group each day thus giving them "something to do" when they were finished with their work.
- I moved my reading area near my desk and had a signal (wearing a scarf) when the students were not allowed to interrupt my group.
- I have a better organizational plan when dealing with many different students at different grade levels with varying needs (use of color-coded folders).
- I used journals for student reflection of daily activities. This is a good connection with parents.
- I used technology to motivate and engage students.
- I learned to take data on children's skills and reassess after breaks to check for regression.
- I learned how to share information and data in a more effective way.
- I learned how to analyze data and use as needed.

Through the Voice of New Teachers...
Reflection Stage

- My students now know how to think critically, how to approach different reading/writing tasks, and how to use specific skills essential to particular genres. They also know how to interact socially in a group, how to approach tough decisions/choices, and how to reflect on their progress.

- It was a great year! There were smooth transitions, learning was rigorous, and the students enjoyed the variety of my lessons as well my enthusiasm. I have learned to change my approach to instruction. I measure my success by their comments and their work.

- I feel my students have not only learned math, but also some life skills that will help them throughout their lives. I think my students and I have developed a good relationship which helps the learning community function well. I measure our success by how daily lessons, assessments and discussions go.

- In the beginning of this year, I was nervous and overwhelmed. "Would I teach them all they need to know?" By the end of this year, I feel they have made so many accomplishments. They are reading and writing! They are confident! I measure their confidence by their skills and their parents' input.

- The students see connections between their lives and the different parts of learning. I flow with the punches better. My responses are more measured.

- I learned that a respectful classroom atmosphere is essential. Critical thinking is fun; it reveals secrets. Language is powerful. I care about my students. I want each one to succeed. I want to collaborate more.

- My students know that they are successful in school because they changed their attitudes. They didn't believe they could "learn how to learn." Their academic grades proved they accomplished this feat. They are also feeling successful because they have new friends, laugh more, feel good about presenting in front of their peers, and our classroom seems like a second home.

- The students are more independent learners, better problem solvers and have increased self-esteem and confidence. They are independent thinkers and think outside the box. They are vested in their own learning and have created a classroom environment together.

Through the Voice of New Teachers...
Anticipation for Next Year

- I will put more responsibility on the students. The students will tell me the process and explain the concepts. I will have rubrics prepared ahead of time for the students. I will decide on finals in September or at the beginning of the course.

- I will prepare for the final exam in September.

- I will expect and accept only the best work from my students.

- I will map the curriculum for the year.

- I want to get more organized. I will read the math and science manuals more in depth. I want to hear what others did to obtain success.

- I will display exemplars.

- I want to be able to be more organized at the beginning of the school year with a long-term plan. Also, I want to be more assertive in becoming a part of my students' lives and of the school community.

- I will take time in the beginning of the year to learn their learning styles so they can be incorporated into lessons.

- I will implement the pages and pages of notes that I kept throughout the year.

- I need to be more organized with meetings/agendas, etc. I also need to be better at follow-through with parents, team members, etc.

- I will have units and essential questions planned well ahead of where I am in my teaching. I also want to have the labs in place for the science classes.

- I want to revisit each unit to backward plan and revise essential questions. I'll look up more supplemental material and collaborate more! I also want to work on inclusion modifications.

- I will set up home visits, attend community events, and look for parental involvement.

Through the Voice of Mentors...
Survival Questions You'll Be Asked

- How do you fill out sick/personal leave forms as well as professional and travel reimbursement forms?
- Who provides instructional materials and books?
- What time does school start?
- Where do I get supplies?
- When are grades due?
- Where is the cafeteria?
- How much is a teacher's lunch?
- How do you find the time?
- Where is the bathroom, the copier, the lunchroom?
- What do I do with this kid?
- How do I get...?
- How do you take attendance?
- What about health insurance?
- How much homework do I give?
- When do we get paid?
- How about fire drills?
- What do I do with all this old stuff?
- When do I turn in lesson plans?
- What do I do with a problem child?
- What are the cafeteria procedures?
- How do we use the classroom phone and voice mail?
- What assessment tools do we use here?
- I've heard three different responses to the same question. Whom do I believe?
- Do I grade everything?

Consult **Chapter VIII, Organizational Systems for You, the Learners, and the Classroom,** in *Why Didn't I Learn This in College?* for assistance with those questions that are not district/school specific and for additional issues to surface with new teachers.

Through the Voice of Veteran Teachers...
What I Wish I Had Known That First Year

- Who was REALLY in charge...the chain of command
- List of district and school personnel to know and how to contact them
- I was not going to accomplish everything!
- Have students bring in waterless hand-sanitizer to keep next to tissues so YOU don't get sick!
- It is all right to say, "HELP!"
- That I did not have to be perfect
- Just ASK!!!
- Awareness of the sports program so I could have gone to watch my students participate
- It's okay to make mistakes because you learn from them!
- A comfort level to know that it's "okay" to ask questions without feeling judged
- Other first year teachers are experiencing similar frustrations
- Calendar of events prior to start of school
- Get to know the custodial workers
- Save things (i.e., examples of projects) to use next year. You won't have to stay as late.
- Acknowledge those who make a difference to me...that is, they reach out to me!
- Child study process/special education referral process
- To be patient and know that it will get better
- How to organize all the paperwork
- What should go into the grade book and what can be left out
- Supervision and evaluation process including the criteria
- Pick your battles
- Which personal items to take home and which to leave in the room
- Organize and sort information as you receive it
- How to be flexible
- Achieve personal/professional balance
- Be their teacher, not their friend or parent
- Do not take it personally
- Maintain confidentiality
- Save receipts for taxes
- Ways/systems for learning and remembering student and colleague names
- Don't spend all your money at the teachers' store. Decorate your room with student work.

Through the Voice of Mentors...
Welcome Aboard Kit Items

Many of these items can be gathered from the school supply room. See page 212 in *Why Didn't I Learn This in College?* for more ideas.

- Daily planner
- Hand sanitizer
- Tissues
- Frequently used phone numbers
- Stickers
- Sharpie markers
- Homework charts
- E-Z up clips or Stikki clips
- Pass sign
- Black, green, and red pens
- Coupon book with no expiration date with coupons for items such as
  - A hug
  - A listening ear
  - One walk around the block
  - One student to be sent to your room
  - One new instructional strategy for...
  - Help with grading one set of papers
  - A shoulder to lean on
  - A cup of coffee or tea
  - Problem solving session
- Chocolate candy
- Band-Aids
- Tylenol
- Tums
- Paper clips
- Tape
- Post-Its
- Pens and pencils
- Stapler
- Glue sticks
- Department list
- Substitute kit or recommended list of contents
- Change for the soda machine
- Map of building with teachers names written in classrooms
- Map of area
- Thank you notes
- Notes to use for correspondence with parents

Adapted from lists generated by Alexandria City Public Schools, VA mentors

Mentoring Calendar

Chapter V

The Mentoring Calendar

The Mentoring Calendar is provided as a tool for all members of the school community. While many of the suggestions can be used by mentors, there are many that the administrative staff, other teachers, parents, and community members can implement or support as part of a comprehensive mentoring program.

No one mentor is expected to implement all the recommendations on The Mentoring Calendar. Actions that match the requirements or expectations of district programs, and those that refer to the responsibility of mentors to be positive representatives of the district and role models for new teachers, are not optional. Other actions are listed as **possibilities for mentors to consider.** In order for mentors to best support the new teachers with whom they should work, they should base additional interactions on continuing dialogue with the new teachers, student data, and professional observations. **Mentors should read through the monthly listings, decide which are appropriate for the teachers they are mentoring, decide who should complete the tasks, and then implement or facilitate the implementation of the actions.**

Mentors in schools on a modified or year-round calendar can use the sequence of actions and interactions but will need to retitle each month to match their school schedule.

Recommendations for each month are organized into eight categories which capture the potential challenges and concerns of teachers new to a school or district. The categories are as follows:

- **Personal:** This section addresses life beyond the work place as well as creating a welcoming work environment where new teachers feel a part of both the learning community and the social fabric of the school.

- **Professional:** This section addresses both the professional development and learning that teachers continue throughout their careers and the human resource issues of contracts, finances, benefits, etc.

- **Curriculum, Instruction, and Assessment:** This section addresses the daunting task of knowing what students are supposed to know and know how to do as a result of the instructional program designed and implemented by their teachers.

- **Organizational Systems:** This section addresses systems for organizing professional papers, instructional materials, student materials, and the classroom.

The Mentoring Calendar

- **Students:** This section addresses systems for getting to know the students as learners and as people, for building a learning community, and for developing a repertoire of ways to deal with unmet expectations that are not grounded in compliance and control but rather in increasing student learning.

- **Colleagues:** This section addresses issues of collegial collaboration including working with the administrative staff, teaching staff, and support staff in professional and productive ways in the interest of student learning.

- **School and School System:** This section addresses the policies and procedures, written and unwritten, for the operation of the organization.

- **Parents and Community:** This section addresses the need to work collaboratively and proactively with parents as partners in their children's education.

An additional feature of **The Mentoring Calendar** is a section entitled **Especially for Special Educators**. It lists recommended mentoring strategies to provide special educators the support they need to deal with unique issues they face in doing their work.

Mentoring Calendar
August
Personal

- Contact new teachers as soon as possible. It is best to contact them, and even meet with them, prior to new teacher orientation or the opening of school work/planning days. If that is not possible, contact them at the earliest opportunity.
- Share as many forms of personal contact information as you are willing to share.
- Make a welcome bag or basket. See list of possible contents on page 85.
- Greet new teachers on first day of orientation and escort them to first meetings.
- If the new teachers are moving into the area, provide information and assistance in locating a place to live, identifying shopping areas, doctors' offices, and city offices.
- If the teachers are new to the area, provide information about recreational facilities including gyms, restaurants, and parks.
- Take or obtain photographs of new teachers, create a **Our New Colleagues** poster, and post it in a prominent place for all staff members to see when they return to school.
- Use old yearbook pictures to create a pictorial display of returning staff members.
- Create a **Who's Who** at your school by putting together a short biography of each staff member, new and veteran. List educational background including degrees, certifications, professional affiliations and appropriate personal information such as hobbies and history. Provide copies to all staff members.
- Plan an off-site meeting of all new teachers and mentors where all can get acquainted and "off-the-record" questions can be answered in an informal but professional way.

Professional

- Explain the induction and mentoring program. Include what they can expect from you and their responsibilities as well. Inquire about their hopes and dreams for their work this year. Use **Tool: In My Mind's Eye** on page 239 to capture their thinking.
- Identify the problems, concerns, and challenges that are the biggest issues for them at this point. Use one of the **Tools: Challenges and Concerns for Novice Teachers** on pages 240-241.

Mentoring Calendar
August continued...

- Discuss professional dress.
- Go over payroll and benefits. If payroll and benefits are explained at the district level, check for understanding; if not covered in other settings, provide sufficient information for the new teacher to make informed decisions about direct deposit, 401Ks, medical plans, etc. This may be the first time a novice teacher has dealt with these issues.

Curriculum, Instruction, and Assessment

- Debrief all district and school curriculum meetings. Some terms and examples may have had no meaning for new teachers; in any case, check for understanding by asking explicit questions that the new teachers can answer only if they understood what was said or written.
- Fill in any gaps in the overview of curriculum not covered by district or school meetings.
- Locate and provide access to, either in hard copy or on-line, district standards, pacing guides and other curriculum documents.
- Use the pacing guide and the district standards to assist the novice teacher in chunking the year. Use **Tools for Instructional Planning** on pages 323-357.
- Based on the year-long outline and the goals the new teachers have for the learning community they want to create, assist the novice teacher in creating detailed plans for the first week of school. See page 187 in **Why Didn't I Learn This in College?**
- Do overview of the standardized testing program as it relates to and is aligned with curriculum and instruction.

Organizational Systems

- Set up a card file, three-ring binder, or online communication system through which you can provide the novice teachers organizational tips throughout the year.
- Point out the classroom organization tips found on pages 222-236 in **Why Didn't I Learn This in College?**
- Explain procedures for attendance, e-mail, voice mail, etc.
- Help clean out "old" stuff in room.
- Check classrooms for furniture and supplies.
- Collect materials needed by new teachers.
- Coordinate with department chair, grade level, or team leader to ensure that the new teachers have what everyone else has.

Mentoring Calendar
August continued...

- Discuss and share examples of bus/hall passes, fire drill sheets, referral sheets. See page 209 in *Why Didn't I Learn This in College?*
- Ensure novice teacher has either a print or on-line calendar. As appropriate, provide one with important dates already placed on it. Go over district and school calendars. Have new teachers write important meeting dates and due dates in either their print or on-line calendars.
- "Trade Spaces." Go into each other's rooms and discuss room arrangement. See pages 237-240 in *Why Didn't I Learn This in College?*

Students

- Go over the student demographics. Describe any recent changes.
- Discuss building a learning community in the classroom. See pages 25-31 in *Why Didn't I Learn This in College?*
- Explore how to establish and implement procedures and routines with students. See pages 29-30 and 224-235 in *Why Didn't I Learn This in College?*

Colleagues

- Work with principal in planning the induction program for your novice teacher. Keep her/him informed of what you are doing as a mentor.
- Explain to colleagues the role they can play in welcoming new teachers and helping them be successful and contributing faculty members.
- Introduce new teachers to all appropriate staff members. See list on page 204 in *Why Didn't I Learn This in College?*
- Explain the support services available and provide a list of the names of providers at the school and district level.
- Identify staff members who have expertise in particular areas and who would be willing to help the new teachers.
- Be explicit about which colleagues will be more than willing to provide strong support.
- Provide new teachers with a map of the school with teacher and staff member names written in their main work area or classroom.

School and School System

- Provide overview of procedures and policies. Use the district's handbook for new teachers if available in print or on-line. If not, see pages 199-202 in *Why Didn't I Learn This in College?* for procedures and policies to consider.

Mentoring Calendar
August continued...

- Provide a map of the school layout and take the new teachers on a building tour. See page 205 in *Why Didn't I Learn This in College?* for points to note.
- If possible, take a tour around the district to other schools which the students have attended or will attend and to district offices. At the very least provide a map of the district with important buildings highlighted.
- Identify whom to call for what at the district level. Provide a list of names and telephone numbers or email addresses.
- Explain which resources will and will not be provided.

Parents and Community

- Assist in planning early home contact.
- Take on tour of community pointing out demographics and local institutions of note.
- Discuss the importance of keeping parents informed about curriculum, course content, and important dates throughout the year.
- Explain how community resources including the school/business partner and other programs outside the school system can provide additional support to the school.
- Explain how email as well as classroom and school web sites are used as communication tools.

Especially for Special Educators

- Provide an overview of the special education services offered in the school and in the district.
- Explain the referral process and pre-referral process used in the district with details about how the process operates in the school.
- Supply a list of key personnel at the school and district, their responsibilities, and contact information for each of them.
- Explain and provide models of paperwork requirements, procedures, and time lines for child study, evaluations, and IEPs.
- Introduce the technology used to prepare IEPs with modeling and coaching to follow.
- Describe in a professional but truthful manner the norms of interaction between general education and special education staff members.
- Provide inventory of supplies and instructional materials available in the department and explain the process for ordering additional supplies and instructional material.

Mentoring Calendar
August continued...

- Assist them in accessing general education curriculum materials including both student texts and teacher's manuals.
- Discuss strategies for early contact with parents and suggest setting up meetings to introduce themselves and to establish a positive context for future interactions.
- Provide an overview of the norms and practices around curricular adaptations, inclusion, and co-teaching.
- Assist the new teachers in reviewing their caseloads and reading IEPs.
- Review accommodation forms and guide the new teachers in completing the forms.
- Discuss with the new special education teachers the best way to introduce themselves and their students to the general education teachers with whom they and the students will be working.
- Either provide or help the new teachers prepare a calendar of when IEPs and TRAs are due.
- Discuss role of teaching assistant, one-on-one aides, and related service providers.
- Check on their experience with and skills for working with paraprofessionals and provide guidance as appropriate.

Mentoring Calendar
September
Personal

- Review August list and complete any points that you were unable to complete in August or that are more appropriately done in September.
- Empathize with all the paperwork and the unending meetings.
- Stop by classroom daily to say hello.
- Put personal notes in their mailboxes.
- Check, without prying, to see that teachers new to the area are happy with the life they are creating beyond the school community. As appropriate, assist in resolving any issues.
- Organize informal and voluntary gatherings for new teachers to network with other new teachers.
- Remember to accompany new teachers to meetings and sit with them in the meetings.

Professional

- Have new teachers complete a self-assessment or needs assessment to help you identify areas of challenge and concern. See pages 242-261.
- Using data from the needs assessment, set collaborative goals for the mentoring relationship. Revisit those goals at least monthly.
- Explain the teacher performance evaluation system by going over the process and the criteria.
- Help new teachers prepare for the first observation cycle by doing some form of peer observation together and discussing the teaching and learning using the district's teacher performance criteria. See pages 308-311 for possible peer observation formats.
- Assist with the start of a portfolio as required for the teacher performance evaluation system. If available, share exemplars created by colleagues.
- Have new teachers do a self-assessment(s) and then establish realistic and focused professional goals for the first quarter. See pages 244-265.
- Keep new teachers apprised of professional development opportunities.
- Remind the new teachers to refrain from discussing private issues with students, parents, or colleagues in the lounge and other public places.
- Be a role model by always speaking professionally about administrative staff, support staff, and other teachers. Refrain from gossip!

Mentoring Calendar
September continued...

Curriculum, Instruction, and Assessment
- If not completed in August, review the learning standards and the pacing guide and help the new teachers plan the first week of school. See page 187 in **Why Didn't I Learn This in College?**
- Provide ready-to-use and field tested lessons or units based on the district's learning standards. Explain the planning process used and select significant components to emphasize.
- Reiterate your "open files" policy.
- Use district lesson plan formats or the lesson and unit design templates in **Chapter X, Tools for New Teachers**, as discussion points for the planning process.
- Discuss interims.
- Revisit curriculum map and/or pacing guide.

Organizational Systems
- Ask how paper-flow management systems are working.
- As appropriate, share the strategies for organizing instructional materials found on pages 210-212 in **Why Didn't I Learn This in College?**
- Share strategies for organizing all the paper work to and from the school and district offices. See pages 207-209 in **Why Didn't I Learn This in College?**
- Go over procedures for collecting fees
- Explain the after school bus system.
- Assist in organizing the classroom as needed. See pages 160-169.
- Provide guidance, and if available, exemplars of substitute folders or kits. See pages 220-221 in **Why Didn't I Learn This in College?** for guidelines.

Students
- Provide new teachers with a calendar of extracurricular events in which their students might be participating. Encourage them to attend a few to get to know their students outside the classroom.
- Brainstorm strategies for learning all students' names by the end of the first week or two of school.
- Discuss community building activities that work well with students of this age in this school. See pages 25-28 in **Why Didn't I Learn This in College?**

Mentoring Calendar
September continued...

Colleagues
- Remind colleagues of their role in seeking out and helping new teachers get established as positive and productive staff members.
- Go over policies, possibilities, and potential pitfalls of working with paraprofessionals.
- Discuss relationships and co-teaching with regular or special educators. See pages 269-287 in *Instruction for All Students*.
- Clarify discussion and decision points at faculty, team, and grade level meetings.
- Share your mentor "To Do" list with the principal.

School and School System
- Review procedures for fire drills and school crisis plans.
- Continue to ask about needed resources.
- Examine how new teachers are managing their time.
- Check on non-instructional duties assigned to new teachers and discourage them from volunteering for additional duties for at least the first semester.
- Verify that the new teachers' voice mail and email systems are functioning smoothly.
- Explain how special education referral and pre-referral process works.
- Arrange for the new teacher to sit in on a child study process as an observer.

Parents and Community
- Ask about parent contacts and how they are going.
- Have new teachers listen in on your parent phone calls.
- Share newsletters and letters you sent home.
- Model "parents as partners" practices and discussions.
- Discuss Back-to-School Night agenda and presentation ideas. See pages 261-262 in *Why Didn't I Learn This in College?*
- Organize a panel of teachers to share Back-to-School Night strategies.

Especially for Special Educators
- Explain district policies about aligning IEP goals with district or state learning standards.
- Model preparing an IEP.
- Co-prepare an IEP.
- Coach the new teachers in the use of technology and specific software programs for IEP preparation.

Mentoring Calendar
September continued...

- Think aloud and model preparing paperwork for an IEP meeting.
- Model an IEP meeting.
- Co-facilitate an IEP meeting.
- Provide contact time and access to district special education coordinators so that new teachers can hear first hand the expectations for them and ask questions that can be answered in the moment.
- Discuss methods of documenting progress on meeting IEP goals and grading policies and procedures for special education students.
- Go over student performance on the previous year's standardized testing and discuss performance in relation to adequate yearly progress.

Mentoring Calendar
October

Personal

- Check on balance of work and life. Reality sets in during October and the long hours of preparation and grading begin to take their toll.
- Place cartoons or inspirational quotes about school, teaching, and students in the new teachers' mailboxes or on their desks.
- Bring a brown bag lunch to share and talk not only about school but the fall weather, sports, movies, and good books to read.
- Take a walk around the block together at lunch or after school.
- Attend a school extracurricular event together.

Professional

- Preview professional development opportunities and make suggestions as appropriate.
- Ensure that the new teachers are feeling informed and ready for the first round of formal observations.

Curriculum, Instruction, and Assessment

- Now that the new teachers know their students and their learning needs, revisit the pacing guide and corresponding lesson plans.
- Do an assessment or have the new teachers complete a self-assessment of how their classroom assessment repertoire is working. Use page 255 in this book, and pages 140-166 in *Why Didn't I Learn This in College?* as resources for this discussion.
- Introduce the new teachers to the cumulative records and the student achievement data on their students. Discuss with them how the student achievement data matches the classroom assessment data and how they can use both data sets to plan instruction.

Organizational Systems

- Review grade book and record keeping systems. Examine the efficiency and effectiveness of current review and grading of student work and the way the information provided on returned papers is used by students and teachers.
- Discuss time management both at school and during the after-school hours.

Mentoring Calendar
October continued...

Students

- Ask the new teachers to share stories about evidence of student learning that has been rewarding.
- Have the new teachers describe how students are becoming more comfortable with each other and with the learning process.
- Discuss concerns about students who are struggling and identify interventions that might work. Use pages 37-42 in *Why Didn't I Learn This in College?* as a resource.
- Go over learning profiles of students identified as special education students and assist the new teachers in scaffolding instruction for those students.
- Be sure that the new teachers are comfortable contacting building and district specialists for assistance. As appropriate, have the new teachers sit in on a meeting you hold with instructional specialists or accompany new teachers to their first meetings with building or district specialists.
- Discuss impact of Halloween, homecoming, and other special events on student learning.

Colleagues

- Check in with other mentors to seek and provide support for the mentoring process.
- Debrief department, grade level, team, and committee meetings. Answer questions about unknown terms or unclear processes. Be prepared to explain the rationale for or history behind comments and decisions.
- Invite the new teachers to join grade level or standards area groups to analyze student achievement data and to discuss how to use the information to inform instructional decisions.
- Arrange a meeting of classroom teachers and the special educators who support the learning of special needs students in the classroom. Design an agenda that helps the two get to know each other on a personal level and for each to better know how to make connections between the two programs for the learners.
- Have a conversation with the principal or other administrators to let them know the support you are providing.

Mentoring Calendar
October continued...

School and School System

- Explain which radio station announces late openings or school closings.
- Explain how teacher and student schedules operate when there are snow days or other emergency late openings or school closings..
- Discuss rationale and procedures around interims and intervention plans.
- Go over end of the grading period procedures and emphasize the importance of completing forms correctly and submitting them in a timely fashion. Explain systems that have worked for others.
- Discuss the school holiday policies with an emphasis on how Halloween is handled.
- Go over field trip procedures.
- Explain how book fairs are organized and why they are held in your school.

Parents and Community

- Explain the norms and procedures for parent conferences.
- Provide appropriate assistance with parent conferences. Use pages 259-260 and 263-264 in *Why Didn't I Learn this in College?* as resource materials.
- Discuss the pros and cons of having student led conferences.
- Share examples of letters and other communication home about conference schedule and purposes.
- Do a room tour and help teacher see the classroom through the eyes of parents. Ensure that learning standards and student work dominate.
- Brainstorm ways to stay on schedule during conferences.
- Discuss what to do should the conference become confrontational.
- If a new teacher is expecting a particularly challenging conference, role play the conference and if necessary, sit in on the conference.
- Suggest that general education teachers collaborate with special educators in planning and holding parent conferences of students they both teach.

Especially for Special Educators

- Review first few IEPs prepared by the new teachers and provide feedback on accuracy and completeness of document.
- Hold a planning conference for an IEP meeting, observe the IEP meeting, and provide feedback about how actual outcomes matched desired outcomes. Discuss implications for next IEP meeting.
- Facilitate the observation by the new teachers of students on their case load in the general education setting.
- Coach the new teachers around collaboration with general education teachers in the planning and holding of parent conferences of students they both teach.

Mentoring Calendar
November

Check October calendar to identify any areas of focus more appropriate for November given your school year calendar.

Personal

- Suggest to the new teachers that they walk out the door for Thanksgiving vacation with no school work in hand and that they use the break to rejuvenate and re-energize themselves with family and friends.
- If this is the new teachers' first major holiday away from family, brainstorm with them what they might do to minimize the loneliness and make the holiday fun and rewarding.
- Warn them that the weeks between Thanksgiving and the winter break are busy both professionally and personally. It is a time for exhaustion and possibly depression because of the seemingly insurmountable tasks to be accomplished.
- Monitor new teachers for fatigue and disillusionment.

Professional

- Check in with the new teachers to see if they need assistance in completing forms or requirements for certification.
- Review first quarter professional growth goals.
- Set professional growth goals for the second quarter.
- Review first quarter mentoring relationship goals and set new ones.
- Remind them to save receipts for tax purposes.
- Review professional development opportunities and requirements.
- Attend a professional development event with novice teacher.
- Co-observe another teacher's lesson and debrief.

Curriculum, Instruction, and Assessment

- Be sure that the new teachers do not fall into the turkey and Pilgrims trap. Help them make plans to maximize meaningful active learning experiences the day before Thanksgiving vacation and to refocus learning following the four-day weekend.

Mentoring Calendar
November continued...

Organizational Systems
- Use Procedural Potpourri found on pages 232-235 and 306-307 in **Why Didn't I Learn This in College?** to review the efficiency and effectiveness of classroom procedures and to identify new procedures to develop.

Students
- Discuss the impact of holidays, the athletic schedule, performing arts productions, and homecoming on school schedule and student learning.
- Assist new teachers in working with students who ask for letters of recommendation to accompany their college applications. Share some examples of letters others have written.

Colleagues
- Continue to engage the new teachers in collegial analysis and discussion of student achievement and classroom assessment data. Use pages 315-318 in this book as resources.
- Provide the principal with a summary of the professional goals set and met during the first quarter. Give an overview of the new teachers' second quarter professional goals and ask for support and resources as appropriate.
- Identify colleagues who would be willing to have the new teachers observe in their classrooms.

School and School System
- Discuss leave policy surrounding the Thanksgiving holiday.
- Ensure that grades are submitted in the appropriate format in a timely manner.
- Go over the spring standardized testing schedule. Provide the new teachers with any informational materials about the testing protocols.

Parents and Community
- If parent-teacher conferences are held in November, see October calendar for guidelines.
- Remind the new teachers that multiple positive and productive parental contacts before report cards are sent home result in far fewer questions about grades.
- Provide guideline for responding to parent questions/concerns about first quarter grades.
- Discuss strategies for dealing with parents who are upset about school issues. Use pages 263-264 in **Why Didn't I Learn This in College?** as a resource.

Mentoring Calendar
November continued...

Especially for Special Educators

- Ensure that new special educators who are the only new special educator in a given building have an opportunity to network with other new special educators in the district.
- Check in with the new special educators to ensure that their system for interacting on a regular basis with each of the general education teachers and other educators working with their students is working. Have them share evidence of successful collaboration.

Mentoring Calendar
December

Check the November and January calendars for areas of focus that may be more appropriate for December given your school calendar.

Personal
- Monitor new teachers for fatigue and disillusionment.
- Help them be aware that conflicting priorities and possible concerns about money, family, and holiday arrangements are normal at this point.
- Escort the new teachers to the staff holiday gatherings at school and escort or arrange for someone to escort them to staff-wide celebrations outside of school.

Professional
- Make some microwave popcorn and watch a videotaped teaching episode with the new teachers. Check your professional library for appropriate videotapes. Analyze the video using your district's teacher performance criteria.

Curriculum, Instruction, and Assessment
- Explain that the days before the winter holiday have the potential to be lost instructional time. Guide them in planning meaningful and engaging learning experiences while being mindful of the conflicting demands on student and family time outside of school. Use pages 66-67 in *Why Didn't I Learn This in College?* as a tool for identifying strategies to engage students in active, meaningful learning focused on essential to know learning outcomes.

Organizational Systems
- Discuss the dilemma of the piles of papers that have accumulated on shelves, in boxes, and on the edge of desks. Give a gift of plastic garbage bags and a set of brightly colored folders or two or three new three-ring binders. Help the new teachers figure out what to throw away and what to file.

Students
- Advise the new teachers that the holidays can be either joyful or stressful for students and that either emotion can negatively impact their focus on school and learning.
- Instruct the new teachers to be sensitive to the religious and ethnic diversity of the students so that they will not make references to only the celebrations in which they participate.

Mentoring Calendar
December continued...

- Let new teachers know not to penalize students for decisions made by adult family members about school attendance by giving high stakes assessments the day before the school holidays.

Colleagues

- Ask colleagues to assist in providing moral support to new teachers who are going through "the slump" and need personal and professional support. See **October/November** sections for suggestions on how to provide them relief and support.
- Remind principal of the needs of new teachers at this time of the year and ask that the administrative staff mobilize to let the new teachers know that they are valued personally and professionally.

School and School System

- Go over policies for holiday decorations, celebrations, and gifts.
- Preview semester exam policies and procedures.
- Provide an overview of semester exam policies and procedures.

Parents and Community

- Alert new teachers about the various religious holidays, rituals, and festivities in which students, parents, and community members engage. New teachers from other areas of the country may well be unaware of all the significant religious observances that occur during this time period.

Especially for Special Educators

- Revisit student performance on the previous year's standardized testing and discuss strategies for insuring adequate yearly progress. Use student work to analyze actual student progress.
- Review systems for documenting student progress and assist in revision or refinement as necessary. Use student work to analyze actual student progress.
- Check for alignment of instruction with IEP goals and the state/district learning standards.
- Pay particular attention to itinerant teachers as they move in and out of your building. While they may have a mentor assigned at another school they may be feeling isolated in your building.

Mentoring Calendar
January
Personal
- Write the new teachers "Welcome Back" notes and put them with balloons or candy bars on their desks or near their mail boxes.
- Meet them for coffee or a beer to debrief the first semester.

Professional
- Review second quarter professional goals.
- Have new teachers do a self-assessment and set new goals for the third quarter.
- Discuss how the mentoring process is working.
- Make plans for the mentoring relationship for the second semester.

Curriculum, Instruction, and Assessment
- Focus on planning practices. Use the **Tools for Instructional Design** on pages 323-355 in this book, Chapter II in *Instruction for All Students,* and Chapter VII in *Why Didn't I Learn This in College?*
- Hold an extensive review of the pacing guide/curriculum map and help the new teachers make necessary adjustments.
- Assist the new teachers in analyzing semester exam and other summative assessment data in order to design and select scaffolding strategies for the third quarter.

Organizational Systems
- The beginning of the second semester is the time to evaluate classroom arrangements, adequacy of resources, success of procedures, use of time, efficiency of routines, and effectiveness of responses to unmet expectations. Use pages 32-42 and 207-250 in *Why Didn't I Learn This in College?*

Students
- Assist new teachers in developing systems for monitoring progress and being aware of students who may be in danger of failing.
- Help them set up intervention plans including proactive support systems.
- Have the students of the new teachers do something nice for them. Perhaps they could make a giant "We Appreciate You" card or bring in an apple, candy or flowers.
- Work with the new teachers to increase their display of student work in the classroom.

Mentoring Calendar
January continued...

Colleagues
- Check in with other mentors and attend the mentor support sessions.
- Update the principal or other administrators on the mentoring process.
- Ensure that new teachers engage in any opportunities to review student work in departmental, team, or grade level groups.

School and School System
- Review grading and reporting procedures.
- Discuss the spring standardized testing schedule.

Parents and Community
- For new teachers teaching semester courses, revisit the August and September calendars for reminders of communication systems that need to be implemented with the parents of the second semester students.
- Discuss with them the advisability of communicating via a newsletter or memo the learning goals of the second semester, the purpose and time lines of any major projects, and any changes that will occur in the learning environment during second semester.

Especially for Special Educators
- Support them in reviewing semester grades and other classroom achievement data.
- Help new teachers review the progress of students on their case loads to see if they are moving toward independence.
- Remind them to review the procedures they are using to communicate with general education teachers. Have them do a self-assessment and decide what practices need to be modified.
- Coach them in establishing relationships and communication systems with any new teachers the students have for the second semester.
- Coordinate a review of IEP and TRA dates for second semester.

Mentoring Calendar
February

Personal

- Celebrate Valentine's Day with a card, a cartoon, or a candy bar; just pick up something at the supermarket checkout stand and toss it in your book bag.
- Help them recognize cabin fever in themselves and their students and react accordingly. Surprise them by putting up a paper palm tree and sharing a CD with Hawaiian music.

Professional

- Notice and comment on appropriate professional dress.
- Review and discuss portfolio entries.
- Assist in planning for supervisory observations.

Curriculum, Instruction, and Assessment

- Explore strategies for checking for understanding. With standardized testing coming up soon, the new teachers may be inclined to rush through material without checking to see if students are learning. Use pages 142-146 in *Why Didn't I Learn This in College?* as resources.
- Check in on the January plans for scaffolding instruction. Ask how it is going and how you can assist. Offer scaffolding strategies that work for you or others.
- Discuss how bell work, openers, and anchoring activities provide opportunities to revisit concepts and information as well as provide opportunities for needed standardized test preparation practice.

Organizational Systems

- Concentrate on the use of time. Use pages 228-231 in *Why Didn't I Learn This in College?* to focus on the use of instructional time and then focus on time-managment beyond the classroom.
- Explore ways to better use technology to manage professional, instructional, and student information. See pages 217-219 in *Why Didn't I Learn This in College?*

Students

- Review the learning profiles of students and identify those who might need to be referred for special services.
- Offer to "borrow" a difficult student for a day.
- Have the new teachers preview standardized testing procedures and processes with students.

Mentoring Calendar
February continued...

Colleagues
- Encourage the new teachers to build in time to meet with their colleagues to examine student work. Help them decide what student work samples to bring to the table.
- Bring the principal up to date on how the mentoring process is working.

School and School System
- Be sure that the new teachers are well informed and have accurate information about scheduling and teaching assignments for the upcoming school year as soon as it is available. Be mindful that rumors may be circulating about possible changes.

Parents and Community
- Ensure that the new teachers remind parents of the upcoming standardized testing. Help them develop a plan for letting parents know what they can do to help create a positive and productive testing environment.

Especially for Special Educators
- Remind these new teachers to review the standardized testing schedule and procedures as they apply to students in the special education programs.
- Help them use class work, individualized testing, literacy assessments, and all other available data to design scaffolding for student success on the upcoming standardized tests.
- Coach them in working with general education teachers in setting up the testing accommodations and modifications identified in IEPs.
- Assist the new teachers in identifying appropriate work study options for their students for the summer and/or fall.
- Inform the new special educators of their role in the preparation of the master schedule for the next year. Assist in the process.

Mentoring Calendar
March

Personal
- Make a Spring Break survival kit with magazines and novels, sun screen, and chocolate candy.

Professional
- Review second quarter professional goals and set new goals for the third quarter. See page 263 for a goal setting and review strategy.
- Use new teacher self-assessments or student work to guide your meetings. See pages 242-261 for new teacher self-assessments and page 262 for a goal setting format.
- Analyze portfolio artifacts and assist in identifying how they are aligned with the teacher performance evaluation criteria. Discuss what else might be included.
- As appropriate, discuss the reduction in force (RIF) process.

Curriculum, Instruction, and Assessment
- Focus on classroom assessment practices. Use the **Assessing Learning and the Instructional Program Self-Assessment** on page 255 in this book, Chapters V and VI in *Instruction for All Students* and Chapter VI in *Why Didn't I Learn This in College?*

Organizational Systems
- Check in with the new teachers on their record keeping systems. Review school reports they need to complete, grade books, attendance logs, and parent contact records as appropriate.

Students
- Remind new teachers that if they demonstrate nervousness or speak disparagingly about standardized tests, their students will pick up on those emotions and comments.
- Encourage them to communicate to students how well the students are prepared for both the content and process of the testing.
- Have them explain once again to students the purpose of these tests and how they are different from their usual classroom assessments.

Mentoring Calendar
March continued...

Colleagues
- Ask the principal, as appropriate, to give you a heads-up about any upcoming teaching assignment decisions for the new teachers so that you can be prepared to support the new teacher in dealing with the changes.
- Discuss how collaboration between general educators and special educators is working and help solve any problems that have surfaced.

School and School System
- Just before standardized testing events, review the policies and procedures for administering the assessments.

Parents and Community
- Review the procedures and processes for parent conferences. Discuss what worked in the fall conferences and what needs to be done differently this time around. Use pages 259-260 and 263-264 in *Why Didn't I Learn This in College?*
- Advise the new teachers to keep parents informed of the learning that is occurring in the classroom. Use pages 256-258 in *Why Didn't I Learn This in College?*
- Remind them to keep parents informed of changes in student work or behavior. Suggest that they make at least as many positive parent contacts as they do negative contacts.

Especially for Special Educators
- Provide guidance on how to plan for transition of students between buildings and programs for the upcoming school year.
- Debrief with them on their roles in the administration of standardized tests and help them think through what they would do differently next year.
- Assist them with establishing secondary transition goals and post-secondary goals as well as identifying needed adult services.

Mentoring Calendar
April
Personal
- Celebrate the arrival of spring by taking a walk around the school grounds together. Enjoy the emerging bulbs and the new leaves on the trees.
- Given that the new teachers are now most likely in the reflection and rejuvenation stage of development, reminisce about the first days of school and how far you have come in working together.

Professional
- Review the effectiveness of the mentoring relationship and discuss how to make the best use of your time, energy, and expertise.
- Respond, as appropriate, to the final evaluation report that new teachers generally receive by April 15th along with information about their employment for the following school year.
- For teachers who received satisfactory evaluation reports, provide guidance in thinking about their professional goals for the following year and help them identify professional development opportunities for the summer.
- In the situations where new teachers receive satisfactory evaluation but face the strong possibility of a reduction in force, help them prepare updated resumes and put together a professional portfolio if they did not already prepare one during the school year.
- Should any new teachers not be rehired for the following year, respond professionally and privately. Do not discuss such matters with other staff members. Offer support to anyone being dismissed so that they can maintain their dignity and finish the school year providing as strong an instructional program as they possibly can.

Curriculum, Instruction, and Assessment
- Identify the concepts and information that students have not yet mastered and discuss how to revisit and reteach those concepts while extending and enriching the learning of those who have already mastered those concepts. Use pages 189-225 in *Instruction for All Students.*
- Encourage the new teachers to offer students more choice in their learning. Use pages 200-204 and 141-143 in *Instruction for All Students.*

Organizational Systems
- Encourage systematic collection and storage of instructional materials and student artifacts that they want to have available for the next school year. Discuss possible collection and storage possibilities.

Mentoring Calendar
April continued...

Students
- Spring fever is an issue for both students and staff. Discuss with the new teachers how to recognize and celebrate the bursts of energy students display and how to channel it into active, meaningful learning experiences.

Colleagues
- Discuss how collegial interactions are going and hold a coaching session around any problem areas.

School and School System
- Debrief the standardized testing that has been completed and discuss what needs to be done differently for the next round of testing.
- Review field trip procedures.
- Preview exam schedule and end-of-the year time lines.

Parents and Community
- Assist the new teachers with any questions about third quarter report cards. Discuss ways they can ensure that the information on the report cards is not a surprise to students or parents but rather a formal confirmation of information previously shared.
- Discuss strategies for dealing with parents who are upset about events at or communication from the school. Use pages 263-264 in *Why Didn't I Learn This in College?* as a resource.

Especially for Special Educators
- Explain summer learning options for students and help the new special educators prepare recommendations to students and/or parents about student participation in those programs.
- Review cumulative folders and confidential folders with the new special educators to help them identify any missing paperwork.
- Provide guidance for setting up communications between this year's special education teachers and next year's special education teachers.

Mentoring Calendar
May

Since the date for the end of the school year varies, review both the May and June calendars for suggestions on mentoring around the close of the school year.

Personal

- Be sure that new teachers are invited to any end-of-the-year staff social events.
- Invite them to accompany you to end-of-the-year concerts or other events such as graduation.
- Be supportive of those who, for whatever reason, are leaving your school.

Professional

- Encourage participation in school and/or district level celebrations of the induction program and the professional accomplishments of new teachers and mentors.
- Discuss summer professional development opportunities.
- Review with the new teachers the professional growth goals they set for the fourth quarter and discuss next steps.
- Ask them to summarize their learning from this year by identifying the key strategies they want to remember for future use. Use pages 267-275, **Lists of Top Ten Tips** as tools.

Curriculum, Instruction, and Assessment

- Provide strategies for staying focused through the end of the school year.
- Discuss the questioning strategies the new teachers are using. Use pages 54-60 in **Why Didn't I Learn This in College?**
- Use student work and the results of classroom assessment to help the new teachers plan engaging and focused end-of-the-year learning experiences.

Organizational Systems

- Assist the new teachers in identifying materials they will need for next year and making plans for obtaining or creating them.
- Coach them in systems for organizing their teaching materials so that they can easily access them next year.

Students

- Remind new teachers that if they demonstrate nervousness or speak disparagingly about standardized tests, their students will pick up on those emotions and comments.

Mentoring Calendar
May continued...

- Encourage them to be positive about how well students are prepared for both the content and process of the testing.
- Be sure that they know which of their students are enrolled in AP classes and will therefore be focused on preparing for and taking AP exams in early May. Advise them to not assign other big projects at that time.
- Graduation, prom, awards assemblies, concerts, and other end-of-the-year activities become the focus for students at this time. Suggest to new teachers that while they want to continue to engage students in meaningful learning that they should also be mindful of the higher number of events taking place outside of school time.

Colleagues

- For new teachers who have a different teaching assignment next year, facilitate the arrangement of observations and/or planning conferences with someone who currently has that teaching assignment.
- If there is a change in teaching assignment, ask colleagues with whom new teachers will be working next year to reach out to the new teachers to welcome them to the team and to share well in advance any instructional and assessment materials the team uses.

School and School System

- Ensure that the new teachers know what they need to do with the May administration of standardized tests.
- Explain how to order supplies for the next school year.
- Go over the end-of-the-year procedures for student and teacher check-out.
- Clarify any confusion about responsibilities for attendance at end-of-the-year ceremonies.

Parents and Community

- Help new teachers identify ways they will let parents see the big picture of what their children have learned and accomplished this year.

Especially for Special Educators

- Assist the new teachers in completing paraprofessional performance evaluations
- Facilitate the review of student work as a measure of student learning. Help new teachers select work samples that will be forwarded to the receiving special education teachers.

Mentoring Calendar
June

Since the date for the end of the school year varies, review both the May and June calendars for suggestions on mentoring around the close of the school year.

Personal

- Celebrate the learning of the new teachers, the mentors, and the students by having dinner or at least a cup of coffee or a glass of wine away from school at a local establishment.
- Write the new teachers a note stating how much you have learned by participating in the mentoring process and from working with them.

Professional

- Join the new teachers in reflecting on their accomplishments this school year. Revisit the goals they set and the dreams they held for the year. Celebrate those accomplishments.
- Ask them to give you feedback on how well the mentoring and induction program have supported them and what might be eliminated, added, or modified. Use the **Induction/Mentoring Program Reflection and Evaluation** on pages 277-280 of this book.
- Complete the mentor's version of the **Induction/Mentoring Program Reflection and Evaluation** on pages 296-299 of this book.

Curriculum, Instruction, and Assessment

- Discuss the pacing of the instructional year and help the new teachers consider what they will do next year to be better able to have students access all the essential understandings and build the appropriate levels of understanding.

Organizational Systems

- Assist the new teachers in designing a system for packing up their own instructional materials for the summer. Be sure that they pull out any materials they will need to use during summer professional development work.
- Advise them about what to leave at school and what to take home with them.

Mentoring Calendar
June continued...

Students
- Suggest an end-of-the-year note for each student celebrating individual and group accomplishments. Given the large number of students secondary teachers and elementary specialists teach in a given year, suggest that they write one that celebrates the learning and growth during the year and give all students a copy.

Colleagues
- If the new teachers are going to have a different teaching assignment in the upcoming school year, suggest that they meet with someone who teaches that grade or class now or make arrangements to meet with that person over the summer.

School and School System
- Go over book count and storage procedures.
- Explain procedures for collecting any necessary fees or fines.
- Provide guidance for completing the technology inventory.

Parents and Community
- Advise new teachers to send thank you notes to parents and community members who have assisted in any way during the school year.

Especially for Special Educators
- Ensure that the new special educators have completed all the necessary paperwork to document student learning, recommendations for instructional opportunities for next year, and placed all documents in the appropriate files.
- Meet with the new special educators for analysis and reflection on professional accomplishments and learning this year. Have them review their systems for managing and using student data, their own organizational systems, and their communication with colleagues and parents.
- Facilitate planning sessions for new special education teachers and the general education teachers with whom they will be working next year. Help them set up summer planning sessions.

Mentoring in a Standards-Based Environment

Chapter VI

Mentoring in a Standards-Based Environment

Standards-Based versus Standards-Referenced

We would all like to believe that we are standards-based in our instructional decision-making and practices but the reality is that few of us can call ourselves **standards-based**. What we can say is that we are all at least **standards-referenced**. That is, many of us refer to the standards to see if we can justify what we had planned to teach based on teachers' manuals, on programs purchased by the district or on what we've have "always" done. Mentors have an important responsibility for being clear about what it means to be standards-based as opposed to standards-referenced so that they can provide appropriate guidance to new teachers. The good news is that most new teachers can readily engage in practices that are **standards-based** because they have no "old habits," units, lessons, or activities to give up.

What Mentors Need to Know About Being Standards-Based

The stages of being **standards-based** are as follows:
- Knowing that the standards exist
- Knowing where to find a copy
- Reading the standards
- Posting the standards
- Occasionally referring to the standards during planning and with students
- Checking to see if what is being taught can be found in the standards
- Beginning to understand the power and focus the standards provide and working to identify the essential understandings that are embedded in and that transcend the standards as they are written in the documents
- Being able to say "I am **standards-based** because I used the standards to design assessments and instruction, and I used student work to judge whether or not the instruction was well designed for this content with these learners."

The first six bullets are more representative of **standards-referenced** than they are of **standards-based.** We have to include the last two bullets before we can say that we are **standards-based.**

Mentoring in a Standards-Based Environment continued...

The Focus Is Always on Student Learning

If we are in fact standards-based, the focus is always on student learning and the statement **"I have so much to cover."** is replaced by **"I need to structure learning opportunities so that all students can learn at a high level."** and **"The analysis of my students' work informs my decision-making about instructional practice."** It is true that the amount of information and the number of skills we and the new teachers are asked to ensure that the learners master is mind-boggling. Given that, we need to be sure that every single learning experience in which the students are engaged is not only an interesting activity, but also the right exercise for moving their learning forward. Just because exercise is next in the textbook or teammates have been using it for years, is not sufficient reason for having students continue to do it. The next exercise, or the long projects, may be just what is called for as the next lesson, but we have to ask the following questions:

- **Is this the right lesson for these students right now?**
- **Given the school-year time frame, is this learning experience worthy of the time it will cost?**
- **Is there another way to approach this learning that might work better for these learners or be more efficient in moving them along?**

Teachers in their first years of teaching find it incredibly difficult to know the answers to these questions, so it is essential that as they move through those first years we help them as they consider these questions.

All Students Are Expected to Achieve at a High Level

At the same time the standards movement was sweeping across the land, IDEA made legally imperative what was already our moral responsibility. We are required to ensure that all students have access to the same rich curriculum and that they all be held to the same level of understanding. The implications for mentors and new teachers alike are huge. The percentage of students who have been labeled as "special needs" and the percentage of English Language Learners (ELLs) is staggering. This mandate and these students are the reason we hear so much about **differentiation of instruction.** While experienced teachers new to the district may be ready for focused mentoring and collaboration around differentiation, novice teachers must first master the incredible knowledge base and complex skills of teaching before they can provide multiple pathways to learning. Mentors need to focus on helping new teachers build solid repertoires of research-based instructional strategies and then gradually coach them in using multiple strategies simultaneously.

Mentoring in a Standards-Based Environment continued...

Using Assessment Results to Inform Practice

Are the students learning? We need to coach new teachers in the gathering and analysis of **preassessment** or baseline data about what students know and can do as they enter the learning experience. We have to help them use that data analysis to design learning experiences at which students can be successful. Few new teachers have had extensive training in the ongoing gathering and use of **formative assessment data** so they need help learning to use every piece of student work, all student responses, and student questions as data sources about how well students are learning. In a standards-based classroom, even **summative assessments** become data sources because we can determine whether or not individual students have mastered or are moving toward mastery of the identified standards. The question we must teach new teachers to ask is not did the students complete all the assignments and do their homework, **but rather, did they learn what they were supposed to learn, did they retain it over time, and can they use it in ways that demonstrate understanding at a high level.**

Standards-Based Planning Process

Planning in a standards-based environment is often described as "beginning with the end in mind." Teachers have always planned with an end in mind. Often though, the end we had in mind was to work our way through the book, chapter by chapter, or through the year, project by project. In a standards-based environment, mentors have to work closely with new teachers to ensure that they understand that the end they should have in mind is not completion of a particular activity or project, chapters in a book, or a packaged program, but is instead mastery of the learning standards identified by the state and the district.

Just like we have a clear picture of that perfect vacation, car, wedding, or ad campaign, we need to have a clear picture of what it looks like when our students are competent in what we want them to know and be able to do. Just as that vacation, wedding, or ad campaign will not happen without an action plan, we need an action plan for guiding our students to be able to demonstrate the learning we have in mind for them. The first step in this planning process, both inside and outside the classroom, is identifying the outcome we want. The second step is creating our vision of what it looks like when we get there. Next we analyze the outcome and vision to figure out what we have to do in the third step in order to accomplish the first and second steps. It makes no sense to start the third step without **THE END** in mind. As mentors we have the opportunity to ensure that new educators begin their professional practice thinking and planning this way.

Mentoring in a Standards-Based Environment continued...

In this chapter the **Guidelines for Unit Design**, a list of concepts to use in forming generalizations and essential understandings, and the **Top Ten Questions to Focus Discussions of the Teaching and Learning Process** provide a big picture look at the key ideas for mentoring in a standards-based environment. These pages elaborate on the four steps in the Standards-Based (SBE) Planning Process. See SBE Planning Process graphic below.

There is an extensive array of best practices to note, suggestions to make, and reflective questions to ask on each of six areas: planning instruction, implementing instruction, assessing instruction, orchestrating a positive learning-centered environment, organizing a productive learning-centered environment, and professionalism and collegial collaboration. There are references to where these issues are discussed in *Why Didn't I Learn This in College?* and *Instruction for All Students* as well as in other recommended print and web resources.

See **Chapter XIII, Tools for Instructional Planning** for templates to use as resources with new teachers. See also **Chapter X, Tools for New Teachers** for self-assessments in each of the six areas listed above. Use these self-assessments with new teachers to help identify areas of focus for professional goal setting. See pages 262-265 for tools to use in goal setting.

Mentors should review their own district teacher performance evaluation criteria to identify alignment with the six areas used in this book and assist new teachers in making explicit connections between the two.

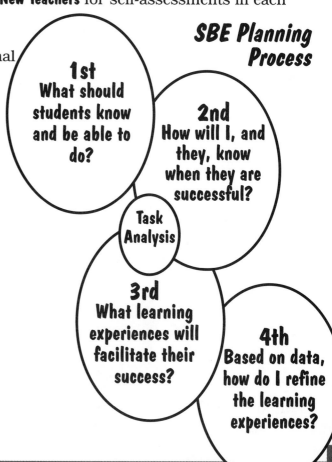

SBE Planning Process

1st What should students know and be able to do?

2nd How will I, and they, know when they are successful?

Task Analysis

3rd What learning experiences will facilitate their success?

4th Based on data, how do I refine the learning experiences?

Guiding Questions for Unit Design in the Standards-Based Classroom

1st STEP: What should students know and be able to do?

1. On which content standard(s) will the students be working?

2. What are the key ideas, major themes, big concepts, or essential understandings embedded in those standards? How are the selected standards related to the essential understandings of the course?

3. If you are using a commercial program or a unit designed by others, what parts of it are aligned or not aligned with the information you presented in #1 and #2? What components need to be added or eliminated?

4. When and where (inside and outside of school) have the students encountered information about and had experience with these key concepts/big ideas before?

2nd STEP: How will I, and they, know when they are successful?

5. What would it look like when students can demonstrate that they understand the big ideas and have the essential skills? Brainstorm some ways students might demonstrate their capacity to use the newly learned concepts/information appropriately in a new situation?

6. Using the ideas generated in #5, what task/products would best demonstrate student understanding? What form should the criteria take? Should you use a rubric, a performance task list, or a checklist? What variables should be listed as criteria?

7. What does a task analysis (the assessment criteria provides the components of the task analysis,) reveal about the skills, the knowledge, and the level of understanding required by the task?

8. Do you already have sufficient preassessment data or do you need to gather more? If so, what method is best to use? What does the preassessment data tell you about the skills and knowledge on which the entire group will need to focus? Are there individual students who will need additional support if they are to have a realistic opportunity to demonstrate mastery? In which areas will they need support?

Guiding Questions for
Unit Design
in the Standards-Based Classroom continued...

3rd STEP: What learning experiences will facilitate their success?

9. How will you "Frame the Learning" so that students know what they are going to be doing, what they will know and be able to do as a result of those activities, how they will be assessed, and how everything they are doing is aligned with the standards?

10. How will you help students access prior knowledge and use it productively, either building on it or reframing their thinking as appropriate?

11. What methods of presentation and what active learning experiences can you use to help students achieve the standard? Could you provide multiple sources of information and exercises that would help all students to make real world connections and use sophisticated thinking skills?

12. What assignments, projects, and homework will help students see the relevance of the learning? How might you provide multiple pathways to learning?

13. What classroom activities/observations, as well as formative quizzes and tests, would provide you and your students information on their progress toward the standard?

14. What materials and resources do you need to locate and organize to provide multiple pathways to learning? How should you organize the classroom and the materials to provide easy student access?

15. What else might you do to to provide challenging and meaningful experiences for both struggling and advanced learners? Are there other human, print, or electronic resources you might consult to refine/review your plan?

Guiding Questions for
Unit Design
in the Standards-Based Classroom continued...

4th STEP: Based on data, how do I refine the learning experiences and/or the assessment?

16. How did students do on the performance task? Were there some students who were not successful? What might account for that? What could you do differently next time?

17. What else do you need to consider in your advance planning the next time you are focusing on this standard?

18. Did all of the activities guide students toward mastery of the standard? Are there activities that need to be added, modified, or eliminated?

19. Overall, was this unit effective for addressing the standard(s)? Are there other standards that you could incorporate into this unit or are there other units of study where you can have the students revisit these standards or essential understandings?

adapted from the Facilitator's Guide and Workbook for *Common Ground in the Standards-Based Education Classroom* prepared by the Northern Colorado BOCES SBE Design Team

Essential Understandings

Use this list of concepts to help new teachers write generalizations or essential understandings. The combination of two or more of these concepts plus the addition of content-specific concepts promotes concept-based teaching and learning rather getting bogged down in facts taught in isolation. By using this approach, you can help new teachers move beyond working through the book page by page. This exercise can also help new teachers design rigorous and authentic assessment tasks.

Stimulus	Individual	Revolution	Organization
Belief	Balance	Renaissance	Attitude
Probability	Communication	Object	Estimation
Values	Number	Community	Message
Change	Interaction	Curiosity	Honor
People	Variables	Challenge	Love
Celebration	Projection	Fairness	Loyalty
Production	Influence	Justice	Reaction
Time	Relationship	Equilibrium	Survival
Space	Knowledge	Economics	Wellness
Order	Limit	Geography	Stamina
Force	Motion	Solution	Fitness
Complexity	Consequence	Tradition	Group
Culture	Music	Reciprocity	Matter
Interdependence	Tension	Stability	Sequence
Perspective	Opinion	Cohesion	History
Scale	Habitat	Disparity	Rotation
Property	Needs	Factor	Success
Behavior	Diversity	Density	Intelligence
System	Wants	Faith	Style
Adaptation	Rhythm	Fantasy	Failure
Structure	Pace	Division	Speed
Role	Conflict	Unity	Truth
Freedom	Pattern	Family	Capacity
Competition	Control	Patriotism	Power
Symbol	Beauty	Parallel	Supply

TOP TEN QUESTIONS
to focus discussions of the teaching & learning process

1. What should **students know and be able to do** as a result of this lesson? How are these objectives related to national, state, and/or district standards?

2. How do **students demonstrate what they know and what they can do?** Are there multiple forms of assessment including **student self-assessment?** What are the **assessment criteria** and what form do they take?

3. How does the teacher **find out** what **students already know (preassessment),** and how does she help them access and use what they know and have experienced both inside and outside the classroom? How do learners not only **build on prior experiences** but **deal with misconceptions and naive understandings** and **reframe their thinking** when appropriate?

4. How are new knowledge, concepts and skills introduced? How is data about the **diversity** of the students and from the **task analysis** used to select from a wide variety of sources and presentation modes?

5. How do students **process (make meaning)** of their learning? What are the key questions, activities, and assignments (in class or homework)?

6. What are the **formative assessments** or **checks for student understanding** during the lesson? How is the data from those assessments used to inform teaching decisions?

7. How is instruction **differentiated** so that the learning experiences are productive for all students?

8. How is the learning framed so that **students know the objectives**, the **rationale** for the objectives and activities, the directions and procedures, as well as the **assessment task and criteria** at the beginning of the learning process?

9. How are opportunities for students to make **real world connections** and to learn and use **varied and complex thinking skills** built into the learning experience?

10. What arrangements/adjustments are made to create a positive and productive **learning environment**? How is **data** being used to make these decisions?

Planning Instruction
Best Practices to Note and Suggestions to Make

> *I noticed that you... You might consider... It is likely to promote student achievement if you... Given that, I suggest you... The district teacher performance criteria state that we are to...*

- Use the **district and state standards** to plan for the year, the unit, and the lesson

- **Use the standards-based planning process to plan and pace for the year**

- **Use the standards-based planning process for units and lessons** by aligning assessments and learning experiences with the standards

- Identify the **essential understandings, key concepts, and big ideas** of the content areas being taught

- **Design summative assessments prior to planning units or lessons**

- Design learning experiences that give students **practices and rehearsals** at the same level of understanding as the level at which the standards/outcomes are written

- Be clear about how any given **lesson/learning experience is directly related** to the standards/outcomes

- State standards in lesson plans

- **Analyze instructional materials** for match to district outcomes

- **Identify supplemental materials** and design learning experiences to **fill any gaps** in standard materials

- Use the **task analysis process** to identify the knowledge, skills, and level of understanding required by the task

- Include knowledge of student **readiness levels, interests, and learning styles** in designing learning experiences

- Build **pauses for processing** into the lesson design and use 10:2 Theory and Wait Time as guidelines

- Plan and write out the **key questions** to ask during a lesson

- Analyze **text structure** and teach students to use **graphic organizers** to represent the thinking processes used by the author and to capture the key information in the text

Planning Instruction
Best Practices to Note and Suggestions to Make continued...

> *I noticed that you... You might consider... It is likely to promote student achievement if you... Given that, I suggest you... The district teacher performance criteria state that we are to...*

- **Align assignments to include homework with standards and assessments** and be purposeful about **examining homework results for evidence of learning**

- Use **Models of Teaching** such as Bruner's Concept Attainment, Hilda Taba's Inductive Model, Aronson's Jigsaw Classroom, and the Inquiry/Problem Solving Model

- Use the skills and competencies laid out in the **SCANS Report** (Secretary's Commission on Achieving the Necessary Skills) in lesson and unit design

- Eliminate lessons and learning exercises that do not move students toward meeting the standards

- **Collaborate /consult with support staff** about special needs students

- **For special educators:**

  ➤ Use knowledge of **medical conditions and medications** and their possible effects on student learning and behavior to plan instruction

  ➤ Use knowledge of **educational disabilities and giftedness** and their effects on student learning needs to individualize instruction

See Chapter II in *Instruction for All Students* and Chapter VII in *Why Didn't I Learn This in College?* for information on planning.

Planning Instruction
Reflections and Questions

> Use these stems with the statements on the previous pages: *How might you...? How do you feel it went when you...? What did you learn from the situation in which you...? What does the data/research tell you about ...?* Additional reflections and questions are listed below.

- Describe your **efforts to master the state standards and the district outcomes** in your field/at your grade level.

- How have you used your **knowledge of state standards and district outcomes to plan, implement, and evaluate, your instructional programs?**

- Describe the factors you consider and the methods you use to formulate **lesson objectives.**

- Describe the factors you consider in lesson and unit design.

- How do you combine **personal practical experience and research** to make instructional decisions?

- What are your systems for ensuring that **instruction focuses on what students need to achieve standards** instead of on what is fun to teach or is readily available in a textbook?

- Explain how **content specific pedagogy** impacts your planning?

- What is the process you use to identify essential understandings and then use those understandings to plan instruction and assess learning?

- Who/what has the **greatest influence on the planning decisions** you make around instruction, assessment, and the environment? Why do you think these are the most influential?

- What are the **key concepts, big ideas, or essential understandings** of the content you are teaching?

- How do you ensure that you present **different points of view and a variety of cultural perspectives?**

- How do you use **preassessment data and/or students' prior knowledge in the planning process?**

Planning Instruction
Reflections and Questions continued...

> Use these stems with the statements on the previous pages: *How might you...? How do you feel it went when you...? What did you learn from the situation in which you...? What does the data/research tell you about ...?* Additional reflections and questions are listed below.

- How do you go about **evaluating teaching resources and materials** for comprehensiveness, accuracy, potential for student engagement, and their match to the learning standards?

- What are the **variables** you consider when planning for **differentiation of instruction**?

- How do you use your knowledge of **Multiple Intelligences theory and learning styles** to design learning experiences that will engage all learners?

- What is the process you use to create **interdisciplinary learning experiences** that help students make connections between the various content areas they are studying?

- When planning for the year, what is your process for ensuring that the **level of student work increases between the fall and the spring?**

- How do you think about what you **plan in relationship to both the entire school year and to the K-12 experiences of learners?**

ASK Framework for
The Study of Teaching and Learning

The **ASK Framework** is presented here with notations of support materials found in *Leading the Learning* (Rutherford, 2003), *Why Didn't I Learn This in College?* (Rutherford, 2002), and *Instruction for All Students* (Rutherford, 2002).

Why Didn't I Learn This in College? is written for novice teachers and their supervisors, mentors, and coaches. The content focuses on planning, instruction, building a learning community, and creating and implementing organizational systems for effective learning in a learning-centered classroom. *Instruction for All Students* builds on that work and extends the study of teaching and learning to include differentiation of instruction, 21st century thinking skills, and collegial collaboration.

Planning Instruction

Standards-Based Teaching, Learning, and Assessment
Instruction for All Students pages 12-13, 16-34
Why Didn't I Learn This in College? pages 172-183

Lesson, Unit, and Course Design
Instruction for All Students Chapter II, pages 15-47
Why Didn't I Learn This in College? Chapter VII, pages 170-190

Learning Styles, Multiple Intelligences, and Brain Research
Instruction for All Students pages 8, 42-43, 119-124, and 198-199

Diversity of Students
Why Didn't I Learn This in College? pages 39-42 and 132

Active Learning
Instruction for All Students Chapter IV, pages 73-111
Why Didn't I Learn This in College? Chapter IV, pages 63-106

Connections to the World Beyond The Classroom
Instruction for All Students pages 9-11, 39-41, 129-134, and 174-187

Integration of the Curriculum
Instruction for All Students pages 35-38

Additional Resources on
Planning Instruction

On the Web
- www.askeric.org
- www.sdcoe.k12.ca.us
- webquest.sdsu.edu
- www.eduhelper.com
- www.nytimes.com/learning
- www.teachers.net

In Print
- *Models of Teaching* by Bruce Joyce & Marsha Well
- *Operators Guide to a Standards-Based Classroom* from Centennial Boces, Longmont, Colorado
- *Instruction: A Models Approach* by Mary Alice Gunter, Thomas Estes, & Jan Schwab.
- *Understanding By Design* by Grant Wiggins & Jay McTighe
- *The Differentiated Classroom: Responding to the Needs of All Learners* by Carol Ann Tomlinson

Planning Instruction

Professionalism & Collegial Collaboration

Implementing Instruction

Organizing a Productive Environment

Assessing Learning & the Instructional Program

Orchestrating a Positive Environment

Implementing Instruction
Best Practices to Note and Suggestions to Make

> *I noticed that you... You might consider... It is likely to promote student achievement if you... Given that, I suggest you... The district teacher performance criteria state that we are to...*

- **Communicate the standards** and learning objectives **in age-appropriate language**

- **Communicate why** what students are learning is **important to know**

- **Communicate how the learning exercises** the students are doing **are related to the learning outcomes**; that is, explain the purpose and relevance of all assignments and learning experiences

- **Communicate how the current lesson is related to and builds on previous lessons**

- **Help students build skills at recognizing how the current lesson is related to and builds on previous lessons**

- **Communicate** to students how their **learning will be assessed**

- **Provide scoring guides** such as rubrics, performance task lists and checklists to students **before they begin working**

- **Provide daily, unit, and semester agendas**

- **Have students access their prior knowledge**

- **Identify student misconceptions and naive understandings**; help students reframe their thinking as appropriate

- Provide or have students provide **connections between what is being learned in the moment with other areas of their study and to life beyond the classroom**

- Present **accurate and current information**

- **Provide multiple illustrations, examples, and comparisons of complex or highly abstract ideas or concepts**

- **Emphasize the key terms/ideas** to be learned

- **Use positive and negative examples** to help identify critical or important attributes

Implementing Instruction
Best Practices to Note and Suggestions to Make continued...

> *I noticed that you... You might consider... It is likely to promote student achievement if you... Given that, I suggest you... The district teacher performance criteria state that we are to...*

- Whenever possible move from **concrete** (props) **to semi-abstract** (pictures) **to abstract** (words and numbers) in presenting new concepts

- **Model thinking aloud**

- **Use analogies, metaphors, and similes**

- **Use physical models and manipulatives**

- **Use Wait Time I and Wait Time II**

- **Use segues at transitions** so students can make cognitive connections between points under study and between various learning exercises

- Have students **make predictions** about what will happen next or about the next steps they need to take

- **Have students process and summarize learning** at meaningful points

- **Have students assess old predictions, make new predictions, make connections, pose questions, and/or identify significant information at processing points**

- Use **10:2 Theory** as a time template for student processing

- **Supplement lectures** with colorful transparencies, Power Point-type presentations, models, charts, graphs, and other **visual aids**

- **Enhance lectures with discussion partners, graphic organizers, learning logs, etc.**

- **Check for understanding** throughout lessons by asking questions students can answer only if they truly understand concepts and/or the reasons for the processes

- **Assign homework** for which students have the prerequisite skills to complete the **work independently with an 80% success rate**

Implementing Instruction
Best Practices to Note and Suggestions to Make continued...

> *I noticed that you... You might consider... It is likely to promote student achievement if you... Given that, I suggest you... The district teacher performance criteria state that we are to...*

- **Assign homework from all four categories**: practice, preparation, extension, and creative to promote both homework completion, learning, and engagement

- **Go beyond recording completion of homework; use successful/unsuccessful completion as formative assessment data to inform teaching decisions**

- Gather and make accessible **multiple sources of information** such as books, magazines, journals, posters, pictures, charts, graphs, maps, and technology

- **Differentiate instruction** by providing a variety of sources, learning processes, and ways to demonstrate learning

- **Use flexible groupings** based on readiness levels, interests, student choice, and learning styles

- **Change strategies as necessary** to meet students' learning needs

- **Integrate content with cross-curricular themes and skills**

Focus on
Rigorous Instruction and Thinking Skills
Best Practices to Note and Suggestions to Make

I noticed that you... You might consider... It is likely to promote student achievement if you... Given that, I suggest you... The district teacher performance criteria state that we are to...

- **Use Bloom's Taxonomy** and the Question and Task Wheel to purposefully design questions and tasks at a variety of cognitive levels

- **Ask all students questions that require higher levels of thinking and probe student answers** for clarification and extension

- **Pose open-ended thought-provoking questions**

- **Name, model, and provide practice of thinking processes** so that students can build and independently access their own thinking skills repertoire

- Have students identify where else a particular thinking skill might be useful and **design tasks so that they use these thinking skills in multiple situations**

- **Teach students** to use journals, learning logs or interactive notebooks to **analyze and reflect on their own learning and the effectiveness of their effort**

- **Use Williams' Taxonomy of Affective and Creative Thinking** to design questions and learning tasks

- **Have students analyze print text, media, and technological souces for reliability and relevance**

- Include opportunities for both **inductive and deductive thinking**

- **Teach skills of inquiry**

- **Teach skills of dialogue and debate**

- Point out, or have students identify, **how ideas are alike and different and how they relate to one another**

- Have students **seek evidence/data to support opinions and generalizations**

- Have students demonstrate **relevant and important connections they are making**

For information on 21st Century Thinking Skills see Chapter IX, pages 217-247, in *Instruction for All Students*.

Planning Instruction

Professionalism & Collegial Collaboration

Implementing Instruction

Organizing a Productive Environment

Orchestrating a Positive Environment

Assessing Learning & the Instructional Program

Focus on
Constructivist Instruction
Best Practices to Note and Suggestions to Make

> *I noticed that you... You might consider... It is likely to promote student achievement if you... Given that, I suggest you... The district teacher performance criteria state that we are to...*

- Encourage **students to talk about ideas with other students**

- Encourage students to **think about how the information they are learning relates to other subjects and their lives beyond the school day**

- Have students **think critically and creatively** by asking questions that have more than one answer

- **Encourage students to think and discuss answers with a partner or a small group before answering in the larger group**

- Help students **explore and build on their ideas**

- Ensure that class time spent on practice exercises and learning the facts leads to **meaningful use of the facts and skills** in the near future

- **Ask students what they already know about a unit before introducing it**

- **Use essential questions and key concepts to** help students organize new information in ways that make sense to them

- Have students **take sides on issues and explain points of view**

- Have students **resolve their differences by discussing their thinking**

- **Encourage students to try solving difficult problems, even before they learn all the material**

- **Allow students to explore topics that excite or interest them**

- Design assessments around **real world applications**

- **Have students help determine how they demonstrate learning and how they are assessed**

Focus on
Small Group Work/Cooperative Learning
Best Practices to Note and Suggestions to Make

> *I noticed that you... You might consider... It is likely to promote student achievement if you... Given that, I suggest you... The district teacher performance criteria state that we are to...*

- Ensure that the work is **rigorous, worthy of the time, and aligned with desired outcomes**
- **Give directions that apply to all in the large group; when directions apply only to certain groups, give directions via task cards at learning centers or as handouts**
- **Model and practice student movement** so that students move quickly and smoothly into groups
- Provide direction and practice so that **students stay with their group** rather than wandering around
- **Encourage students to help each other answer questions and solve problems** rather than relying on the teacher to answer all questions and solve all problems
- Monitor whether or not all students in the groups are **working on the task equally and adjust accordingly**
- **Consider assigning roles** to students **and rotating those roles** so that all students are given the opportunity to develop the skills necessary for success in that role
- **Intervene in both academic and process situations** as appropriate while allowing students to resolve issues when possible
- **Offer responses that promote student solving of problems** rather than teacher solving of problems
- **Build in individual accountability** rather than relying on group grades.
- **Use flexible grouping;** consider readiness, gender, learning style, interests, and student choice as variables
- **Answer questions with a question**
- Teach, model, and review the **interaction/social skills** needed for successful work and learning
- Have students review the **effectiveness and efficiency of the group process and make plans for improvement**

See pages 46-47 in *Instruction for All Students* for information on cooperative learning and pages 243-250 in *Why Didn't I Learn This in College?* for information on small group work.

Planning Instruction

Professionalism & Collegial Collaboration

Implementing Instruction

Organizing a Productive Environment

Assessing Learning & the Instructional Program

Orchestrating a Positive Environment

Focus on
Literacy Instruction Across the Curriculum
Best Practices to Note and Suggestions to Make

> *I noticed that you... You might consider... It is likely to promote student achievement if you... Given that, I suggest you... The district teacher performance criteria states that we are to...*

- Create a **text-rich environment** by collecting, displaying, and using a wide variety of books, magazines, posters, etc., in the classroom

- Provide opportunities for **students to locate, organize, and use information from various sources** to answer questions, solve problems, and communicate ideas

- **Use diverse fiction and non-fiction sources** to include many authors and perspectives, as well as children's and young adult literature

- **Teach reading as a process of constructing meaning** through the interaction of the reader's prior knowledge and experiences, the information presented in the text, and the context/purpose of the reading

- **Teach affixes, prefixes, and common roots** used frequently in the content area

- Identify **independent, instructional, and frustration reading levels** of groups and individuals and plan assignments accordingly

- Provide opportunities for students to:
  - **Speak** for a variety of purposes and audiences
  - **Listen** in a variety of situations to information from a variety of sources
  - **Write** in clear, concise, organized language that varies in content and form for different audiences and purposes
  - **Read** various materials and texts with comprehension and critical analysis
  - **View, understand, and use** nontextual visual information (NJ Core Curriculum)

See Chapter V: Surprise! You're A Reading Teacher! in *Why Didn't I Learn This in College?*

Planning Instruction

Professionalism & Collegial Collaboration

Implementing Instruction

Organizing a Productive Environment

Assessing Learning & the Instructional Program

Orchestrating a Positive Environment

> *I noticed that you... You might consider... It is likely to promote student achievement if you...   Given that, I suggest you...   The district teacher performance criteria state that we are to...*

- Provide a **balanced literacy program** that includes reading to students, reading with students, independent reading by students, writing for and with students, and writing by students

- **Analyze and evaluate instructional materials** by considering readability, content, length, format, cultural orientation, and illustrations/visuals

- Use a reading approach aligned with the **No Child Left Behind Act of 2001** to include **phonemic awareness, phonics, vocabulary development, reading fluency, including oral reading skills and reading comprehension strategies.**

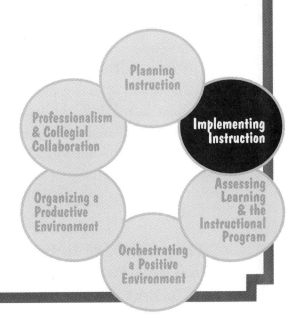

Focus on
Instruction in Inclusive Classrooms
Best Practices to Note and Suggestions to Make

I noticed that you... You might consider... It is likely to promote student achievement if you... Given that, I suggest you... The district teacher performance criteria state that we are to...

- **Task analyze** all assignments and assessments

- Provide **special education students with an expanded curriculum** including communication skills, oral language development, social/behavior skills, motor skills, and self-advocacy skills

- Include **explicit instruction that is structured, sequential, and cumulative** in the development of skills

- **Break complex tasks into simpler parts** and then put the complex task back together

- **Use backward chaining**

- **Use think alouds** and then guide students in using the skills or processes modeled in the think aloud

- In co-teaching situations
  - ➤ Ensure that all professional interactions between the general education and special education teachers cause the two to be seen by all as equal partners rather than having the special educator appear to function as a paraprofessional
  - ➤ Consider the messages about teacher roles and relationships sent in parent communication
  - ➤ Be clear about who is taking responsibility for which parts of the planning
  - ➤ Decide in advance how the lesson will be structured and who will do what
  - ➤ Share responsibility for developing procedures, expectations, and grading/critiquing students' work
  - ➤ Decide who will do which tasks in an equitable way

See *Instruction for All Students* pages 281-284 and *Why Didn't I Learn This in College?* pages 39-44.

Planning Instruction

Professionalism & Collegial Collaboration

Implementing Instruction

Organizing a Productive Environment

Assessing Learning & the Instructional Program

Orchestrating a Positive Environment

Focus on
Differentiation of Instruction
Best Practices to Note and Suggestions to Make

> *I noticed that you... You might consider... It is likely to promote student achievement if you... Given that, I suggest you... The district teacher performance criteria state that we are to...*

- Keep learning and assessment for all students focused on **essential to know concepts and skills** as identified in state and district standards

- **Differentiate instructional support systems but not expectations for student learning**

- Ensure that learning experiences and types and degree of teacher support are selected based on a **task analysis,** which includes an analysis of the **skills and knowledge embedded in the task** plus the **level of understanding** required by the task

- Use an analysis of **student readiness/background knowledge levels, interests** and **information processing styles** to identify appropriate learning experiences and teacher-support systems

- **Provide sources of information** at various reading levels, in different languages, and in varying formats to match the needs of learners

- **Engage all students** in **meaningful tasks** that provide balance between skill building and meaning making

- Provide **a balance of student and teacher choice** of working conditions, sources of information, methods of processing learning, and demonstrating that learning

- Use a variety of instruction approaches to include **individual, small group, and whole class instruction**

- **Use flexible grouping;** create groups based on a variety of factors, including readiness levels and interests

- **Give students precise, public, and prior guidelines for assignments, performance tasks, assessments, and behavior**

- **Provide models or exemplars of products and teach and model processes**

For information on differentiation of instruction see Chapter VIII, pages 189-215, in *Instruction for All Students.*

Focus on
Sheltered Instruction
Best Practices to Note and Suggestions to Make

> *I noticed that you... You might consider... It is likely to promote student achievement if you... Given that, I suggest you... The district teacher performance criteria state that we are to...*

- Be thoughtful and purposeful in the use of **academic/school related language** such as direction giving and content-specific vocabulary

- Be mindful of **slang or colloquialisms** in teacher and classmates' speech

- Use **concrete objects, models, and demonstrations** to support instruction

- Provide **visual cues** to support understanding

- Build in **movement, rhythm, and repetition** to support retention

- **Analyze and evaluate instructional materials** considering readability, content, length, format, cultural orientation, and illustrations/visuals

- Use the **writing strategies included in balanced literacy programs,** such as shared writing, interactive writing, guided writing, and short independent writing sessions in early years of developing English language skills

- Use what is known about students' families, cultures, and communities as a basis for **connecting instruction to students' personal experiences**

- **Provide multiple perspectives,** including attention to students' personal, family, and community experiences and cultural norms

- **Ask questions as simply and concisely as possible**

- **Ask questions that require more than one-word answers**

- Encourage all students to **answer in complete sentences** so that second language learners hear the answer in context and learn the rhythm of the English

- **Use wait time** before calling on any student and after any student answers so that processing and any necessary translation can occur

- **Ask second-language learners to retell, paraphrase, and summarize** discussion and reading points to promote comprehension and fluency

Focus on
Sheltered Instruction
Best Practices to Note and Suggestions to Make continued...

> *I noticed that you... You might consider... It is likely to promote student achievement if you...   Given that, I suggest you...   The district teacher performance criteria state that we are to...*

- **Assign roles in small group work** to ensure that second-language learners are active participants
- **Break complex tasks into simpler parts** by providing second-language learners with oral directions one step at time until they can follow two-and three-part directions independently

See Chapter V, pages 109-135 in *Why Didn't I Learn This in College?*

Implementing Instruction
Reflections and Questions

Use these stems with the statements on the previous pages: *How might you...? How do you feel it went when you...? What did you learn from the situation in which you...? What does the data/research tell you about ...?* Additional reflections and questions are listed below.

- How do you find out **what students already know** about what they are about to read/study?

- How do you ensure that students access what they know and **have experiences with both inside and outside the classroom** as it related to what they are about to read/study?

- How do you help them not only **build on prior experiences** but **reframe their thinking** when appropriate?

- Describe how you provide opportunities for students to make **real-world connections** from their learning.

- Describe two or three situations when you **adjusted instruction based on student questions, misconceptions, naive understandings, or interests.**

- Given your current student population, describe how you **select the presentation modes** to use in introducing new material.

- How do presentation modes and learning experiences move from **concrete to abstract?**

- Describe how you **create, access, select, and adapt materials** and equipment to facilitate learning.

- What are the ways in which you use **technology as a learning tool?**

- How do you **select the examples, stories, and props** for use in introducing, reinforcing, or extending understanding of new information?

- How do you **ensure that the explanations or examples are relevant** and that the **references have meaning** for students?

- What might you do to **extend and expand the thinking** of students ready to and/or interested in going beyond what is planned?

Planning Instruction

Professionalism & Collegial Collaboration

Implementing Instruction

Organizing a Productive Environment

Assessing Learning & the Instructional Program

Orchestrating a Positive Environment

Implementing Instruction
Reflections and Questions continued...

> Use these stems with the statements on the previous pages: *How might you...? How do you feel it went when you...? What did you learn from the situation in which you...? What does the data/research tell you about ...?* Additional reflections and questions are listed below.

- How do you use **technology as a learning tool?**

- What do you know from your own learning experiences about the fact that **"one size of learning does not fit all?"**

- What do you know about your **struggling, resistant, or reluctant learners** that you need to address up front?

- Describe the various ways you **configure small groups and the variables you consider in those configurations?**

- How is the **rationale for grouping explained to students?**

- How do you **plan the questions** you use to:
  - ➤ initiate discussions and keep them on track?
  - ➤ pique student curiosity?
  - ➤ help students make connections?
  - ➤ check for understanding?
  - ➤ cause students to think critically by evaluating credibility of sources and strength of evidence, to consider alternative viewpoints, and to challenge the obvious?

- How do you **reconcile differentiation of instruction with holding all students to the achievement of high standards?**

- What instructional strategies do you have in your **repertoire for helping students who do not grasp/understand the content or process the first time** it is presented and practiced?

- Describe how you vary **your role as instructor, facilitator, coach, or audience** in your interactions with students.

Planning Instruction

Professionalism & Collegial Collaboration

Implementing Instruction

Organizing a Productive Environment

Assessing Learning & the Instructional Program

Orchestrating a Positive Environment

ASK Framework for
The Study of Teaching and Learning

The **ASK Framework** is presented here with notations of support materials found in *Leading the Learning* (Rutherford, 2003), *Why Didn't I Learn This in College?* (Rutherford, 2002), and *Instruction for All Students* (Rutherford, 2002).

Why Didn't I Learn This in College? is written for novice teachers and their supervisors, mentors, and coaches. The content focuses on planning, instruction, building a learning community, and creating and implementing organizational systems for effective learning in a learning-centered classroom. *Instruction for All Students* builds on that work and extends the study of teaching and learning to include differentiation of instruction, 21st century thinking skills, and collegial collaboration.

Implementing Instruction

Framing the Learning
> *Instruction for All Students* pages 52-53
> *Why Didn't I Learn This in College?* pages 48-51

Dealing with Naive Understandings and Misconceptions
> *Instruction for All Students* pages 49, 55, 100-101, 102-103, 105, 109-111
> *Why Didn't I Learn This in College?* pages 68. 78, 81-82, 89, 98, 100,

Communicating Purposes, Expectations, and Directions
> *Instruction for All Students* pages 52 and 115
> *Why Didn't I Learn This in College?* pages 48 and 227

Using a Repertoire of Strategies, Materials, and Resources
> *Instruction for All Students*...the book!
> *Why Didn't I Learn This in College?*...the book!

Designing Rigorous Questions and Assignments
  Aligned with Desired Outcomes
> *Instruction for All Students* pages 114-145
> *Why Didn't I Learn This in College?* pages 54-60

Promoting Connections and Meaning Making
> *Instruction for All Students* pages 73-111 and
> pages 129-134
> *Why Didn't I Learn This in College?* pages 63-106

Framework for
The Study of Teaching and Learning

Planning Instruction

Professionalism & Collegial

Implementing Instruction

Organizing a Productive Environment

Assessing Learning & the Instructional Program

Orchestrating a Positive Environment

Additional Resources on
Implementing Instruction

- *Classroom Strategies That Work* by Robert Marzano, Debra Pickering and Diane Pollack

- *The Skillful Teacher* by Jon Saphier and Bob Gower

- *Activators* by Jon Saphier and Mary Ann Haley

- *Summarizers* by Jon Saphier and Mary Ann Haley

- *Strategies that Work* by Stephanie Harvey and Anne Gouvis

- *The Art of Teaching Reading* by Lucy McCormick

- *Mosaic of Thought* by Ellin Oliver Keene and Susan Zimmerman

- *Put Reading First* from the National Institute for Literacy. Download at www.nifl.gov

- *Literature Circles* by Harvey Daniels

Assessing Learning
and the Instructional Program
Best Practices to Note and Suggestions to Make

> *I noticed that you... You might consider... It is likely to promote student achievement if you... Given that, I suggest you... The district teacher performance criteria state that we are to...*

- **Go beyond grading student work to critiquing and analyzing student work** to see which components of the standards are at mastery, which are progressing, and which are in need of teaching and reteaching

- **Select assessment tools from a wide range of options** including, but not limited to, paper and pencil assessments

- Do a **preassessment** as part of the planning for a unit of study

- **Design rubrics, performance task lists, and checklists** that articulate in precise language performance and assessment requirements

- **Provide students with clear criteria and exemplars** of processes and products before they begin the work

- **Check for understanding** across all students by using signal cards, slates, think pads, choral responses, and circulation and adjust instruction accordingly

- **Provide formative rehearsals for summative assessments at appropriate levels of thinking**

- **Design and give assignments, to include homework, that provide practice and rehearsals and then analyze the results**

- Include **student self-assessment of products and of the effectiveness of the effort**

- **Teach students** to give each other feedback through **peer editing and review**

- **Use every assignment as data** on what to teach next and to whom and in what ways

- **Engage students in the design of assessment criteria**

- Have **students score anonymous work** to help them understand what the scoring criteria look like in student work

Planning Instruction

Professionalism & Collegial Collaboration

Implementing Instruction

Organizing a Productive Environment

Assessing Learning & the Instructional Program

Orchestrating a Positive Environment

Assessing Learning
and the **Instructional Program**
Best Practices to Note and Suggestions to Make continued...

> *I noticed that you... You might consider... It is likely to promote student achievement if you... Given that, I suggest you... The district teacher performance criteria state that we are to...*

- **Structure individual accountability in group work**
- **Monitor impact of teacher behavior** on student success and **modify behavior, plans, and instructional strategies accordingly**
- Describe the **criteria and/or the techniques you use to determine the effectiveness of your instruction**
- **Compare desired outcomes with actual outcomes and adjust plans accordingly**

See Chapter VI, pages 137-167 in *Why Didn't I Learn This in College?* and Chapter VI, pages 147-171 in *Instruction for All Students.*

Assessing Learning
and the Instructional Program
Reflections and Questions

Use these stems with the statements on the previous pages: *How might you...? How do you feel it went when you...? What did you learn from the situation in which you...? What does the data/research tell you about ...?* Additional reflections and questions are listed below.

- How do you use **the results of classroom assessments** such as tests and performance tasks to plan future instruction?

- How do you use **informal assessment information to make instructional decisions?**

- How do you use **standardized test results to make decisions** about the instructional program?

- How do you ensure that the **classroom assessments** you select or design are **valid measures of the district outcomes?**

- Describe the **process used for development of the evaluation criteria.**

- How do you **communicate assessment information to students, other staff, and parents?**

- **How would students describe the evaluation process?**

- How do you **provide opportunities for students** to set goals and assess progress?

- **How are initial attempts to use new processes and information used in establishing the final grade?**

- Describe how you **teach students to assess their own performances.**

- How do you ensure that the **feedback** you provide is **focused on specific points** on which students can improve or correct?

- How do you **give feedback/present data** to students about performance so that they can to react to that data and develop skills of self-adjustment?

- How do you ensure that **students are learning and growing from the grading, critiquing, and correcting** you do?

- Describe how you **demonstrate to students how to do the task or project and/or provide them examples of products.**

Planning Instruction

Professionalism & Collegial Collaboration

Implementing Instruction

Organizing a Productive Environment

Assessing Learning & the Instructional Program

Orchestrating a Positive Environment

Assessing Learning and the Instructional Program
Reflections and Questions continued...

> Use these stems with the statements on the previous pages: *How might you...? How do you feel it went when you...? What did you learn from the situation in which you...? What does the data/research tell you about ...?* Additional reflections and questions are listed below.

- How do you **monitor the balance between negative and positive feedback?**

- Describe the **performance of three students** who demonstrated little learning from the preassessment to the summative assessment. What kinds of errors did they make and what did you do before the next learning experiences to help them improve their efforts and their learning?

- Describe how you collect and use information from **classroom interactions, questions, and analysis of student work as formative assessment data.**

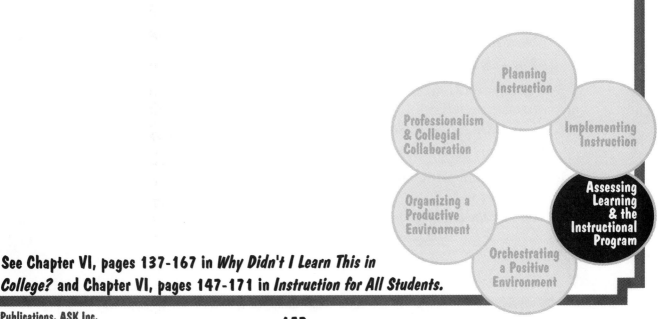

See Chapter VI, pages 137-167 in *Why Didn't I Learn This in College?* and Chapter VI, pages 147-171 in *Instruction for All Students.*

ASK Framework for
The Study of Teaching and Learning

The **ASK Framework** is presented here with notations of support materials found in *Leading the Learning* (Rutherford, 2003), *Why Didn't I Learn This in College?* (Rutherford, 2002), and *Instruction for All Students* (Rutherford, 2002).

Why Didn't I Learn This in College? is written for novice teachers and their supervisors, mentors, and coaches. The content focuses on planning, instruction, building a learning community, and creating and implementing organizational systems for effective learning in a learning-centered classroom. *Instruction for All Students* builds on that work and extends the study of teaching and learning to include differentiation of instruction, 21st century thinking skills, and collegial collaboration.

Assessing Learning & the Instructional Program

Additional Resources for Assessing Learning And the Instructional Program

- *Understanding by Design* by Grant Wiggins and Jay McTighe
- *Performance Based Learning & Assessment* by Educators in Pomeraug Regional School District 15

Planning Instruction

Professionalism & Collegial Collaboration

Implementing Instruction

Organizing a Productive Environment

Assessing Learning & the Instructional Program

Orchestrating a Positive Environment

Positive Learning-Centered Environment
Best Practices to Note and Suggestions to Make

I noticed that you... You might consider... It is likely to promote student achievement if you... Given that, I suggest you... The district teacher performance criteria state that we are to...

- **Learn student names and information about each one** early in the year
- **Greet students at the door with a smile and a handshake**
- **Use student names in examples**
- Make a strong effort to **interact in a positive way with each student each day**
- Develop a system for **monitoring the nature and frequency of your interactions with students**
- Create opportunities for **students to learn about themselves and each other**
- **Be knowledgeable** about the fads, fashions, music, hobbies, sports, and other recreational activities that are **of interest to your students**
- **Display student work** both in the classroom and in public areas; **identify the standard of learning the work represents**
- **Teach students how to set and work toward learning goals**
- Encourage students to **ask for and get help from one another**
- Encourage students to **monitor their own academic progress**
- Set up conditions where **students can assess the effectiveness of their learning habits**
- Teach students to **self-assess the appropriateness and effectiveness of their social skills**
- **Model respect** in words spoken, voice tone, eye contact, and in body language
- **Use music, books, posters, and pictures from different cultures**
- **Practice equity and explain to students the difference between equity** (get what you need when you need it) **and equality** (all get the same thing at the same time)

Planning
Instruction

Professionalism
& Collegial
Collaboration

Implementing
Instruction

Organizing a
Productive
Environment

Assessing
Learning
& the
Instructional
Program

Orchestrating
a Positive
Environment

Positive Learning-Centered Environment
Best Practices to Note and Suggestions to Make continued...

> *I noticed that you... You might consider... It is likely to promote student achievement if you... Given that, I suggest you... The district teacher performance criteria state that we are to...*

- Role-play situations with students to **identify appropriate and inappropriate behavior**
- **Provide student choice** of learning process, teach them to make good choices, and analyze whether or not the choices were the best for the learner
- **Explain the reason why you are doing what you are doing or making the decision you are making**
- **Change strategies to meet students' needs rather than expecting students to change to meet teacher needs** (Centennial BOCES)
- Take advantage of opportunities to **use humor**
- Remind yourself that you are a **role model**
- Develop a repertoire of ways to **encourage your students**
- **Reinforce students' attempts to solve problems and exert effort**
- Make it a practice to **recognize effective effort**
- **Resolve behavioral issues privately** with minimum disruption of instruction
- **Avoid sarcasm and ridicule**
- **Promote intrinsic motivation** (I did it!) **rather than extrinsic motivation** (you did it so you get a sticker or piece of candy)
- Show interest in students' lives beyond the classroom by **becoming involved in student activities**
- **Monitor student attributions and use attribution retraining** with those who make external attributions
- **Demonstrate respect for students as individuals** with different personal and family backgrounds and a wide range of skills, talents, and interests.

Orchestrating a Positive Learning-Centered Environment
Reflections and Questions

Use these stems with the statements on the previous pages: *How might you...? How do you feel it went when you...? What did you learn from the situation in which you...? What does the data/research tell you about ...?* Additional reflections and questions are listed below.

- How do you **engage students in establishing conditions that promote learning for all?**

- How do you provide for **different roles in group work**, and how do you ensure that the students carry out those roles?

- What processes do you use to **ensure that students apply and use information rather than simply memorizing facts or processes?**

- How do you **engage students in problem identifying and solving?**

- How do you help students learn to **use collaboration and communication skills in learning situations?**

- How do **students demonstrate enthusiasm, interest, and involvement in their learning?**

- How is **student interest measured?**

- How do you **help students recognize and develop skills to accommodate their own learning styles?**

- How do you **involve students in creating and evaluating their own organizational systems?**

- How would you handle/how have you handled **difficult human relations or a communications problem?**

- How do you **engage students in "ownership" of the classroom** and its smooth operation?

- Describe how you **gather and use information about students' experiences, interests, learning behaviors, needs, and progress from parents, professional colleagues, and the students themselves.**

Planning Instruction

Professionalism & Collegial Collaboration

Implementing Instruction

Organizing a Productive Environment

Assessing Learning & the Instructional Program

Orchestrating a Positive Environment

Positive Learning-Centered Environment
Reflections and Questions continued...

Use these stems with the statements on the previous pages: *How might you...?*
How do you feel it went when you...? *What did you learn from the situation in*
which you...? *What does the data/research tell you about ...?* Additional
reflections and questions are listed below.

- How do you **purposefully build on students' interests, needs, and levels of understanding?**

- What opportunities do you provide for **meaningful student choice?**

- How and when do you **build in opportunities for students to reflect on their learning and on the effectiveness of their efforts?**

- How do you use your understanding of **Multiple Intelligences theory and learning styles to help students understand their own and others' learning strengths and needs?**

- How do **students share their work with others?**

- In what ways do you use **your knowledge of group dynamics** to orchestrate the environment in the classroom?

Framework for
The Study of Teaching and Learning

The **ASK Framework** is presented here with notations of support materials found in *Leading the Learning* (Rutherford, 2003), *Why Didn't I Learn This in College?* (Rutherford, 2002), and *Instruction for All Students* (Rutherford, 2002).

Why Didn't I Learn This in College? is written for novice teachers and their supervisors, mentors, and coaches. The content focuses on planning, instruction, building a learning community, and creating and implementing organizational systems for effective learning in a learning-centered classroom. *Instruction for All Students* builds on that work and extends the study of teaching and learning to include differentiation of instruction, 21st century thinking skills, and collegial collaboration.

Orchestrating A Positive Learning-Centered Environment

Building a Community of Learners
Why Didn't I Learn This in College? Chapter II pages 7-44

Having and Communicating High Expectations to All Students
Instruction for All Students page 252
Why Didn't I Learn This in College? pages 13-17

Using Attribution Theory to Reframe Belief Systems
Instruction for All Students page 253
Why Didn't I Learn This in College? pages 18-19

Building Capacity Through Learning How to Learn Strategies
Instruction for All Students pages 254-258
Why Didn't I Learn This in College? pages 150-158

Using Errors and/or Lack of Background
Knowledge and Skills as Learning Opportunities
Instruction for All Students pages 254-257
Why Didn't I Learn This in College? pages 127-131

Building in Reflection & Metacognition
Instruction for All Students pages 81-84, 170-171, and 224-227
Why Didn't I Learn This in College? pages 19, 81-82, and 150-158

Planning Instruction

Professionalism & Collegial Collaboration

Implementing Instruction

Organizing a Productive Environment

Assessing Learning & the Instructional Program

Orchestrating a Positive Environment

Positive Learning-Centered Environment

Developing Thinking Skills for the 21st Century
  Instruction for All Students Chapter IX
  Pages 217-247

Building Appropriate & Positive Personal
  Relationships with Students
  Why Didn't I Learn This in College? pages 20-35
  Instruction for All Students pages 281-284

Additional Resources for Creating a
Positive Learning-Centered Environment

- *For Our Students, For Ourselves* video from McCrel

- *The Skillful Teacher* by Jon Saphier and Robert Gower

- *Control Theory in the Classroom* by William Glasser

- *Discipline with Dignity* by Richard Curwin and Allen Mendler

- *Beyond Discipline: From Compliance to Community* by Alfie Kohn

- *People Skills* by Robert Bolton

- *T.E.T.* by Thomas Gordon

Productive Learning-Centered Environment
Best Practices to Note and Suggestions to Make

> *I noticed that you... You might consider... It is likely to promote student achievement if you... Given that, I suggest you... The district teacher performance criteria state that we are to...*

- Use **flexible room arrangements** to match instructional objectives and desired student interaction

- **Identify room arrangements that work best in small-group work, whole class discussion, and testing**

- **Teach students to help you arrange/rearrange the student desks/tables quickly and safely**

- Arrange the room so that you can **move around the room with ease**

- **Reduce distance and barriers** between you and your students

- When working with a small group, position yourself so that you can **monitor other students at work**

- **Rotate duties among students** on a scheduled basis

- **Identify needed routines and procedures to ensure maximized learning time**

- **Explain, model, and practice routines and procedures** so that they can be regularly used by students and teacher without need for further explanation

- **Plan and use a short and relevant exercise for students to engage in as they enter the classroom** (These are called sponges, bell ringers, starters, fillers or anchoring activities.)

- **Be sure you have students' attention before beginning instruction or giving directions**

- Use high-results attention moves such as **wait time, the look, proximity, and circulation**

- **Provide practice and processing time**

- **Post the agenda and the learning outcomes** on the board, overhead or chart in the same place each day

- **Explain the work to be done and how to do it**

Planning Instruction

Professionalism & Collegial Collaboration

Implementing Instruction

Organizing a Productive Environment

Assessing Learning & the Instructional Program

Orchestrating a Positive Environment

Productive Learning-Centered Environment
Best Practices to Note and Suggestions to Make continued...

> *I noticed that you... You might consider... It is likely to promote student achievement if you... Given that, I suggest you... The district teacher performance criteria state that we are to...*

- Check to be sure **students know before they start work what to do and how to do it**

- Repeat and stress complex directions and difficult points; **write out steps to any process having three or more steps**

- **Repeat or rephrase questions and explanations** students do not understand or have students do so for each other

- **Use known or easy content to teach a new process, and use a known process to introduce or teach difficult new material**

- **Assist students in developing organizational systems** that work for them

- Teach students how to use **graphic organizers, mnemonics, and visualizations**

- **Teach students note-taking and reading strategies**

- **Provide opportunities for students to use a variety of learning strategies and to learn which works best for them** so that they can become independent learners

- Build in **movement**

- **Teach students to identify text structure and to use the appropriate graphic organizers** to capture key information

- **Warn students of upcoming transitions**

- **Match the pace of the instruction with the complexity of the concepts being studied and with the amount of unfamiliar vocabulary**

- **Mass practice at the beginning** of new learning and follow-up with **distributed practice throughout the learning**

- After practice of small chunks, **move quickly to meaningful use of the information and skills**

Productive Learning-Centered Environment
Best Practices to Note and Suggestions to Make continued...

> *I noticed that you... You might consider... It is likely to promote student achievement if you... Given that, I suggest you... The district teacher performance criteria state that we are to...*

- **Write directions for classwork and homework** on board, chart, or transparency

- **Use flexible grouping** determined by such variables as readiness levels, interest, information processing styles, student choice, and, on occasion, random order

- Stay focused on learning; **do not let "off-the-mark" behavior or backtalk take you off track**; notice and deal with it when it fits your agenda

- **Identify the causes of inattentive or disruptive behavior and match your response to the perceived cause**

- **Wait** to hold discussions about inattentive or disruptive behavior, or unmet expectations, **until both of you are calm**

- **Focus on future behavior** rather than on past behavior

- **Include students in developing procedures for handling inappropriate behavior or unmet expectations**

- Use **logical consequences** directly related to the behavior

- Use a **clearly articulated range of consequences** for unmet expectations based on the quality, intensity, and frequency of the action

- **Organize supplies, equipment, and papers** so that they are easily accessible; eliminate clutter

Planning
Instruction

Professionalism
& Collegial
Collaboration

Implementing
Instruction

Organizing a
Productive
Environment

Assessing
Learning
& the
Instructional
Program

Orchestrating
a Positive
Environment

Productive Learning-Centered Environment
Reflections and Questions

> Use these stems with the statements on the previous pages: *How might you...? How do you feel it went when you...? What did you learn from the situation in which you...? What does the data/research tell you about ...?* Additional reflections and questions are listed below.

- How do you **involve students in creating and evaluating their own organizational systems?**

- How would you handle/how have you handled **difficult human relations or a communications problem?**

- **What systems do you use to manage time and keep yourself organized?**

- How do you **organize materials and equipment to facilitate learning?**

- What **classroom routines do you use to enhance student time on meaningful tasks?**

- **How well are the routines/procedures you have established working?** What data do you have to support your evaluation of the effectiveness of your routines/procedures?

- How do you **engage students in "ownership" of the classroom** and its smooth operation?

- Describe your **record-keeping procedures-** which ones are working well and which ones are you working to improve?

- **How are you using technology to track student performance?** What do you see as logical next steps in using technology as an organizational tool?

- How do I/you **ensure consistent communication with students, colleagues, parents, and the community?**

- What issues are the focus of your **"mental movies"** when you are rehearsing/reviewing your plans for an upcoming lesson?

- Describe your thinking about **resource allocation to include time, space, materials, and attention** to ensure active and equitable learning for all.

ASK Framework for
The Study of Teaching and Learning

The **ASK Framework** is presented here with notations of support materials found in *Leading the Learning* (Rutherford, 2003), *Why Didn't I Learn This in College?* (Rutherford, 2002), and *Instruction for All Students* (Rutherford, 2002).

Planning Instruction

Professionalism

Organizing a Productive Environment

Implementing Instruction

Assessing Learning & the Instructional Program

Orchestrating a Positive Environment

Why Didn't I Learn This in College? is written for novice teachers and their supervisors, mentors, and coaches. The content focuses on planning, instruction, building a learning community, and creating and implementing organizational systems for effective learning in a learning-centered classroom. *Instruction for All Students* builds on that work and extends the study of teaching and learning to include differentiation of instruction, 21st century thinking skills, and collegial collaboration.

Organizing
A Productive Learning-Centered Environment

Creating and Using Organizational Systems for Professional and Instructional Materials
> *Why Didn't I Learn This in College?* pages 195-221

Developing and Implementing Organizational Systems for Learners and the Classroom (Space, Time, Procedures, Transitions, Gaining Attention)
> *Instruction for All Students* pages 258-264
> *Why Didn't I Learn This in College?* pages 221-252

Proactively Addressing the Needs of Reluctant and Resistant Learners
> *Instruction for All Students* pages 265-266
> *Why Didn't I Learn This in College?* pages 32-52

Additional Resources on Organizing
A Productive Learning-Centered Environments

- *The Skillful Teacher* by Jon Saphier and Robert Gower
- *What to Do With The Kid Who...* by Kay Burke
- *Discipline with Dignity* by Richard Curwin and Allen Mendler

Professionalism and Collegial Collaboration
Best Practices to Note and Suggestions to Make

> *I noticed that you... You might consider... It is likely to promote student achievement if you... Given that, I suggest you... The district teacher performance criteria state that we are to...*

- Use the **district mission and vision statements, the district learning standards, and the criteria for professional performance as benchmarks** for professional practice
- Demonstrate knowledge about and use of **current state and federal laws** regarding special services students
- **Consult with and inform appropriate personnel around legal questions**
- **Keep your grade book updated and legible**
- **Maintain accurate attendance records**
- **Inventory** school property, books and instructional materials and **maintain accurate records**
- **Perform duties** such as restroom supervision, lunch duty, hall duty, and bus duty **as assigned**
- **Use clear, concise, and grammatically correct language in oral and written communication**
- **Submit reports correctly and on time**
- **Attend required meetings**
- **Be prompt to and attentive at staff, departmental, and team meetings**
- **Participate and contribute at staff, departmental, and team meetings**
- **Provide substitute with thorough instructional plans** and notes on classroom procedures
- **Develop and make accessible emergency substitute plans**
- **Handle situations involving staff members in a professional manner**
- **Implement decisions made by groups** in which teacher served or was represented

Planning Instruction

Professionalism & Collegial Collaboration

Implementing Instruction

Organizing a Productive Environment

Assessing Learning & the Instructional Program

Orchestrating a Positive Environment

Professionalism and Collegial Collaboration
Best Practices to Note and Suggestions to Make continued...

> *I noticed that you... You might consider... It is likely to promote student achievement if you... Given that, I suggest you... The district teacher performance criteria state that we are to...*

- **Maintain Internet access safeguards** appropriate to age level and as identified by the district

- **Use discretion in handling confidential information and difficult situations**

- **Ensure that supportable facts,** rather than rumors or insinuations, **are discussion points in conversations and conferences**

- **Be available for conferences with parents**

- **Seek out parents** and make parents feel comfortable contacting you and interacting with you **as a partner in their child's education**

- **Teach parents** about the instructional program and your approach to learning through newsletters and evening academic events that feature student work and expected standards

- **Collaborate with special education teachers/general education teachers** to facilitate the learning of students with IEPs

- **Seek out and use professional expertise** for assistance and guidance in supporting students with intellectual, emotional or physical challenges

- **Serve as a school representative** when asked to do so

- **Serve as a catalyst for constructive change**

- Demonstrate responsibility in **attendance and punctuality** as required by school policy

- Always be **professionally groomed and attired**

- **Express views and ideas to others in a professional manner** that is respectful of the possibility and probability of different perspectives

Planning Instruction

Professionalism & Collegial Collaboration

Implementing Instruction

Assessing Learning & the Instructional Program

Organizing a Productive Environment

Orchestrating a Positive Environment

Professionalism and Collegial Collaboration
Best Practices to Note and Suggestions to Make continued...

> *I noticed that you... You might consider... It is likely to promote student achievement if you... Given that, I suggest you... The district teacher performance criteria state that we are to...*

- **Align professional development work with school and district goals**
- **Adjust classroom practice as a result of professional learning** completed independently, in collaboration with colleagues, and/or sponsored by the school or district
- **Work with colleagues across grade levels to align curriculum and decrease redundancy**
- **Recognize that collegial sharing is essential to the learning process** for both students and educators
- **Use all available resources** accessible locally, at the state level, nationally, and technologically
- **Use communication skills that demonstrate an awareness of cultural, gender, and generational differences**
- **Assess group dynamics and productivity and adjust own behavior to maximize the outcomes of the work**

Professionalism & Collegial Collaboration
Reflections and Questions

> Use these stems with the statements on the previous pages: *How might you...?*
> *How do you feel it went when you...? What did you learn from the situation in
> which you...?   What does the data/research tell you about ...?* Additional
> reflections and questions are listed below.

- Describe ways that you have **shared new ideas and your expertise with colleagues.**

- Describe your efforts to **foster collegial collaboration among school staff.**

- How do you **initiate/create opportunities to be a resource** to other teachers?

- How have you **contributed to the development and implementation of district, school, department or team programs and goals?**

- Describe the **professional development opportunities in which you have been engaged**; explain how and why you chose those particular professional development activities.

- **How have you integrated what you have learned** through participation in professional development opportunities into your practice in ways that impacted student learning and achievement?

- What opportunities have you sought to **mentor a colleague**, whether a new teacher or a teacher attempting to learn a new technique or area of content?

- How do you use **school-based specialists, district personnel and resources, and professional organizations** to support student achievement?

- How do you **coordinate your efforts** with other staff members?

- How do you keep abreast of **new developments in your field?**

- Describe your own **collaboration and co-teaching involvement?**

- How does your lesson and unit design process reflect the **beliefs, vision, and mission of the district?**

- What opportunities exist for **community members to view student work and provide feedback?**

- Describe how your practice demonstrates your belief that **all the students belong to all of us.**

Planning
Instruction

Professionalism
& Collegial
Collaboration

Implementing
Instruction

Organizing a
Productive
Environment

Assessing
Learning
& the
Instructional
Program

Orchestrating
a Positive
Environment

Professionalism and Collegial Collaboration
Reflections and Questions continued...

> Use these stems with the statements on the previous pages: *How might you...?*
> *How do you feel it went when you...? What did you learn from the situation in*
> *which you...? What does the data/research tell you about ...?* Additional
> reflections and questions are listed below.

- Describe **instructional materials you have designed/developed** yourself or in collaboration with others; describe the process you used in development.

- Describe how you have **sought out grant programs** to enhance your instructional program.

- Describe situations in which you have **piloted materials/programs**; what did you learn from that process?

- Describe the ways you are involved with **student activities as a spectator, active supporter, sponsor, or initiator.**

- What are the ways that you ensure that **parent partnership** goes beyond volunteering and includes decision-making?

Framework for
The Study of Teaching and Learning

The **ASK Framework** is presented here with notations of support materials found in *Leading the Learning* (Rutherford, 2003), *Why Didn't I Learn This in College?* (Rutherford, 2002), and *Instruction for All Students* (Rutherford, 2002).

Why Didn't I Learn This in College? is written for novice teachers and their supervisors, mentors, and coaches. The content focuses on planning, instruction, building a learning community, and creating and implementing organizational systems for effective learning in a learning-centered classroom. *Instruction for All Students* builds on that work and extends the study of teaching and learning to include differentiation of instruction, 21st century thinking skills, and collegial collaboration.

Professionalism and Collegial Collaboration

See *Leading the Learning* pages 122-126 for ideas to try, best practices to note, suggestions to make, questions to ask, and related resources.

The Ways We Collaborate: Consultant, Collaborator, and Coach
Leading the Learning pages 190-198

Formats for Collaboration and Job Embedded Learning
Leading the Learning pages 11-61
Instruction for All Students Chapter XI, pages 270-287

Peer Observation
Leading the Learning pages 39-40
Instruction for All Students pages 277-280

Mentoring
Leading the Learning pages 51-55
Instruction for All Students pages 285-286

Co-Teaching
Instruction for All Students pages 281-284

Professional Responsibilities
Why Didn't I Learn This in College? pages 195-209

Parents as Partners
Why Didn't I Learn This in College? Chapter IX,
pages 253-266

Additional Resources for
Professionalism and
Collegial Collaboration

- *Results Driven Professional Development* by St. Vrain
  Valley Office of Professional Development
- *Cognitive Coaching* by Art Costa and Bob Garmstron
- *Mentoring Matters* by Laura Lipton and Bruce Wellman

Planning
Instruction

Professionalism
& Collegial
Collaboration

Implementing
Instruction

Organizing a
Productive
Environment

Assessing
Learning
& the
Instructional
Program

Orchestrating
a Positive
Environment

Peer Observation Possibilities

Chapter VII

Why Peer Observation?

Most state departments of education strongly recommend or even require that a peer observation component be included in district induction programs; this responsibility is usually given to mentors. The rationale behind the inclusion of peer observations in the induction process is that all teachers can learn much by observing expert teachers and by being observed, participating in reflective conferences about the observation, and in receiving feedback from a trained observer. While this practice is valuable for all teachers, it is especially important for teachers new to teaching and teachers new to a district or school.

Novice Teachers

Although most novice teachers participated in student teaching experiences, for one reason or another that experience may or may not have been a valuable one. One reason is that the student teacher works in a classroom where the productive learning environment and positive learning community have already been established by the supervising teacher. The student teacher has no way of knowing what all went on to create the environment in which he is working. Secondly, student teaching often occurs in one grade level or one content area class and the first teaching assignment may not only be in another grade level or content area, it may be in another demographic setting where multiple variables seem to negate all the learning that occurred in the student teaching experience. Thirdly, there may have been a mismatch between student teacher and supervising teacher because of differences in learning and teaching styles, lack of skills on the part of the supervising teacher for working with adult learners, or even a reluctance to have a student teacher in the first place. The most significant factors limiting the novice teacher's capacity to take what they experienced in the student teaching experience and use it in their own classroom are that they quite simply were not in charge and did not have the sense of urgency that being totally and completely responsible for the learning of the students, the organizing of the classroom, communicating with colleagues and parents, and completing the multiple administrative tasks that are part of the job.

Alternative Certification Programs

Today many of the teachers new to our schools have not had a student teaching experience. They are entering the profession through alternative certification programs. They bring great experiences from other fields and add greatly to the richness and diversity of our teaching staffs. The question we want to ask is not focused on how they were prepared to teach, but how well. They are usually quite knowledgeable about the content they are to teach and may well be skilled at orchestrating and organizing learning experiences for adults, but they have had

Why Peer Observation?

few opportunities to spend the day with classrooms full of children. We need to provide them with multiple opportunities to see experts working in such classrooms and to receive coaching and feedback about how they are doing in their own classrooms.

Experienced Teacher New to the District, School, or Team

Experienced new teachers who join us each year need opportunities to master the nuances of working in the district and school. They need not only information about how the school operates and the rationale for those actions, they need to see how they play out in classroom practice. Variables to consider in structuring peer observations with experienced teachers entering a school district are as follows:

- philosophy of district and school
- school culture
- financial realities of the district
- degree of collaboration between teachers, departments, grade levels, and schools
- how inclusion is implemented from both a student and teacher perspective
- demographics of staff and student body
- socio-economics of school and district
- role parents and community play in the educational process
- size of school and size of district
- location of school: urban, suburban or rural
- impact of influx of students who speak a language other than English as their first language
- the use of data to inform teaching practices
- the teacher performance evaluation system
- possibly different grade or subject assignment

These factors which influence our professional work create a strong case for these new but experienced teachers to spend time planning with mentors, observing, being observed, and analyzing and reflecting what is seen and heard.

Often new teachers do not know what we are talking about when we describe how to implement a certain action in the classroom. There are several ways to help them move forward in both their understanding of what we are talking about and to increase the likelihood that they will try it in their own classrooms. When the new teacher has a knowledge base about what needs to be done but is not skillful at doing it, an effective way to learn a new technique is to see someone else use it. The new teacher may observe the mentor teacher in his or her classroom or have the mentor teacher come into his own classroom and use the technique with the new teacher's students.

Why Peer Observation?

In this chapter we will explore multiple ways to engage in peer observations. Some involve true peer coaching and others are simply peer poaching!

Peer observation possibilities discussed are as follows:
- New teacher observes mentor
- Mentor arranges demonstration teaching by expert teacher
- New teacher shadows teachers or students
- New teacher and mentor observer together
- Co-teaching by mentor and new teacher
- Videotaping and analysis of mentor teaching
- Videotaping and analysis of new teacher teaching
- Viewing and analyzing videotaped classroom episodes
- Observations beyond the classroom

Peer Observation Possibilities

There are many ways for new teachers to gather the data needed to participate in data-driven discussions about teaching and learning. Observing and analyzing shared teaching and learning episodes is one of the mot powerful. Some of those observations may result in peer coaching opportunities and others provide "peer poaching" opportunities. The difference is, of course, in the purpose of the observation. Are the new teachers to reflect on and analyze their own teaching and receive feedback from an expert coach or are the new teachers on a mission to gather new ideas, explore how others apply strategies in their classroom, and then make plans to use the approaches and strategies in their own classrooms.

New Teacher Observes Mentor

One way to break down potential barriers to the peer observation process is to invite the new teacher into your own classroom. One objective of any peer observation process for new teachers is to communicate the value the staff places on collegial collaboration and that fact that classroom doors are open to others at all times.

If you ask the new teacher to complete a needs assessment before or close to the beginning of school, that needs assessment can give you clues as to what would be interesting and useful to the new teacher. See **Chapter IX, Tools for New Teachers** for needs assessments and self-assessments. The observation can be a quick ten minute visit or, as appropriate, a complete class session. It is important that the observation be debriefed. This provides you an opportunity to model analytical and reflective practice and gives the new teacher a chance to ask you questions about not only the observed teaching and learning but also about the decision-making that went into how the learning experiences were orchestrated.

Mentor Arranges Demonstration Teaching by Expert Teacher

In those situations where a visit to your own classroom would not provide the new teacher with the experience they need, arrange a visit to the classroom of another teacher who has the teaching expertise and the class composition the new teacher needs to see.

New Teacher Shadows Teachers or Students

A shadowing experience is appropriate in many situations. If the new educator is one who works in a specialized setting that may or may not include a traditional classroom, shadowing a teacher throughout an entire day may be a powerful learning experience for the new teacher. The Teaching and Learning Center in Greece Central School District, New York, provides teachers the

Peer Observation Possibilities

opportunity to engage in the shadowing process. Topics on which the teachers focused on 2003-2004 included standards-based instruction, literature circles, autism, framing a lesson, student engagement and active learning strategies, inclusive education, rigor, and integration of literacy into the content areas. See new teacher comments on page 191 in the Through the Voice of New Teachers ...Reactions to Shadowing Experiences and the Shadow Day Program application on page 192. The questions on this form are aligned with the professional development and school improvement goals of the district.

New Teacher and Mentor Observe Together

There is a possibility that when new teachers observe other teachers they may not know the most important teacher and student actions to notice. When new teachers and mentors observe together the mentor can point out significant events and assist the new teacher in analyzing the cause and effect of what is occurring. These observations can be either a lengthy observation of one teacher or a series of short visits to multiple teachers. These short visits are called walk-throughs, learning walks, and quick visits. See **Chapter XI, Tools for Peer Observation and Data-Driven Discussions** for resources in planning and reflecting on these observations.

Co-Teaching by Mentor and New Teacher

Planning and co-teaching together in one or the other's classroom provides an extraordinary learning opportunity for not only the new teacher but the mentor as well. It may be possible for the teachers to combine their classes for a joint lesson. See **Chapter XII, Tools for Instructional Planning** for multiple lesson planning formats to use in planning the co-teaching experience.

Mentor Observes New Teacher

A mentor's observation of the new teacher is the most used peer observation format in mentoring programs. Participating in one or more of the other possibilities discussed here prior to the mentor observing the new teacher may make this format less intimidating. Informal drop-in visits can pave the way for the longer more structured observations. This format provides the opportunity for new teachers to experience the observation process used by the school in the teacher supervision and evaluation program. Because those formal observations begin relatively early in the year, mentors need to move quickly in establishing trust, inviting the new teacher into their own classrooms, and organizing other forms of peer observation. One important goal of any mentoring relationship should be establishing the norm of "public teaching."

Peer Observation Possibilities

Videotaping and Analysis of Mentor Teaching

If geography and time are issues, videotaping can help solve the problem. It may be that in the near future we will be using video streaming to transmit and then analyze the teaching and learning occurring in our classrooms. If a video camera is frequently used in the classroom both teacher and students quickly get used to having it there and are able to go about business without being aware of its presence. Mentor modeling of this process is most likely necessary before new teachers will be willing to videotape and analyze themselves.

Videotaping and Analysis of New Teacher Teaching

This approach to peer observation is one that can be used by teachers working together in the same building or in different parts of the state. While the video will not be of professional quality, a camera set up on a tripod in the back corner of the room can provide a lens on teaching and learning that can serve as the focus of mentor-new teacher discussions of classroom practice. Even an audiotape can provide data for analysis of classroom work.

Viewing and Analyzing Videotaped Classroom Episodes

An easy way for mentor and new teacher to share a teaching and learning experience is for them to view a videotape of a third teacher teaching. Visit www.ascd.org for a list of videotapes appropriate for mentor and new teacher analysis. The Lesson Collection series features 12 to 20 minute classroom episodes across all grade levels and content areas. In addition to segments filmed in the classroom the teacher featured in the video explains his or her thinking and often explains what preparation work was necessary to have students learning as they are seen learning.

Observations Beyond the Classroom

Most educators have responsibilities beyond the classroom. Counselors, reading specialists, and media center specialists may need a different form of peer observation such as structured interviews and shadowing. New teachers have responsibilities for parent teacher conferences, staffings for special education, Back--to-School Night, and co-curricular activities and coaching. They need coaching and feedback on these professional responsibilities. Mentors need to identify ways to observe and coach new teachers in these roles.

Peer Observation Possibilities
Observations Beyond the Classroom

Teacher responsibilities beyond the classroom include parent teacher conferences and Back-to-School Night, staffings for special education placement, IEP meetings, and co-curricular activities and coaching. Novice teachers may not have had any opportunities to observe or participant in this type of meetings and experienced teachers new to the district may find that protocols for these meetings are quite different from those they experienced in other districts. Mentors can provide a valuable support system by observing, modeling, or co-facilitating such meetings.

Parent Teacher Conferences

These conferences can cause great fear for novice teachers and difficult conferences can cause concern for even the most experienced teachers. Guidance counselors, psychologists, and special educators spend a great deal of time interacting with parents so have a strong need for support with this responsibility. Planning, modeling, observing with coaching and feedback or co-facilitating by mentors can provide strong support for those leading parent teacher conferences for the first time, leading a first conference with a translator, or dealing with volatile situations. See pages 259-265 in *Why Didn't I Learn This in College?* for concrete suggestions for productive parent teacher conferences. In these conferences, be sure that all involved understand the issue of confidentiality.

Staffings for Special Education

Local regulations and procedures vary greatly from school system to school system so peer observation and coaching around these meetings should be a priority of mentors. Mentor support around the decision-making and practice of special educators, counselors, social workers, and psychologists is important throughout the year but is especially important at the beginning of the school year. With the passing of IDEA, co-teaching is often the norm; as a result, general education teachers also spend a significant amount of time preparing for and participating in these meetings. Mentors need to work with all new teachers to ensure that they are knowledgeable about the law and regulations, the requirements for student identification, the services that are available as well as the interventions to try before making a referral, and that they have developed strong communication skills for working with colleagues and parents.

Observations Beyond the Classroom

Back-to-School Night

These events provide one of the most important public examinations of our practice. While it may be impossible to arrange a peer observation of a Back-to-School Night, mentors can role play such a meeting and could videotape themselves conducting a Back-to-School night and use the videotape the following years as an electronic peer observation tool. See pages 261-262 in *Why Didn't I Learn This in College?* for guidance to share with new teachers.

Co-Curricular Activities and Coaching

While academic achievement and learning is the primary goal of schooling, the teaching staff supports not only the academic growth of students but also contributes to their affective, social, and physical growth. This work often occurs outside the classroom in club meetings, auditoriums, and on playing fields. In most instances experienced coaches and club sponsors provide the necessary mentoring. Be sure, however, to check with the new teachers to see how that component of their professional day is going.

Peer Observation Possibilities
Learning Walks/Walk-Throughs Together

Walk-throughs are informal brief classroom visitations that may be used for generic data gathering or focused on particular teaching and learning behaviors.

Several education researchers and consultants have written about and advocated the use of these brief and more frequent classroom visits or observations. **Dr. Carolyn Downey** of San Diego State University and **Dr. Lauren Resnick**, Director of the Learning Research and Development Center at the University of Pittsburgh, have focused their work around the power of increasing the frequency of classroom observations by supervisors. Dr. Resnick's efforts have been focused on various stakeholders participating in **Learning Walks** to look for conditions that would promote student achievement of high standards while Dr. Downey has focused on walk-throughs as a component of data gathering in the supervision and evaluation process. **The New Teacher Center**, at the University of California Santa Cruz, calls the short but frequent observations **Quick Visits** in its training program for mentors.

What to Notice During Walk-Throughs: The Experts Say ...
Ellen Moir, Executive Director, and the staff at the New Teacher Center suggest that the focus of the **Quick Visit** should be as follows:
- **Content:** What are the students learning?
- **Strategies:** How are they learning/practicing/applying skills, knowledge and concepts?
- **Alignment:** How does this learning correlate to district standards and to the needs of the students?
  How does this work help students meet performance standards?
  How have student needs been assessed?
  Does the pacing match student needs?
  How is instruction differentiated?

Dr. Resnick recommends that observers
- Look at the work in which students are engaged
- Examine student work displayed in the classroom
- Talk to students
- Talk with the teacher

Walk-Throughs Together

What to Notice: Looking at Student Work

Another area of focus for walk-throughs could be around the kind of work students are doing at the time of the walk-through. Data collected could include:
- Type of task (note taking, reading, collaborating, listening, etc.)
- Knowledge students were expected to master or demonstrate in the task
- Skills students were expected to be using or demonstrate mastery of
- Level of thinking required of the students in completing the task

What to Notice: Using District Performance Criteria as the Focus

Use the district criteria to identify areas of focus for learning walks/walk-throughs. See **Tools for New Teachers** for self assessments which can be used to identify areas of focus. Short classroom visits might focus on:
- A complete set of criteria as identified by the district, the induction program, or a professional development program
- One or two areas of focus as selected by the district, the mentor, the teacher, or a combination thereof
- One or two variables across all the classrooms in the school/district

What to Notice: A Collaborative Approach

Use the **T-Chart** provided on page 328 to collaborate with the new teacher in generating lists of look-fors or to further personalize and quantify district performance criteria. If you are working with multiple new teachers or using a team mentoring approach, the **Graffiti** strategy described on page 79 of *Why Didn't I Learn This in College* provides a way for groups to generate lists of look fors and listen fors during walk-throughs. Place an area of focus at the top of the chart and use a large T-Chart to capture the ideas of the group.

Processing What is Observed

Pause after each classroom visit to have a chat in the hallway about what you noticed. You may carry a clipboard to record key observations so that you can discuss patterns as you continue to observe in other classrooms or at the end of the walk-through session. See **Tools for Peer Observation** for forms to use for data collection during learning walks, walk-throughs, and observations.

Through the Voice of New Teachers...
Our Shadowing Experiences

I found this experience to be amazingly valuable. I think that it would be beneficial to make this shadowing a mandatory part of Teacher's First for the next year. Even though it is hard to find time for these kinds of activities, they are what have the most impact on my teaching practices.

This shadowing experience was valuable because...

- I learned so many practical applications for instructional delivery. I also observed two teacher librarians that have excellent classroom management skills that I am trying to model.

- The teacher I shadowed helped me make important connections between the intermediate and middle school 12:1:3 programs. We exchanged many ideas about differentiation of instruction.

- I was able to see how a teacher with the same job title and similar responsibilities implements particular strategies, modifications, and techniques to meet student needs. Since there are very few Autism Consultant Teachers in the District, it was extremely helpful to see how team meetings are run, how my Shadow Teacher organizes her day to provide services to students and teachers, what expectations are for students at "lower grade," how specific behavioral difficulties are handled, etc.

- It helped me to know that I want to continue doing my job. I saw great teaching and terrific reflection techniques. I also took with me some valuable resources.

- It enabled me to "pause" for a day and reflect on my practice. The focused day-long discussion with my colleagues was invaluable!

- I was able to observe lessons similar to those that I teach, but at a different age/grade/developmental level. I came away with several ideas that I will modify.

- This experience allowed me to gain a clearer understanding of the types of special education programs available at our schools. I feel I can speak more knowledgeably to fellow staff members and parents.

- It helped to increase my knowledge of the third grade level expectations. Also, I have more first-hand knowledge that I can share with my second grade parents.

- I saw how I could present a lesson in a different and more effective method. Also, I got many valuable ideas for future lessons.

- I had the opportunity to see different methods of helping students research and organize long-term projects. The experience also allowed me to talk with other teachers and brainstorm ways of approaching different historical topics.

Marguerite Dimgba, Director, Teaching and Learning Center, Greece Central School District, NY

Shadow Day Program

The Greece Teaching and Learning Center is sponsoring the Shadow Day Program. The goal is to have a teacher "shadow" an experienced Greece Central School District teacher for one day or a half day to gain valuable insight in the teaching profession. After a discussion with the appropriate building administrator or Department of Curriculum and Instruction director, the teacher should select a focus for the learning for the day (i.e. Differentiated instruction, inclusion, etc.). This focus should be related to the school improvement plan. The administrator is asked to recommend an outstanding teacher who excels in the chosen focus area and to sign off on the bottom of this form.

The teacher needs to:
- Meet with the appropriate administrator to discuss focus and which teacher to shadow.
- Schedule a mutually acceptable day with the "Shadow Teacher."
- Notify the principal if the visitation will occur in a different building.

1. Name: _____

   Your school: _____ Date of visitation:_____

2. Who are you going to shadow? _____

   At what school? _____

   Why did you select this person to shadow? _____

   _____

3. Do you need a substitute for the day? (Circle one) Yes or No

   How long do you need a sub? (Circle one) Full Day or Half Day

4. Which standards/benchmarks will you focus on for the day? _____

   _____

5. What is the skill/area you want to enhance? How does this relate to your school improvement plan?

   _____

   _____

Principal's Signature _____ Date _____

The Mentor &
The Formal Observation Process

Mentors are not involved in the formal observation process in a supervisory capacity but they do have an important role in understanding the rationale for and the process of the system well enough to be able to explain how it works and why it is set up the way it is. For a variety of reasons, many veteran teachers have their own emotional baggage with the supervisory and evaluation process. Since an important role of the mentor is to represent the district in the best possible light it may be necessary for some mentors to be explicit in examining their own experiences with past evaluations and in identifying how they will be positive about the process in discussing it with teachers new to the district. In the best case scenario this is not an issue for mentors but, unfortunately there are those who find themselves in districts where best practice in supervision and evaluation is not always the norm.

Mentors can support new teachers with the observation component of the supervision and evaluation process. It may be that either explaining the process or it may be that the mentor needs to do a "mock" formal observation process with the new teachers. Hopefully the on-going mentoring observations and data driven discussions provide sufficient practice with the process of planning for, conducting, and reflecting on classroom teaching and learning. If that is not the case then it may be important to "practice" the formal observation process which usually includes a pre-observation conference, an observation of at least thirty minutes, a post-observation, and a written report. In most districts teachers "in the cycle" are observed two to three times a year; the majority of supervision and evaluation systems are structured so that novice teachers and teachers new to the district are to be observed during each of the first three years and veteran teachers every three or four years.

The movement towards performance standards for students and the evolution of best practice in classroom assessment has led to clearly articulated performance standards for teachers and to assessment of teacher performance that is more integrated into the fabric of school life rather than being the event it has often been in the past. Mentor use of these performance criteria with new teachers promotes that integration.

Few supervisors or teachers feel that the time and energy invested in the formal observation process provides anywhere near the opportunities for professional growth that face-to-face interactions with each other and colleagues provide. It is here that the mentor can play such an important role because the opportunities and expectations for observations and face-to-face discussions based on data gathered during the observation are built into the mentoring program.

Data-Driven Discussions

Data-Driven Discussions
How Will You...
How Did You Help Students Learn?

"Feedback is information about how we did in light of what we attempted." If we can agree that **"what we are attempting"** is always increased student learning, then we know how to focus the feedback we give and the questions we ask. That focus alone would change the way we mentor teachers. The first question asked should always be, **"How did you help students learn?"** rather than "How do you think it went?" While the latter may have the same intent, it is not as explicit.

We want the teachers whom we are mentoring to learn to self-assess, to know when to ask for coaching, and then to be able to self-adjust in order to promote student learning. To do this, mentors need incredible knowledge and skill to orchestrate conferences and other data-driven discussions. While some of us do this work quite well intuitively, as Madeline Hunter said, "Intuition is no substitute for competence!" We never know when a mentoring "teachable moment" will occur. Both carefully planned conferences and informal hallway conversations can have powerful influence on teacher decision making and classroom practice. To that end we need to be purposeful about identifying sources of data, appropriate data to discuss, and about building skills for engaging in data-driven discussions.

Chapter III, New Teachers as Colleagues and Learners focuses on adult learning theory, information processing styles, and generational differences. This chapter focuses on **data sources, conference approaches, and strategies for engaging new teachers in formal and informal data-driven discussions.**

> **"Feedback is information about how we did in light of what we attempted. Intent vs. effect. Actual vs. ideal performance. The best feedback is highly specific, descriptive of what we did and did not do in light of standards, and occurs in both a timely and ongoing way. Think of the best feedback systems: computer games, your shower faucets, or tasting the meal as you cook. Or recall how often the music or tennis coach provides a steady flow of feedback to show you how your actions cause this or that result.... What feedback most certainly isn't is praise and blame or mere encouragement."**
>
> **Grant Wiggins**

Data-Driven Discussions
Data Possibilities

Just as teachers gather assessment data about student learning in many ways, mentors can gather data about the work and the impact of new teacher work on student learning in a variety of ways. Listed below are some, but certainly not all, possible data sources which can provide focus for initial or ongoing discussions, observations, and self-assessment.

- **Planning conferences**
- **Peer Observations**
- **Informal observations**
  - ➢ parent/teacher conferences
  - ➢ professional development events
  - ➢ professional meetings
- **Reflective conferences**
- **Student work**
- **Student achievement data**
  - ➢ state
  - ➢ district
  - ➢ classroom assessments
  - ➢ longitudinal rubrics
  - ➢ grade distribution reports
- **Journals**
- **Self-Assessment**
- **Teacher work**
  - ➢ year, unit, and daily lesson plans
  - ➢ action research
  - ➢ review of records, such as plan book, grade book, teacher-prepared materials, grading policy
  - ➢ teacher logs/records of after school assistance provided to students
  - ➢ substitute plans
  - ➢ teacher's parent conference notes, phone logs
  - ➢ written communication initiated by the teacher, such as notes, memos, letters, and newsletters to parents, students, and colleagues
  - ➢ documentation of involvement in school and professional activities
- **Portfolios**
- **Conversations**

Data-Driven Discussions
Planning Conferences

Planning conferences provide opportunities to gather data, establish context, and interact as new teachers. The time spent in planning conferences provides a tremendous opportunity for the mentor to be an instructional change agent. The planning conference provides the ultimate **"teachable moment."**   It is hard to imagine a better time to help teachers shape their thinking or to learn more about instructional decision-making.

Stand-Alone Planning Conferences

Planning conferences can be held when there is no intention of following up with an observation. The sole purpose, in this instance, can be simply to plan a lesson, unit, or map out a semester or course. These conferences may include small groups or teams rather than being one-on-one interactions.

Planning Conferences Prior to an Observation

Information to discuss with new teachers prior to mentor observations:
- What students are supposed to know and be able to do as a result of the learning experiences to be observed
- How those outcomes relate to district standards, benchmarks, and indicators
- How student learning will be assessed in both formative and summative ways
- How the learning experiences in which the students will be engaged are related to what they are supposed to learn, to prior lessons, and to the big picture of the unit and the year
- The sequence of the lesson
- How data has been used to determine the best course of action
- What learning difficulties have been and are expected to be encountered and the plans for dealing with those problems
- Any other contextual information
- Any special areas of focus, as well as rationale for that focus, as identified by the mentor or by the teacher

The Top Ten Questions to Focus Discussions of the Teaching and Learning Process on the next page provide discussion starting points for planning conferences.

TOP TEN QUESTIONS
to Focus Discussions of the Teaching & Learning Process

1. What should **students know and be able to do** as a result of this lesson? How are these objectives related to national, state, and/or **district standards?**

2. How do **students demonstrate what they know and what they can do** with what they know? Are there multiple forms of assessment including student **self-assessment?** What are the **assessment criteria** and what form do they take?

3. How do you plan to **find out** what **students already know (preassessment)** and help them access what they know and have experienced both inside and outside the classroom? How do the learners not only **build on prior experiences** but **reframe their thinking** when appropriate?

4. How are new knowledge, concepts, and skills to be introduced? Given the **diversity of the students** and the **task analysis**, what **options for sources of information and presentation modes** are used?

5. How do students **process (make meaning of) their learning?** What key questions, activities, and assignments (in class or homework) promote retention, understanding and transfer?

6. What are the **formative assessments** or **checks for student understanding** during the lesson? How is data from those assessments used to inform teaching decisions?

7. How is **instruction differentiated** so that the learning experiences are productive for all students? Are students encouraged to **process** and **demonstrate learning** in different ways?

8. How is the learning framed **so that students know the objectives**, the **rationale** for the objectives and activities, the directions and procedures, the **assessment task and criteria,** as well the connection of the lesson and the activities to the standards and to life beyond the classroom.

9. How are opportunities for students to make **real world connections** and to learn and use the **varied and complex thinking skills** built into the learning experiences?

10. What adjustments are made in the **learning environment** and in **instruction** so that all students can work and learn efficiently? How is **data** used to make these decisions?

Data-Driven Discussions
Reflective Conference Approaches

Much has been written about approaches to conferencing. Although a variety of terms have been used to describe conference approaches, an examination of the approaches reveals that they are far more alike than they are different. Following a review of those approaches and the terms used over time, the recently introduced terms **consulting, collaborating, and coaching** are used to describe the repertoire of approaches mentors can use.

Although it often appears from the way descriptions of conferencing approaches are written that each conference is conducted using only one approach or another, that is not the reality. The reality is that once the full repertoire of approaches is part of the mentor's knowledge and skill base, the mentor is able to move smoothly from one approach to another throughout any one conference. This means that in addition to skillfulness with conference approaches, the previously discussed communication skills play an important role in knowing how and when to switch approaches.

Glickman, Gordon, and Ross-Gordon

Glickman, Gordon, and Ross-Gordon describe four approaches to conferencing and feedback:

- Directive-Control: The supervisor tells the teacher what to do **(Consulting)**
- Directive-Informational: The supervisor lists the options and asks for input from the teacher **(Collaborating)**
- Collaborative: The supervisor and teacher work together to share information and options for actions and as partners make a plan **(Collaborating)**
- Nondirective: The supervisor facilitates the teacher's thinking so that the teacher can make a plan for herself **(Coaching)**

They contend that the approach should be selected to match the teacher's level of development, expertise, and willingness to change.

Implications for Mentors

Almost all mentor reflective conferences will use the last three approaches described above. While the nondirective approach is the end goal of the mentoring process, the reality is that the mentor may often, especially with novice teachers, need to list options of strategies to try and, may in some situations, need to explicitly tell the novice teacher what to try. This latter approach is the least desirable. Mentors should have as a goal to lead new teachers to be able analyze data, identify problems and possibilities and make an appropriate plan of action.

Data-Driven Discussions
Reflective Conference Approaches
Hersey and Blanchard

Hersey and Blanchard in their *Situational Leadership* model provide four approaches to promoting change in behavior based on a person's **readiness and willingness** to change:

Direct	Clearly communicate what change must be made, as well as the timelines for change. Careful use of this approach may be appropriate in a few instances with novice teachers. This approach is almost always used by supervisors when teacher performance is below the district standards. Extensive follow-up to ensure follow-through is essential. **(Consulting)**
Recommend	Clearly communicate the need to change or improve behavior or techniques, but allow flexibility for the teacher to select from the options presented by the supervisor or mentor. The need for change is strong and follow-up to ensure follow-through is important. **(Collaborating)**
Facilitate	Discuss possible changes, but leave the decision open. Usually used to promote teacher decision making and/or repertoire building. Follow-up is in the form of support and encouragement. **(Collaborating and coaching)**
Delegate	Leave the decision about what to change up to the teacher. Provide support, feedback, and recognition. Typically used with highly skilled, knowledgeable, and reflective teachers. Follow-up is in the form of encouragement and support. **(Coaching)**

Implications for Mentors

This business model is an important part of the knowledge base of a positive and productive mentor. While many new teachers may be **willing** to do whatever is expected of them, they do not have the **readiness level** that comes with time, analysis, reflection, and repertoire building. Mentor decisions through the lens of this model are closely aligned with teacher decisions about differentiation of instruction. Different scaffolding is needed for different teachers.

Recommending and facilitating are probably the most appropriate approaches to use in mentoring interactions. Few novice teachers can be described as highly skilled, knowledgeable, and reflective so delegating is not an appropriate entry point. Care must be taken with novice teachers as they mature during the first

Data-Driven Discussions
Reflective Conference Approaches

years of teaching and with new experienced teachers to analyze their willingness and readiness to refine decision making and adjust teaching practices. When they are ready and willing to do their own thinking, mentors need to be ready to use the delegating approach.

Blase and Blase

In their research at the University of Georgia, the Blases identified five conference strategies that promote teacher growth.
- make suggestions
  - ➤listen before making suggestions
  - ➤extend teachers' thinking
  - ➤use examples and models
  - ➤give teacher choice about which suggestion to implement
  - ➤encourage teachers to take risks
  - ➤give suggestions both orally and in writing
- give feedback
  - ➤make feedback nonjudgmental/nonevaluative
  - ➤include infrequent constructive criticism
  - ➤use praise
  - ➤use collaborative approach
  - ➤be available for further discussion of feedback
  - ➤include student learning and behavior
- model
- use inquiry and open-ended questions
- solicit teacher opinion

Implications for Mentors

Blase and Blase interviewed teachers to find out what conferencing behaviors best promoted professional growth. The behaviors described above are aligned with coaching and collaborative approaches to mentoring. While it may be fastest to use a consulting mode and tell new teachers what to do, mentors should exercise caution about being too directive. Unasked for advice often falls on unhearing ears, so it is advisable to orchestrate the mentoring discussions so that the new teacher asks for advice.

Data-Driven Discussions
Reflective Conference Approaches

Costa and Garmston

Costa and Garmston recommend that we focus more on teacher decision-making and less on teacher behavior. This belief system requires that supervisors and mentors need strong coaching skills that can help others mediate their own thinking about their decision making. Their model of coaching, which they call Cognitive Coaching, is the most sophisticated form of coaching and requires skillful and well-trained coaches. The three goals of cognitive coaching are as followes:

- establishing and maintaining trust, including
  - ➤trust in self
  - ➤trust between individuals
  - ➤trust in the coaching process
- facilitating mutual learning
- enhancing growth toward holonomy which they define as individuals acting autonomously while simultaneously being interdependent within a group. The five states of mind in holonomy are:
  - ➤efficacy
  - ➤flexibility
  - ➤craftsmanship
  - ➤consciousness
  - ➤interdependence

Implications for Mentors

Reading Art Costa and Bob Garmston's book, *Cognitive Coaching: A Foundation for Renaissance Schools*, and/or attending one of the Cognitive Coaching workshops would be a great learning experience for any mentor. To observe Art Costa, Bob Garmston, one of their consultant group members, or someone who has developed skills through the Cognitive Coaching workshops is an awe-inspiring experience. They have fine-tuned this important component of our repertoires to an extraordinary level. Learning and becoming skilled at the process is time consuming, requires a strong commitment to the process, and is well worth the effort.

Data-Driven Discussions
Reflective Conference Approaches

Lipton and Wellman

Laura Lipton and Bruce Wellman, building on their work with Costa and Garmstron, present a continuum of interactions in their book, *Mentoring Matters, A Practical Guide to Learning-Focused Relationships*. It is these terms that are elaborated on in the following pages.

- **Consult**
  - ➢Most directive interaction
  - ➢provide information and expert counsel
  - ➢balance support with challenge
  - ➢offer options
- **Collaborate**
  - ➢promote mutual learning
  - ➢facilitate mutual growth
  - ➢ create mutual respect
- **Coach**
  - ➢least directive stance
  - ➢mediate thinking
  - ➢nonjudgmental interactions
  - ➢support
  - ➢reflection and inquiry

Implications for Mentors

Mentors need to develop an understanding of and build skillfulness at each of the three types of interactions. They then need to develop skillfulness at determining when to use which approach. With practice mentors can learn to move fluidly from one approach to another as the situation demands.

Data-Driven Discussions
Consulting, Collaborating, and Coaching

Coaching and mentoring involve a variety of strategies that fall along a continuum. When partners use **consultation** strategies, one partner is the expert giving advice to the other (learner). In **collaboration**, both partners share expert and learner roles. **Coaching**, through questioning, facilitates thinking, planning, and reflecting around classroom practice.

Mentoring and Coaching Approaches	Consultation	Collaboration	Coaching
Purpose	Give advice to... • clarify goals • plan for, observe, and provide feedback about teaching practice • improve teaching practice • create resources • provide follow-up	Plan, observe, provide feedback, and refine instructional strategies to... • expand the knowledge base of both partners • improve practice and student learning results • share resources and expertise • develop collegial, professional relationships and diminish professional isolation	Help new teachers think about and reflect on their professional work and its impact on student learning,
Roles	A mentor or coach who... • provides formal or informal opportunities to plan, observe, and reflect on professional practice • clarifies problems and successes • gives advice regarding solutions, resources, or changes in practice when needed	Mentors and new teachers who as colleagues... • enter a partnership targeting areas of their practices for examination and then providing and receiving feedback • collaborate as critical friends to improve teaching and student learning	A mentor or coach who... • asks insightful questions to coach a partner's decision-making and reflective process • helps a colleague examine the relationship between perceptions, attitudes, thinking, and behaviors that will affect student learning
Knowledge	The mentor or coach... • is a skillful teacher or administrator • is able to describe or demonstrate effective teaching/administrative strategies • has a thorough understanding of the curriculum being taught • practices good listening and communication skills • is sensitive to other's needs • is effective in establishing rapport	The mentor and new teacher... • plan for and focus on developing skills and/or improving practice • practice good listening and communication strategies • are sensitive to each other's needs • are open to observation of and feedback on their teaching practice • are effective in establishing rapport	The mentor or coach... • is a good role model • is effective in establishing rapport • practices good listening and communication strategies • asks appropriate questions

Data-Driven Discussions
The Coaching Conference

Outcomes for the Teacher

The teacher becomes more reflective, and more aware of the cause and effect of behaviors, and more conscious of the decision-making process used.

Mentor Behaviors

- actively listen (see **Communication Strategies for Coaching** on page 208)
- be non-judgmental
- encourage self-awareness
- encourage self-reflection
- use data, as appropriate

When the Coaching Approach is Used

- The teacher has the **knowledge, skills, and attitudes** to think through the decision making process, and, with coaching, arrive at own conclusions about what needs to be done.
- This is the default approach. Start with coaching and return to coaching whenever possible.

Essential Components of the Coaching Conference Sequence

- Teacher explains issues or situation
- Mentor checks for understanding
  - ➢So you are saying that ...
  - ➢You think that..."
- I think I understand that you want to...
- Mentor clarifies and probes for specificity and to identify the real problem
  - ➢What exactly did you want to occur?
  - ➢What do you think could be the cause?
  - ➢What do you mean by ...?
  - ➢What does it look like when that is happening?
  - ➢What would it look like if it were working?
- Teacher identifies problem and considers options as mentor facilitates thinking
- Teacher decides what to try and makes an action plan
- Mentor verifies plan and sets follow-up meeting

Data-Driven Discussions
Communication Strategies for Coaching

Attentive Silence

This adult **wait time** allows both parties to process what has been said, to collect their thoughts, to review notes, and to figure out and formulate next points of discussion.

Acknowledgment Responses

These responses are given to indicate that you are paying attention to what is being said. They are accompanied by head nodding, eye contact, and a posture matched to that of the teacher. When talking with a very reflective teacher, the vast majority of your responses may be acknowledgment responses. Interestingly enough, when the conversation or conference is over, the teacher may well say, "Thank you for your help," because what she needed to do was think out loud.

Examples of acknowledgment responses are: **"I see." "That's interesting." "Hmmm."**

Paraphrasing and Summarizing

When paraphrasing, you check for understanding and summarize what the teacher said. You attempt to capture the essence of the feelings and content of the statement and paraphrase them in an abbreviated form. You make no inferences. In order to avoid adding your own voice, think of paraphrasing and summarizing as a parallel to the way you paraphrase to be sure you have the correct directions to a party.

Reflecting Meaning and Feelings

With this strategy, you add inferences about what you think the teacher is saying. For example, a teacher might say, "That lesson was a big success. The kids really got it!" You might respond, "You are feeling pretty good about the learning results you got!" If you are on the mark, the teacher response might be, "Yes! They did so much better than they have before!" If you are off the mark, the teacher might respond, "No, but they at least knew what to do." You make an effort to ensure you are interpreting the right emotion and that the words you heard conveyed the meaning the person meant to send.

Questions That Promote Teacher Thinking*

Costa and Garmston write that when you coach you attempt to move the teacher with whom you are working to a new place. Carefully crafted questions can help you do that. Examples of questions that are likely to promote teacher thinking are found on the next page.

*Costa and Garmston name pause, paraphrase, and probe as three key skills of cognitive coaching.

Data-Driven Discussions
Questions That Promote Teacher Thinking

Questions that promote teacher thinking are open-ended; there is not one correct answer. They are not leading, accusatory, or nosy. We ask these questions to...

- **initiate a discussion and keep discussions on track**
- **focus on new concepts or a different aspect of a concept**
- **facilitate flexible thinking**
- **challenge the obvious**
- **break down complex tasks and issues**
- **consolidate previous discussions and experiences**
- **explore possible next steps**

Question Starters

- What do you need to do next?
- Based on what you know, what can you predict about...?
- Does what... said make you think differently about...?
- How do you decide...?
- How does... tie in with what we have discussed before?
- Suppose... what then?
- How does this match what you thought you knew?
- What might happen if...?
- When have you done something like this before?
- What sort of impact do you think...?
- How would you feel if...?
- How did you come to that conclusion?
- How about...? What if...?
- Tell me what you mean when you...
- What do you think causes...?
- When is another time you need to...?
- What do you think the variables/issues/problems are?
- What were you thinking when...?
- Can you think of another way you could do this?
- Why is this one better than that one?
- How can you find out?
- How is... different (like)...?
- What have you heard about..?
- Can you tell me more?
- What else do you see?
- How does that compare with...?

Data-Driven Discussions
Reflective Conference Question Menu
Question Selection

Mentors should plan the questions they want to use with novice teachers based on what they know about the attitudes, skills, and knowledge of the novice teacher as well as the learning and information processing style of the teacher.

Also see **Chapter VII, Mentoring in a Standards-Based Environment** for more specific questions.

- How does what you and your students worked on today fit in the context of the unit on which you are working?
- How did you go about finding out if your students had the background knowledge and skills required to be successful on this lesson?
- How did you decide what instructional strategies to use?
- What are the variables, beyond completion of assignments, that you consider in determining whether or not the students have learned what you wanted them to learn?
- What do you think worked and did not work in this lesson? Why do you say that?
- When you teach this lesson again, what will you do differently?
- As you look back on this lesson, how do you think it went? What happened to make you think this way?
- What do you remember about your actions during the lesson? How did what you actually did match what you had planned? Why do you think that is the case?
- What do you remember about student work and behavior during the lesson? How did their actions and work match what you hoped/expected would happen?
- How successful were the students in moving toward competency with the standard? What is your data?
- What do you think caused some students to not "get it?"
- What did you notice that caused you to...?
- What did you learn from this conversation that may influence your future thinking and planning?
- From your perspective, was the learning objective clear and significant? What evidence can you provide?
- What percentage of the students mastered the objective? What evidence can you provide?
- What work did the students do to achieve the objective, and did that work add up to a quality learning experience? How do you measure that?
- To what extent were the students actively involved in the construction of meaning? What evidence can you provide?
- How do you explain students' success or lack of success?
- How will your practice change as a result of this reflection together?

Data-Driven Discussions
The Collaborative Conference

Outcomes for Teacher

Mutually agree on next steps in learning or refining a new technique, identify problems, develop solutions to problems

Mentor Behaviors

- focus on the teacher's agenda
- guide problem solving process
- explore pros and cons of solutions
- keep discussion focused on problem solving

When the Collaborative Approach Is Used

The mentor and the teacher are equally engaged in determining the next steps. The teacher has a positive **attitude** about his own capacity and the capacity of his students and, while knowledgeable and skillful, seeks to have even more **knowledge** and develop more **skills**.

Essential Components of the Collaborative Conference Sequence

- Identify the problem, issue, or concern from the teacher's perspective through sharing of data and questioning
- Check for understanding of the issues
- Brainstorm possible solutions
- Weigh alternatives
- Agree on a plan and a follow-up meeting to assess if solution is working and plan next steps

See the next page for a description of the **Six-Step Problem Solving Process,** which is widely used for individual and group problem solving.

Skills for Collaborative Problem Solving

- active listening
- "I-messages" or assertive messages
- brainstorming
- consensus building

For information on these prerequisite skills see *People Skills* by Robert Bolton.

Data-Driven Discussions
The Six-Step Problem Solving Method

Step One: Identify the Problem

A great deal of time is spent solving the wrong problem. Often people try to "fix" a symptom rather than get to the problem. Once the problem can be written in a problem statement that says, "The problem is that...", write a goal statement describing what a successful remedy would accomplish. It may be that the problem is so big and complex that the components of the problem may need to be tackled one at a time.

Step Two: Generate Potential Solutions

This step calls for divergent thinking and brainstorming. The goal is to generate as many potential solutions as possible. Consider doing individual brainstorming before you share ideas. Do not judge solutions as they are generated, but jot them down for later consideration as a solution or as a component of the solution. Do not stop too soon. Often the best ideas come toward the end of the brainstorming because ideas begin to be integrated.

Step Three: Evaluate the Solutions

Some suggested solutions may need to be eliminated because of the time, energy, or money they would require. Others may be eliminated because of policies and rules. After those have been eliminated, examine the remaining possibilities and rank them by a criteria you design. Identify the two or three solutions that have the best potential and analyze them further as to how feasible it would be to implement them and the possible impact each might have.

Step Four: Select a Solution to Try

In this step the teacher decides which solution to try. If the solution involves the assistance of other people, they will need to be consulted as to their willingness to participate. Once a solution is identified, decide on the criteria to be used to evaluate the effectiveness of the solution after the implementation.

Step Five: Make a Plan and Implement It

Using the description of the ideal situation, the solution selected to try, the time frame for implementation, and the criteria to be used to evaluate the effectiveness of the solution, make an action plan and implement it.

Step Six: Evaluate the Solution

Use the criteria established in step five to decide whether or not the solution is working and determine if the plan should be modified. Use the problem solving process to plan any needed modifications.

Data-Driven Discussions
The Consulting Conference

Outcomes for Teacher
- learns new techniques
- perfects a technique
- changes a behavior
- develops a plan for change
- determines next steps

Mentor Behaviors
- inform
- direct
- model
- give advice
- critique
- make suggestions
- give instruction for change

Glickman, Gordon, and Ross-Gordon identify two consulting options
- mentor tells the teacher what to do
- mentor lists options and asks the teacher to choose from those options

See pages 132-135 in the *21st Century Mentor's Handbook* for suggestions to make.
See *Why Didn't I Learn This in College?* and *Instruction for All Students* for detailed information and directions for suggested instructional, assessment, and organizational strategies.

When the Consulting Approach Is Used
The mentor or coach has a predetermined notion of what should happen and believes that the teacher does not have, in the moment, the knowledge, skills, or attitudes to determine what needs to be done.
It may be that the teacher...
- does **not have knowledge** about the topic under discussion
- is **not skilled** at identifying and solving problems
- has **little commitment** to teaching or student learning
- is doing something that is potentially harmful to students

OR

The teacher explicitly asked for the mentor to provide expert advice. Some novice teachers are comfortable asking for advice and others feel a need to demonstrate

Data-Driven Discussions
The Consulting Conference continued...

competency without assistance. Either situation can be a valuable learning experience or a mentoring challenge. When time is of the essence or the request for a suggestion or direction on how to proceed is about a new set of circumstances, simply telling the new teacher what to do can be the most efficient and effective. If, however, the novice or new teacher continuously asks what to do, the mentor has to take care to not become an enabler. It is in these situations that the mentor needs to implement collaborative and even coaching approaches whenever possible by asking questions such as...

- What have you tried so far?
- What options are you considering?
- What have you seen others doing in this situation?
- What does the data tell you?

It is in those situations where the novice teacher does not ask for advice or does not listen to advice of the mentor, that superior communication skills and decision making skills are required by the mentor. Advice given without rationale or data, given publicly, given too often, or given the wrong way, in the wrong place, and at the wrong time ensures that the advice will not be followed and the relationship may be damaged.

Essential Components of the Consulting Conference Sequence
- Mentor or teacher identifies the problem(s)
- Mentor or teacher shares data that supports the conclusion that the problem exists
- Mentor offers solutions...may or may not ask for teacher input
- Solution identified by both parties
- A follow-up plan and meeting are established

Data-Driven Discussions
Mentoring Reflective Conferences
Key Points to Remember

1. Never lose sight of the essential goal of all mentoring conferences: **teacher growth and increased student learning** no matter how well things are going.

2. Decide on conference approaches based on the **attitude, skills, and knowledge** of the teacher around the issues to be discussed. It is highly likely that more than one approach will be used in a conference.

3. Plan **agenda and questions** carefully so that the interactions move the teacher toward the goals of the conference. Avoid leading questions.

4. Be conscious of the **time available** for the conference and pace accordingly. Do not be drawn off track into interesting, and perhaps even important, conversations for which this is not the appropriate forum.

5. In all mentoring conversations and conferences, use language from the **professional performance criteria** so that those criteria become part of the shared language.

6. Use coaching as the **default strategy**. Start with coaching and return to coaching whenever possible.

7. Tie **feedback** to teaching or content standards, previous conversations, or staff development offerings.

8. Use **student work, student achievement data, or data** gathered from multiple sources to support question selection, opinions, suggestions, or directives.

9. Check for **understanding, agreement, and commitment**.

10. **Follow-up and follow-through**. Ensure that agreements reached and the commitments made result in action. Follow-through by providing the resources and support promised.

11. Avoid **killer statements and communication stoppers!**

12. Match style and word choice to the teacher's **information processing style**.

13. Use **feedback, encouragement, and praise** appropriately.

Data-Driven Discussions
Looking at Student Work
Data-Driven Decision Teams (3-D Teams)

In an effort to help new teachers use data to make solid instructional decisions, meet with them once or twice a month to review and analyze student work. The analysis, reflection, and collegial collaboration provides a framework for decision-making about future instruction. This practice is a particularly useful tool in schools where teachers are striving for consistency across classrooms in a standards-based learning and assessment environment.

Mentors should actively participate in the process by bringing student work from their own classrooms. Hanson, Silver and Strong, in descriptions of their Authentic Achievement Teams, suggest that teachers bring six pieces of students' work. They further recommend that the samples represent different achievement levels or different levels of success on a particular assignment. For example, two might be from the top third of a class, two from the middle, and two from the bottom. An alternative approach would be to **analyze the work of "regular" students and that of second language learners, advanced learners, or inclusion students.** It is also helpful to bring copies of any directions given to the students and to identify the learning standards addressed by the assignment.

New teachers and mentors can collaboratively agree to analyze the work of their students around the same set of criteria, or each teacher can indicate the questions, concerns, and criteria to be considered for that set of student work. In either case, the outcomes of the discussion might be directed toward:

- checking for **validation** about the appropriateness of the work for the developmental stage of the students
- checking to ensure that the task is **aligned** with district standards
- checking for **consistency** of opinion about the assessment and evaluation of the work
- possible **adjustments** in teacher directions and **support** for all/some of the students

Using Longitudinal Rubrics

Work with the new teachers to teach them how to monitor learning over time. Use district or teacher developed rubrics to track students progress by marking the rubric in a different color each quarter. Lead the new teachers in discussions about what the data means and pose questions as to next steps in working with each student.

Data-Driven Discussions
Looking at Student Work
Writing Rubrics Using Student Work

This process is a productive way to engage new teachers in collegial discussions about student work and to establish consistency across teachers with whom they work. Conversations about what work does and does not meet the standards of performance not only establish consistency, the new teachers leave the table with rubrics ready for classroom use. Follow this process:

- Ask the new teachers to bring a set of student papers to analyze.
- Collaboratively sort the work into broad categories: **excellent, okay,** and **needs work**.
- Identify two or three strong examples of each category.
- Start with the **excellent** examples and list the attributes that make them excellent.
- Continue the process with the **okay** and **needs work** examples.
- Write these attributes into a holistic rubric.
- Be sure that an attribute listed in any one category is also listed in the other two. If you want to turn your holistic rubric into an analytical rubric, sort by attributes and assign a rating to each of the attributes.
- Have all participants in the discussion use the rubric in their classrooms and come together again to discuss how it worked and to identify needed revisions.
- Try scoring work from each other's classes using the rubric.

Data-Driven Discussions
Student Achievement Data

Given that using student achievement data to guide instructional practice is not an option, it is essential that mentors work with new teachers to build their skillfulness with analyzing and using data. The first component of the data analysis process mentors need to engage in is convincing new teachers that data is a friend and not an enemy. A second lesson, a difficult one for all educators, is figuring out which data is most important, and then deciding what to do with the data we obtain when we analyze student achievement data.

In some instances, the analyses listed below are provided by the district; in that case, the question becomes, what to do with the data. Any of these analysis approaches can be instructive for both novice and experienced teachers new to the district.

- Identify and analyze general **trends or patterns** observed. These patterns might be:
  - Identify percentage or number of advanced proficient, proficient, and not proficient
  - Disaggregate data by **demographics** such as gender, ethnicity, time in district, English language proficiency, students on IEPs, and free and reduced lunch (required by No Child Left Behind Act of 2001)
  - Compare current data to **data from past assessments** at this grade level
  - Complete a **longitudinal** comparison of the work of individuals or groups of students over time
- **Analyze data by subsets** such as specific standards, benchmarks, or indicators. See the **Item/Indicator Analysis** template on page 317.
- **Cause and effect analysis**
  - Analyze how and when the assessed concepts, facts, and processes were taught
  - Consider which strategies were used
  - Consider what materials were used
  - Consider how much time was allocated
  - Consider the level of thinking the students/student groups now use and the level required by the assessment
  - Review the alignment of the learning experiences with the knowledge, skills, and level of thinking required by the assessment task
  - Ask what changes need to be made the next time these points are taught or to whom they should be retaught
  - See the **Cause and Effect Analysis** template on page 318.

Data-Driven Discussions
Student Achievement Data

- **Compare classroom assessment data and external assessment data**
- **Do an item analysis**
  - ➤ Which items were missed by most students
  - ➤ Which items were missed by highest performing students
  - ➤ Which items were missed by almost proficient students
  - ➤ Which items were missed by special needs students
  - ➤ Which items were missed by second language learners
- **Create tables that show the data by students, by subgroup, by item, or broader categories such as benchmarks or standards**

Following the data analysis, work with the new teachers to identify baseline data for which targets will be set. After targets are identified assist the new teachers in making action plans.

Data-Driven Discussions
Journals

Journals can serve as a valuable mentoring tool and an invaluable record for new teachers of their growth over time. They help answer the **so what** and **what if** questions about the events of our professional work. If it appears that the new teacher's information processing is one that would value the journaling process, a journal with a cover representative of the local area would make a wonderful "welcome aboard" gift.

Dialogue Journals

A dialogue journal is one in which two people conduct a written dialogue. If you use paper and pen the journal can be dropped off on each other's desks or placed in mailboxes for ease of transfer. A dialogue journal can, of course, be kept in a traditional journal book format, be a printout of computer entries or be kept electronically. When geography or time constraints limit the frequency of face-to-face interactions these journals can be a productive way to fill the gaps. They are effective if response turnaround time is quick, if the two parties trust one another, and this form of communication matches the information processing styles of both parties.

Entries in the dialogue journals can help the mentor know where the new teacher is in terms of the stages of development identified by the New Teacher Center at Santa Cruz (see pages 67-68) or the mentor can do a Concerns-Based Adaption Model (CBAM) analysis of the comments and questions asked by the new teacher. The National Academy of Sciences has a good description of CBAM at www.nas.edu/rise/backg4a.htm.

On-Line Journals

When mentors and new teachers are not located in the same hallway, same school, or even within the same school district, technology comes to the rescue. Teachers in rural areas or in content areas for which there are few teachers need a support system that is organized a bit differently from other new teachers. Many state departments of education have set up on-line mentoring systems as has the Troops to Teachers organization. Lesson plans can easily be sent back and forth with validations or suggestions for revision. The beauty of this type of mentoring is that it can occur in the early morning hours, in the late evening hours, and even on weekends.

Data-Driven Discussions
Journals

Journal Organization

Journals can be organized chronologically or thematically. Teachers might decide to sort their journal entries by areas of performance used by the district's supervision and evaluation system. This is an especially wise approach if the journals are to become part of a portfolio.

Possible entries or sections:
- first impressions
- survival questions
- ideas to remember
- goals and action plans
- brainstorming instructional strategies
- success or problems with a lesson or units
- parent-teacher conferences
- professional development experiences
- collegial collaboration
  - with team members, grade level partners or departmental colleagues
  - with other new teachers
  - with mentors
- interactions with individual students or the entire class
- daily thinking...aha's and questions, general musings
- responses to discussions, professional development opportunities, or professional readings
- working with parents as partners
- data analysis
- set priorities and schedules
- identify and solve problems
- record and evaluate practices and effectiveness of effort
- planning for next year

Data-Driven Discussions
Self-Assessment

Because of the complexity of teaching, new teachers most often operate in a reactive mode. Mentors need to assist new teachers in moving from being reactive in their decision-making to being proactive. One effective way to accomplish this is to engage new teachers in on-going self-assessment and support adjustments in new teachers' practice.

The use of self-assessment as part of the mentoring process is best promoted by mentor modeling of the process. Be purposeful in thinking aloud about your decision-making and about the results of your teaching decisions. It is easy for all teachers to be so driven to prepare for the next class or to be swamped with students' papers to grade that reflective and analytical opportunities are lost or postponed. Mentors should guide new teachers in setting realistic professional growth goals aligned to student needs. See **Chapter X, Tools for New Teachers** for templates for goal setting and for tracking goals and action plans.

Self-assessment can take many forms. There are times when the self-assessment takes a written form such as a needs assessment, survey, questionnaire, or checklist. Other forms of self-assessment are natural outcomes of action research, examination of student work, dialogue journals, videotape critiques, and portfolio preparation. See **Chapter X, Tools for New Teachers** for over a dozen self-assessment instruments.

One powerful way to construct a self-assessment for new teachers is to use the district's teacher performance criteria in a continuum format to identifiy the areas of professional practice on which new teachers need or want to focus their professional growth. See the next two pages for excerpts from such a continuum developed by educators in Monson. Massachusetts.

Professional Practice Profile Self-Assessment

Directions: The Massachusetts Professional Practice Profile is divided into five areas:

- **Plans Curriculum and Instruction**
- **Delivers Effective Instruction**
- **Creates a Positive and Productive Environment**
- **Promotes Equity and an Appreciation of Diversity**
- **Meets Professional Responsibilities**

Each area is broken down into standards and each standard has descriptors/indicators and examples of evidence. Read the listed standards and mark where you think you are on the continuum for each standard - **Not Yet, Work in Progress,** or **In Place and Functioning Smoothly.** You may choose to color code or date your marks on the continuum so you can see changes over time. Use the **Reflection** at the end of each section to summarize where you think you are.

Plans Curriculum and Instruction

1. Draws on content of the relevant curriculum framework to plan activities addressing standards that will advance students' level of content knowledge and skills.

Not Yet	Work in Progress	In Place and Functioning Smoothly

2. Plans sequential units of study that make learning cumulative, connect learning across disciplines, and are based on the learning standards within the frameworks.

Not Yet	Work in Progress	In Place and Functioning Smoothly

3. Draws on results of formal and informal assessments and knowledge of human development to plan learning activities appropriate for the range of students within a classroom.

Not Yet	Work in Progress	In Place and Functioning Smoothly

4. Integrates technology and media in the management of the work of teaching and in student learning.

Not Yet	Work in Progress	In Place and Functioning Smoothly

5. Uses information in Individual Education Plans (IEPs), 504 Plans, and District Curriculum Accommodation Plans (DCAP) to plan strategies for integrating students with special needs into regular classrooms.

Not Yet	Work in Progress	In Place and Functioning Smoothly

Reflections: What are my strengths in planning curriculum and instruction? Which characteristics need strengthening or improvement? What is the data?

Promotes Equity and an Appreciation of Diversity

1. Acts on the belief that all students can master a challenging curriculum and includes all students in the range of academic opportunities and in higher order thinking.

Not Yet	Work in Progress	In Place and Functioning Smoothly

2. Assesses the significance of student differences in performance levels, learning styles, cultural heritage, language, socio-economic backgrounds, and physical and emotional disabilities and adapts classroom activities appropriately.

Not Yet	Work in Progress	In Place and Functioning Smoothly

Reflections: What are my strengths in promoting equity and an appreciation of diversity? What standards need strengthening or improvement? What is the data?

Louise Thompson, ASK Group Consultant, in collaboration with the Monson, MA Supervision and Evaluation Process Revision Committee Standards/Indicators from *Teaching Matters*, a MASSPARTNERS Position Paper

Data-Driven Discussions
Planning and Reviewing Lesson Plans

Data-driven discussions about the planning process should be the primary focus of mentor-new teacher interactions. Being skilled at writing clear and focused lesson plans does not guarantee that new teachers can implement their plans in a way that engages all students in meaningful learning. Without such a plan, however, the likelihood of the design and delivery of lessons that are rigorous, coherent, engaging, and aligned to the district standards is greatly decreased. As mentors we need to be sure that new teachers understand that they cannot rely on textbook publishers or the designers of curriculum programs as the sole source of their lesson plans. They need to know from the very first that no matter how thorough the support provided by text and curriculum manuals, it is teacher decision-making and actions in the classroom that determine whether or not students will learn at high levels.

In some school districts teachers are asked to submit lesson plans for the upcoming week. Often the process is only an accountability check rather than an examination of rigor, coherency, potential for engagement, and the alignment with district standards. This form of lesson plan review does not help new teachers identify what is working, what is not working, or what has the highest probability of working better. Mentors need to focus on instructional decision-making with both novice and experienced teachers whether or not lessons plans are submitted for formal review.

As the new teachers progress through the year, their lesson plans and planning process should reflect a use of the suggestions that have been the focus of earlier conversations, observations, and conferences. Mentors need to keep a log of the areas discussed so that they can note and celebrate progress and revisit the areas needing more attention.

In some school districts teachers are asked to have their lesson plans out and available in their classrooms for observers whenever they come into the classroom. A quick scan of the lesson plans is a valuable tool for mentors because it provides immediate context for what is being observed. Knowing the intent of the learning exercises helps frame the questions you ask the students, the way you listen to teacher comments, the way you analyze the learning environment, and the way you interact later with the teacher.

If there is not a required format for lesson plans, see **Chapter XIII, Tools for Instructional Planning** for a variety of formats to share with new teachers. Also see **Chapter VII, Mentoring in a Standards-Based Environment** for suggestions to make and reflective questions to ask and **Chapter X, Tools for New Teachers** for self-assessments to use with new teachers.

Data-Driven Discussions
Standards-Based Unit Planning and Review

Discussions about unit planning and peer reviews of units are a good choice for mentors of experienced teachers new to the district. Hundreds of teachers each year use the components listed below to design standards-based units during ASK Group workshops. They design units, think through (and, in the workshops, write out) all the components, teach the unit, and in an informal peer review process, present their plan, student work, and planned revisions to colleagues. Although not all teachers have the opportunity to engage in this level of collaborative work in workshop settings, mentors can certainly orchestrate such discussions at the school level.

Points to Note in the Design and Review of Standards-Based Units

- Addresses district **standards, benchmarks, and indicators**

- Includes an assessment or **set of assessments** that allow students to demonstrate what they know and what they can do with what they know

- Incorporates **preassessment, formative and summative assessment** components

- Uses assessment strategies that allow students to demonstrate what they know in different ways

- Provides **public and precise criteria** for success that is to be communicated to learners prior to beginning the work; if possible, exemplars are also provided

- Includes a thorough and detailed **task analysis** of the standards, benchmarks, and/or indicators and of the assessment task

- Includes **instructional strategies that address the knowledge and skills identified by the task analysis**

- Includes instructional strategies that **frame the learning** and learning experiences that help students **make connections** and process their learning in ways that promote retention and transfer to new situations

- Provides **accommodations and differentiation** for a wide range of learners

- Includes plans for revision based on **data and analysis of student work**

- Reveals evidence of **collegial collaboration** in planning, implementing, and/or revising the unit

See **Chapter XIII, Tools for Instructional Planning** in this book. Also see pages 16-34 in *Instruction for All Students* and pages 171-188 and pages 282-288 in *Why Didn't I Learn This in College?*.

Data-Driven Discussions
Classroom Assessments

New teachers have most likely not had extensive training around the selection or design of **traditional assessments**. They may have had minimal instruction in **performance assessment**. Mentors may find that new teachers are lacking the necessary knowledge and skills to assess the appropriateness of either traditional or performance assessments and in designing or selecting criteria to assess student work.

This lack of knowledge and skills may lead to poor student performance on either classroom or external assessments. Assessment and grading seems to be the most private of teaching acts; it needs to be much more public so that all teachers, but especially new teachers, ask for and receive feedback on the **alignment of their assessments** with district standards, the clarity and construction of the questions, and the congruency with what was taught. It is quite possible for teachers to find fault with student study habits when in fact the rehearsals and practices were not well matched to the level of understanding required for success with the assessment task.

The **task analysis** of classroom assessments is an important focal point for data-driven discussions with new teachers. Often they follow the order of lessons presented in the basal text, the purchased program, and even the district curriculum without analyzing what skills, knowledge, and level of understanding is needed for student success. When that happens, there is a strong chance that the learning experiences are not explicitly selected to provide rehearsals and practices with the component parts of the task; that increases the likelihood that students will be unable to demonstrate competency with the learning standards in the classroom and on standardized tests.

An additional problem facing new teachers is that whatever instruction that they have had on assessment was most likely focused on **summative or final assessments**. They may not have internalized, or even have been introduced to, the understanding that **formative assessment** is integrated with instruction and that every student response or non-response, every student question as well as every student assignment, in class or homework, provides assessment data.

See pages 255, 329, 331-333 in this book and pages 140-166 in *Why Didn't I Learn This in College?* and pages 149-171 in *Instruction for All Students* for resource materials to use in data-driven discussions about classroom assessment.

Data-Driven Discussions
Portfolios

Many districts require portfolios as a part of their teacher performance evaluation systems. While portfolios provide a wonderful opportunity for teachers to demonstrate both the depth and breadth of their expertise and their commitment to analysis and reflection, preparing a portfolio can be a daunting task for busy classroom teachers, especially new teachers. Interestingly enough it is not the collection of artifacts that seems daunting; it is the reflection on the significance of the artifacts. If your district requires portfolios, it is essential that you support the new teachers in the preparation of their portfolios with interim checkpoints along the way. This can minimize the panic as the due date approaches and reduce the probability that new teachers will stay up all night putting the finishing reflective touches on their portfolios. For those who are naturally reflective and inclined to keep a journal or log, a portfolio is an excellent choice. For those who are not so inclined, it may be a painful experience. Mentor-new teacher discussions of portfolio contents and the significance of the artifacts throughout the year can ease the process and promote the professional growth portfolios are designed to elicit.

As new teachers are building their portfolios it is important that they understand that throughout the year they are creating a **working portfolio** in which they place all the artifacts they identify. As they are gathering artifacts, it makes sense for them to organize their portfolios around the areas of professional performance or domains identified by the school district. You might suggest that they set up a crate with a hanging file folder for each area of performance as one way to begin collecting and sorting artifacts. Later they can select the prime artifacts to include in a presentation portfolio. The use of an artifact checklist or index card file to track what is being collected can help identify gaps and help new teachers begin to think more purposefully about what data needs to be gathered to fully represent the work in each area. The final **presentation portfolio*** should include a rationale for each piece in the portfolio explicitly tying it to one of the teaching standards, an analysis of its usefulness, and a reflection on how it represents accomplishment in terms of student learning and professional growth.

*Portfolios are the basis of certification by the National Board for Professional Teaching Standards (NBPTS). See **www.nbpts.org** for lengthy and detailed directions and exemplars of their requirements in each discipline.

Data-Driven Discussions
Portfolio Artifact Possibilities

- Anecdotal records
- Audiotapes of student work
- Awards and certificates
- Bulletin board displays of student work (photos)
- Class newspapers
- Classroom assessments
- Collaborative efforts
- Computer use for organization
- Computer use for instruction
- Course syllabus
- Extracurricular/co-curricular documentation
- Grant proposals/grants received
- Lesson and unit plans
- Letters of recommendation
- Individualized plans
- Interest inventories
- Interviews with students, teachers and parents
- Journals
- Letters to parents
- Letters from parents
- Letters of recommendation

- Observation reports
- Organizational strategies
- Performance evaluations
- Philosophy statement
- Pictures and photographs
- Problem-solving logs
- Professional development plans
- Professional development organized and led
- Professional organizations
- Professional readings list
- Publications
- Resume
- Rubrics and performance assessment task lists
- Self-assessments
- Student achievement goals, action plans, and results
- Student work
- Teacher-made instructional materials
- Use of professional learning documentation
- Videotapes

Tools for
New Teachers

Chapter IX

Tools for New Teachers

In Your Minds's Eye: Page 239

- Use this tool with new teachers to have them create a mental image of what they hope to accomplish this school year.
- Save their written reflections to return to them at the end of the school year and use them as the focus of celebration of what has been accomplished.
- Use the statements as "ends in mind" to help the new teachers plan for the first week of school.
- Review the statements on a quarterly basis to facilitate quarterly goal setting.

Needs Assessment: Challenges and Concerns: Pages 240-241

- Use this open-ended tool to have new teachers list the challenges and concerns that they have already identified. The eight categories cause them to sort through their concerns and categorize them.
- Use this tool as a log of comments made by new teachers as you interview them at one of the first meetings.
- As a mentor identify the actions that you can take immediately to satisfy concerns.
- Collaboratively rank order the categories or entries within a category and tackle the problem.
- See **Chapter III, Mentor-New Teacher Interactions**, pages 43-59 for potential responses to identified needs.

Needs Assessment: Challenges and Concerns with Rankings: Pages 242-243

- Use this checklist tool to have new teachers indicate which of the listed challenges and areas of concern are most important to them in the present and which are potential areas of focus in the future.
- Use this "select a response" tool rather than the open-ended tool described above when new teachers indicate that they cannot create a list of their concerns.
- Use the items selected on this needs assessment as the first areas of focus for your mentoring work.
- See **Chapter III, Mentor-New Teacher Interactions**, pages 43-59 for potential responses to identified needs.

Self-Assessment: Planning Instruction: Pages 244-245

- Use this tool to help new teachers focus their thinking on the planning process. Their responses will help you know where to start conversations about planning.
- Turn the statements into questions to ask the new teachers and engage in discussions around ones of interest on those in need of clarification.
- Use **Chapter IX, Tools for Instructional Planning** to facilitate the discussions.
- See Chapter VII in *Why Didn't I Learn This in College?* and Chapter II in *Instruction for all Students.*

Tools for New Teachers

Self-Assessment: Implementing Instruction Pages 246-247

- Use this tool to help the new teachers gather baseline data about their repertoire of instructional strategies.
- Have the new teachers identify one or two areas on which to focus their repertoire refinement and assist them in that refinement.
- Upon review of the self-assessment, conversations, and observations collaboratively identify areas of focus.
- Use this tool with experienced new teachers to identify areas of interest. Collaboratively agree on an approach or strategy that both new teachers and mentors can use in their classrooms and discuss following use.
- See the tables of contents of *Instruction for All Students* and *Why Didn't I Learn This in College?* for page references on the listed items.

Self-Assessment: Rigorous Instruction and Thinking Skills: Page 248

- Use this tool to help new teachers check the level of thinking they are asking students to use. Help them align the level of questions and tasks with the level of thinking identified in the learning standards.
- See pages 54-60 in *Why Didn't I Learn This in College?* and pages 212-247 in *Instruction for All Students* for resources to use in support of this survey.

Self-Assessment: Constructivist Instruction: Page 249

- Use this tool to help new teachers design instruction that is learning-centered rather than teacher-centered.
- If new teachers are telling rather than teaching, have them identify one or two strategies on this self-assessment to try using in their instruction.
- See page 75 in *Instruction for All Students* for another self-assessment on use of meaningful and engaging active learning strategies.

Self-Assessment: Small Group Work: Page 250

- Use this tool to help new teachers identify critical components of successful small group work on which they need to concentrate.
- Have them identify the variables on which they need to work in order to improve the quality of student work in small groups and cooperative learning exercises.
- See pages 243-250 in *Why Didn't I Learn This in College?* for resources.

Tools for New Teachers

Self-Assessment: Literacy Instruction: Page 251

- Use this tool with all new teachers to help them analyze the process of integrating literacy in all content areas.
- See Chapter V in *Why Didn't I Learn This in College?* for reading strategies for new teachers to use with elementary and secondary schools.

Self-Assessment: Inclusive Classrooms: Page 252

- Use this tool with all general education teachers to identify some basic instructional tips for working with special education students and their teachers.
- See pages 281-284 in *Instruction for All Students* and pages 39-44 in *Why Didn't I Learn This in College?*

Self-Assessment: Differentiated Instruction: Page 253

- Use this tool with experienced teachers new to the district to assist them in identifying the components of a differentiated program they would like to further integrate into their instructional design.
- Be cautious about asking novice teachers to do this level of instructional planning. They need to build knowledge and skill about the content they are expected to teach and the learning needs of their students before they can differentiate instruction. Suggest instead that they concentrate on accessing prior knowledge, helping students make real world connections, and using formative assessment data to make instructional decisions.
- See pages 39-42 in *Why Didn't I Learn This in College?* for resources on working with students with special needs. See pages 191-215 in *Instruction for All Students* for resources on differentiation.

Self-Assessment: Sheltered Instruction for ELLs: Page 254

- Use this tool with new teachers who have second language learners in their classroom. Have them identify areas of focus for their professional growth and skill building.
- After new teachers have completed this self assessment, have a discussion about how these strategies are actually good strategies to use with all students.
- See pages 115-135 in *Why Didn't I Learn This in College?* for resource material.

Tools for New Teachers

Self-Assessment: Assessment: Page 255

- Use this tool to help new teachers expand their thinking about formative and summative assessment and to identify areas of professional growth.
- As new teachers complete this self-assessment do a terminology check to be sure that they know what the statement is asking them to do. For unclear components of the assessment continuum provide exemplars of teacher and student work such as rubrics, performance task lists, grade and content area appropriate examples of student work, student self-assessments, and methods for examining student work.
- See pages 147-171 in *Instruction for All Students* and pages 137-168 in *Why Didn't I Learn This in College?* for rationales, resources, and strategies to suggest to new teachers as components of their assessment repertoire.

Self-Assessment: Positive Learning-Centered Environment: Pages 256-257

- Use this tool with novice teachers as soon as possible. The items listed surface teacher-student and student-student interactions that can be implemented the first day of school.
- Use this tool with experienced teachers new to the district when the demographics of this district are different from the demographics of their previous districts.
- Re-visist this self-assessment whenever there is a challenge or concern about the functioning of the classroom as a learning community.
- See pages 10-35 and 243-250 in *Why Didn't I Learn This in College?* for resources.

Self-Assessment: Productive Learning-Centered Environment: Pages 258-259

- Use this tool with novice teachers as soon as possible. Provide assistance in selected areas through coaching, modeling, and peer observation.
- As you work with this tool point out that the focus is on setting up a productive learning environment, not on control and compliance.
- See pages 210-242 in *Why Didn't I Learn This in College?* for resource materials for organizing a productive learning-centered environment.

Self-Assessment: Professionalism/Collegial Collaboration: Pages 260-261

- Use this tool to assist new teachers in identifying those behaviors and characteristics valued by the school district.
- See pages 270-287 in *Instruction for All Students* for an array of ways for new teachers to collaborate with colleagues in the interest of student learning.
- See pages 206-209 in *Why Didn't I Learn This in College?* for reference materials on meeting professional responsibilities and collaboration and pages 253-264 on working as partners with parents.

Tools for New Teachers

Professional Growth Plan: Page 262
- Use this tool after each self-assessment.
- Align the professional growth goals to the district performance criteria.
- Revisit the goals on a regular basis, use data such as teacher work or student work, and celebrate accomplishments.

3-2-1 Goal Setting and Reflection: Page 263
- Use this tool to reflect on previous goals and to set new goals. It provides a place for new teachers to indicate how their mentors can assist them in the attainment of their new goals.
- Concurrently use the **Mentor Tool 3-2-1 Goal Setting and Reflection** as a model for life-long learning and professional goal setting.

Professional Growth Plan Reflection and Goal Setting: Page 264-265
Use this tool as an alternative reflection and goal setting tool. It is useful with new teachers who learn best by more reflective writing.

Home Run/Strike Log: Page 266
- Suggest the use of this log on a daily basis as an efficient way to record key events.
- This tool is useful for those new teachers who do not wish to keep a reflective or dialogue journal but feel a need to, or are required to, keep an ongoing record of their work.

My Own Top Ten 10 Top Lists: Pages 267-275
- Suggest the use of these tools as a thorough but efficient way for new teachers to capture key ideas to use again the following year. The areas addressed are:
  - Planning and Pacing
  - Assessment
  - Instruction
  - Organizing Professional, District, and School Documents
  - Organizing Myself and My Teaching Materials
  - Organizing My Learners and Their Materials
  - Orchestrating a Positive Learning-Centered Environment
  - Organizing a Productive Learning-Centered Environment
  - Working with Parents as Partners

New Teacher Tools

My To Do List to Be Ready for the Opening of School: Page 276
- Have new teachers use this form to list what they want to do to start the year more efficiently the following year.

Induction/Mentoring Program Reflection and Evaluation: Pages 277-281
- Use this tool and the corresponding mentor tool on pages 296-299 to provide feedback to each other and the district on how the mentoring program has worked this year.

In Your Mind's Eye...

Picture you, your students and the classroom learning environment at the end of the school year. What would students know and be able to do as a result of having spent the school year with you? How will they be different? How will you be different? How would the classroom learning community be functioning? How will you measure your and their success? Use this paper to describe what you hope to see and hear happening at the end of the school year. During our work together, we will try to design and implement plans that can make your hopes and dreams a reality.

New Teacher Needs Assessment
Challenges and Concerns

Personal	Professional

Curriculum, Instruction, and Assessment	Organizational Systems for Teacher and Classroom

New Teacher Needs Assessment
Challenges and Concerns

Students	Collegial Interactions and Collaboration

School and School System Policies and Procedures	Parents and Community

New Teacher Needs Assessment

Please rate each item below to indicate your level of concern about or interest in that topic at this time.

Possible Ratings
- 1 for a low level of concern or interest at this time
- 2 for a moderate level of concern or interest at this time
- 3 for a high level of concern or interest at this time

Personal

_____ Making living arrangements
_____ Locating gyms and recreational facilities
_____ Getting to know people

Professional/Human Resources

_____ Payroll, benefits, and investment information
_____ Certification and tenure requirements
_____ Teacher performance evaluation system
_____ Professional development opportunities
_____ Professional organizations

Curriculum, Instruction, and Assessment

_____ District and state learning standards
_____ Planning for instruction using the SBE planning process
_____ Building a repertoire of instructional strategies
_____ Differentiation of instruction
_____ Assessing student learning (formative and summative)
_____ Using student work and achievement data to inform instruction
_____ Going from rubrics to grades

Organizational Systems for the Classroom

_____ Setting up the classroom
_____ Classroom organizational systems
_____ Organizing my time and work

Getting to Know and Working with Students

_____ Getting to know the students
_____ Creating a learning community
_____ Working with students to establish norms and rules
_____ Diagnosing student needs
_____ Teaching diverse learners
_____ Motivating students
_____ Assisting student with special needs

New Teacher Needs Assessment

Collegial Interactions and Collaboration

_____ Establishing a professional relationship with the administrative staff
_____ Working as a member of a grade level, interdisciplinary, or departmental team
_____ Working with my mentor
_____ Co-teaching and collaboration between general and special education teachers
_____ Working with a paraprofessional

School and School System Policies and Procedures

_____ Understanding my legal rights and responsibilities as a teacher
_____ School and district policy handbooks
_____ Completing administrative paperwork
_____ Administration of standardized achievement tests
_____ Obtaining instructional resources and material
_____ Ordering materials and supplies
_____ Use of district and school library, media, and technology resources

Parents and Community

_____ Establishing positive home contact
_____ Working with parents as partners
_____ Working with parents of special needs students
_____ Back-to-School Night
_____ Parent conferences
_____ Grading and reporting student learning

Planning Instruction
New Teacher Self-Assessment and Goal Setting

_____ Use the district and state standards to plan for the year, the unit, and the lesson

_____ Use the standards-based planning process to plan and pace for the year

_____ Use the standards-based planning process for units and lessons by aligning assessments and learning experiences with the standards

_____ Identify the focus of the content areas being taught

_____ Design summative assessments prior to planning units or lessons

_____ Design learning experiences that give students practices and rehearsals at the same level of understanding as the level at which the standards are written

_____ Communicate how any given lesson/learning experience is directly related to the standards

_____ State standards in lesson plans

_____ Analyze instructional materials for match to district outcomes

_____ Identify supplemental materials and design learning experiences to fill any gaps in standard materials

_____ Use the task analysis process to identify the knowledge, skills, and level of understanding required by the task

_____ Include knowledge of student readiness levels, interests, and learning styles in designing learning experiences

_____ Build pauses for processing into the lesson design and use **10:2 Theory** and **Wait Time** as guidelines

_____ Plan and write out the key questions to ask during a lesson

_____ Analyze text structure and teach students to use graphic organizers to represent the thinking processes used by the author and to capture the key information in the text

_____ Align assignments to include homework with standards and assessments and be purposeful about examining homework results for evidence of learning

Planning Instruction

Professionalism & Collegial Collaboration

Implementing Instruction

Organizing a Productive Environment

Assessing Learning & the Instructional Program

Orchestrating a Positive Environment

Planning Instruction
New Teacher Self-Assessment and Goal Setting

_____ Use Models of Teaching such as Bruner's Concept Attainment, Hilda Taba's Inductive Model, Aronson's Jigsaw Classroom, and the Inquiry/Problem Solving Model

_____ Use the skills and competencies laid out in the SCANS Report (Secretary's Commission on Achieving the Necessary Skills) in lesson and unit design

_____ Eliminate lessons and learning exercises that do not move students toward meeting the standards

_____ Collaborate/consult with support staff about special needs students

For special educators:

_____ Use knowledge of medical conditions and medications and their possible effects on student learning and behavior to plan instruction

_____ Use knowledge of educational disabilities and giftedness and their effects on student learning needs to individualize instruction

See Chapter II in _Instruction for All Students_ and Chapter VII in _Why Didn't I Learn This in College?_ for information on planning.

Implementing Instruction
New Teacher Self-Assessment and Goal Setting

____ Communicate the standards and learning objectives in age-appropriate language

____ Communicate why what students are learning is important to know

____ Communicate how the learning exercises the students are doing are related to the learning outcomes; that is, explain the purpose and relevance of all assignments and learning experiences

____ Communicate how the current lesson is related to and builds on previous lessons

____ Help students build skills at recognizing how the current lesson is related to and builds on previous lessons

____ Communicate to students how their learning will be assessed

____ Provide scoring guides such as rubrics, performance task lists, and checklists to students before they begin working

____ Provide daily, unit, and semester agendas

____ Have students access their prior knowledge

____ Identify student misconceptions and naive understandings; help students reframe their thinking as appropriate

____ Provide or have students provide connections between what is being learned in the moment with other areas of their study and to life beyond the classroom

____ Present accurate and current information

____ Provide multiple illustrations, examples, and comparisons of complex or highly abstract ideas or concepts

____ Emphasize the key terms/ideas to be learned

____ Use positive and negative examples to help identify critical or important attributes

____ Whenever possible move from concrete (props) to semi-abstract (pictures) to abstract (words and numbers) in presenting new concepts

____ Model thinking aloud

____ Use analogies, metaphors, and similes

____ Use physical models and manipulatives

____ Use **Wait Time I** and **Wait Time II**

Planning Instruction

Professionalism & Collegial Collaboration

Implementing Instruction

Organizing a Productive Environment

Assessing Learning & the Instructional Program

Orchestrating a Positive Environment

Implementing Instruction
New Teacher Self-Assessment and Goal Setting Continued

____ Use segues at transitions so students can make cognitive connections between points under study and between various learning exercises

____ Have students make predictions about what will happen next or about the next steps they need to take

____ Have students process and summarize learning at meaningful points

____ Have students assess old predictions, make new predictions, make connections, pose questions, and/or identify significant information at processing points

____ Use **10:2 Theory** as a time template for student processing

____ Supplement lectures with colorful transparencies, Power Point-type presentations, models, charts, graphs, and other visual aids

____ Enhance lectures with discussion partners, graphic organizers, learning logs, etc.

____ Check for understanding throughout lessons by asking questions students can answer only if they truly understand concepts and/or the reasons for the processes

____ Assign homework for which students have the prerequisite skills to complete the work independently with an 80% success rate

____ Assign homework from all four categories: practice, preparation, extension, and creative to promote both homework completion, learning, and engagement

____ Go beyond recording completion of homework; use successful/unsuccessful completion as formative assessment data to inform teaching decisions

____ Gather and make accessible multiple sources of information such as books, magazines, journals, posters, pictures, charts, graphs, maps, and technology

____ Differentiate instruction by providing a variety of sources, learning processes, and ways to demonstrate learning

____ Use flexible groupings based on readiness levels, interests, student choice, and learning styles

____ Change strategies as necessary to meet students' learning needs

____ Integrate content with cross-curricular themes and skills

Planning Instruction

Professionalism & Collegial Collaboration

Implementing Instruction

Organizing a Productive Environment

Assessing Learning & the Instructional Program

Orchestrating a Positive Environment

Rigorous Instruction & Thinking Skills
New Teacher Self-Assessment and Goal Setting

____ Use Bloom's Taxonomy and the Question and Task Wheel to purposefully design questions and tasks at a variety of cognitive levels

____ Ask all students questions that require higher levels of thinking and probe student answers for clarification and extension

____ Pose open-ended thought-provoking questions

____ Name, model, and provide practice of thinking processes so that students can build and independently access their own thinking skills repertoire

____ Have students identify where else a particular thinking skill might be useful and design tasks so that they use these thinking skills in multiple situations

____ Teach students to use journals, learning logs or interactive notebooks to analyze and reflect on their own learning and the effectiveness of their effort

____ Use Williams' Taxonomy of Affective and Creative Thinking to design questions and learning tasks

____ Have students analyze print text, media, and technological sources for reliability and relevance

____ Include opportunities for both inductive and deductive thinking

____ Teach skills of inquiry

____ Teach skills of dialogue and debate

____ Point out, or have students identify, how ideas are alike and different and how they relate to one another

____ Have students seek evidence/data to support opinions and generalizations

____ Have students demonstrate relevant and important connections they are making

For information on 21st Century Thinking Skills see Chapter IX, pages 217-247 in *Instruction for All Students*.

Constructivist Instruction
New Teacher Self-Assessment and Goal Setting

____ Encourage students to talk about ideas with other students

____ Encourage students to think about how the information they are learning relates to other subjects and their lives beyond the school day

____ Have students think critically and creatively by asking questions that have more than one answer

____ Encourage students to think and discuss answers with a partner or a small group before answering in the larger group

____ Help students explore and build on their ideas

____ Ensure that class time spent on practice exercises and learning the facts leads to meaningful use of the facts and skills in the near future

____ Ask students what they already know about a unit before introducing it

____ Use essential questions and key concepts to help students organize new information in ways that make sense to them

____ Have students take sides on issues and explain points of view

____ Have students resolve their differences by discussing their thinking

____ Encourage students to try solving difficult problems, even before they learn all the material

____ Allow students to explore topics that excite or interest them

____ Design assessments around real world applications

____ Have students help determine how they demonstrate learning and how they are assessed

Small Group Work/Cooperative Learning
New Teacher Self-Assessment and Goal Setting

_____ Ensure that the work is rigorous, worthy of the time, and aligned with desired outcomes

_____ Give directions that apply to all in the large group; when directions apply only to certain groups, give directions via task cards at learning centers or as handouts

_____ Model and practice student movement so that students move quickly and smoothly into groups

_____ Provide direction and practice so that students stay with their group rather than wandering around

_____ Encourage students to help each other answer questions and solve problems rather than relying on the teacher to answer all questions and solve all problems

_____ Monitor whether or not all students in the groups are working on the task equally and adjust accordingly

_____ Consider assigning roles to students and rotating those roles so that all students are given the opportunity to develop the skills necessary for success in that role

_____ Intervene in both academic and process situations as appropriate while allowing students to resolve issues when possible

_____ Offer responses that promote student solving of problems rather than teacher solving of problems

_____ Build in individual accountability rather than relying on group grades.

_____ Use flexible grouping; consider readiness, gender, learning style, interests, and student choice as variables

_____ Answer questions with a question

_____ Teach, model, and review the interaction/social skills needed for successful work and learning

_____ Have students review the effectiveness and efficiency of the group process and make plans for improvement

Planning Instruction

Professionalism & Collegial Collaboration

Implementing Instruction

Organizing a Productive Environment

Assessing Learning & the Instructional Program

Orchestrating a Positive Environment

See pages 46-47 in _Instruction for All Students_ for information on cooperative learning and pages 243-250 in _Why Didn't I Learn This in College?_ for information on small group work.

Literacy Instruction Across the Curriculum
New Teacher Self-Assessment and Goal Setting

_____ Create a text rich environment by collecting, displaying, and using a wide variety of books, magazines, posters, etc., in the classroom

_____ Provide opportunities for students to locate, organize, and use information from various sources to answer questions, solve problems, and communicate ideas

_____ Use diverse fiction and non-fiction sources to include many authors and perspectives, as well as children's and young adult literature

_____ Teach reading as a process of constructing meaning through the interaction of the reader's prior knowledge and experiences, the information presented in the text, and the context/purpose of the reading

_____ Teach affixes, prefixes, and common roots used frequently in the content area

_____ Identify independent, instructional, and frustration reading levels of groups and individuals and plan assignments accordingly

Provide opportunities for students to:

_____ Speak for a variety of purposes and audiences

_____ Listen in a variety of situations to information from a variety of sources

_____ Write in clear, concise, organized language that varies in content and form for different audiences and purposes

_____ Read various materials and texts with comprehension and critical analysis

_____ View, understand, and use nontextual visual information (NJ Core Curriculum)

_____ Provide a balanced literacy program that includes reading to students, reading with students, independent reading by students, writing for and with students, and writing by students

_____ Analyze and evaluate instructional materials by considering readability, content, length, format, cultural orientation, and illustrations/visuals

_____ Use a reading approach aligned with the No Child Left Behind Act of 2001 to include phonemic awareness, phonics, vocabulary development, reading fluency, including oral reading skills and reading comprehension strategies.

See Chapter V: Surprise! You're A Reading Teacher! in _Why Didn't I Learn This in College?_

Instruction in Inclusive Classrooms
New Teacher Self-Assessment and Goal Setting

_____ Task analyze all assignments and assessments

_____ Provide special education students an expanded curriculum including communication skills, oral language development, social/behavior skills, motor skills, and self-advocacy skills

_____ Include explicit instruction that is structured, sequential, and cumulative in the development of skills

_____ Break complex tasks into simpler parts and then put the complex task back together

_____ Use backward chaining

_____ Use think alouds and then guide students in using the skills or processes modeled in the think aloud

In co-teaching situations:

_____ Ensure that all professional interactions between the general education and special education teachers cause the two to be seen by all as equal partners rather than having the special educator appear to function as a paraprofessional

_____ Consider the messages about teacher roles and relationships sent in parent communication

_____ Be clear about who is taking responsibility for what parts of the planning

_____ Decide in advance how the lesson will be structured and who will do what

_____ Share responsibility for developing procedures, expectations, and grading/critiquing students' work

_____ Decide who will do which tasks in an equitable way

Planning Instruction

Professionalism & Collegial Collaboration

Implementing Instruction

Organizing a Productive Environment

Assessing Learning & the Instructional Program

Orchestrating a Positive Environment

See _Instruction for All Students_ pages 281-284 and _Why Didn't I Learn This in College?_ pages 39-44.

Differentiation of Instruction
New Teacher Self-Assessment and Goal Setting

_____ Keep learning and assessment for all students focused on essential to know concepts and skills as identified in state and district standards

_____ Differentiate instructional support systems but not expectations for student learning

_____ Ensure that learning experiences and types and degree of teacher support are selected based on a task analysis that includes an analysis of the skills and knowledge embedded in the task, plus the level of understanding required by the task

_____ Use an analysis of student readiness/background knowledge levels, interests and information processing styles to identify appropriate learning experiences and teacher support systems

_____ Provide sources of information at various reading levels, in different languages, and in varying formats to match the needs of learners

_____ Engage all students in meaningful tasks that provide balance between skill building and meaning making

_____ Provide a balance of student and teacher choice of working conditions, sources of information, methods of processing learning, and demonstrating that learning

_____ Use a variety of instructional approaches to include individual, small group, and whole class instruction

_____ Use flexible grouping; create groups based on a variety of factors, including readiness levels and interests

_____ Give students precise, public, and prior guidelines for assignments, performance tasks, assessments, and behavior

_____ Provide models or exemplars of products; teach and model processes

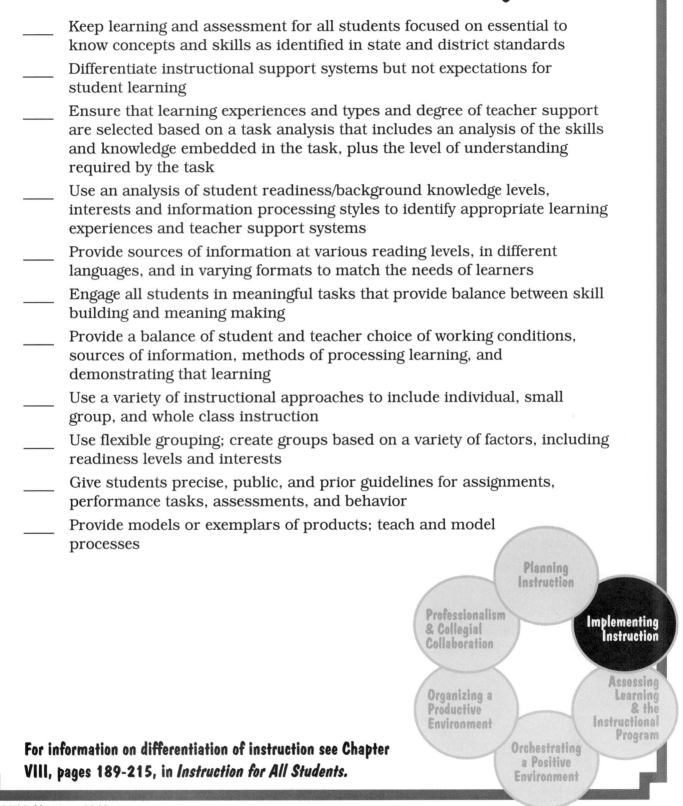

For information on differentiation of instruction see Chapter VIII, pages 189-215, in _Instruction for All Students._

Sheltered Instruction for ELLs
New Teacher Self-Assessment and Goal Setting

_____ Be thoughtful and purposeful in the use of academic/school related language such as direction giving and content-specific vocabulary

_____ Be mindful of slang or colloquialisms in teacher and student speech

_____ Use concrete objects, models, and demonstrations to support instruction

_____ Provide visual cues to support understanding

_____ Build in movement, rhythm, and repetition to support retention

_____ Analyze and evaluate instructional materials considering readability, content, length, format, cultural orientation, and illustrations/visuals

_____ Use the writing strategies included in balanced literacy programs, such as shared writing, interactive writing, guided writing, and short independent writing sessions in early years of developing English language skills

_____ Use what is known about students' families, cultures, and communities as a basis for connecting instruction to students' personal experiences

_____ Provide multiple perspectives, including attention to students' personal, family, and community experiences and cultural norms

_____ Ask questions as simply and concisely as possible

_____ Ask questions that require more than one-word answers

_____ Encourage all students to answer in complete sentences so that second language learners hear the answer in context and learn the rhythm of the English

_____ Use **Wait Time** before calling on any student and after any student answers so that processing and any necessary translation can occur

_____ Ask second language learners to retell, paraphrase, and summarize discussion and reading points to promote comprehension and fluency

_____ Assign roles in small group work to ensure that second language learners are active participants

_____ Break complex tasks into simpler parts by providing second language learners oral directions one step at time until they can follow two and three part directions independently

Planning
Instruction

Professionalism
& Collegial
Collaboration

Implementing
Instruction

Organizing a
Productive
Environment

Assessing
Learning
& the
Instructional
Program

Orchestrating
a Positive
Environment

Assessment of Learning and the Instructional Program
New Teacher Self-Assessment and Goal Setting

____ Check for understanding across all students by using signal cards, slates, think pads, choral responses, and circulation, and adjust instruction accordingly

____ Select assessment tools from a wide range of options including, but not limited to, paper and pencil assessments

____ Do a preassessment as part of the planning for a unit of study

____ Design rubrics, performance task lists, and checklists that articulate in precise language performance and assessment requirements

____ Provide students with clear criteria and exemplars of processes and products before they begin the work

____ Provide formative rehearsals for summative assessments at appropriate levels of thinking

____ Design and give assignments, to include homework, that provide practice and rehearsals and then analyze the results

____ Include student self-assessment of products and of the effectiveness of the effort

____ Go beyond grading student work to critiquing and analyzing student work to see which components of the standards are at mastery, which are progressing, and which are in need of teaching and reteaching

____ Teach students to give each other feedback through peer editing and review

____ Use every assignment as data on what to teach next and to whom and in what ways

____ Engage students in the design of assessment criteria

____ Have students score anonymous work to help them understand what the scoring criteria looks like in student work

____ Structure individual accountability in group work

____ Monitor impact of teacher behavior on student success and modify behavior, plans, and instructional strategies accordingly

____ Compare desired outcomes with actual outcomes and adjust plans accordingly

Planning Instruction

Professionalism & Collegial Collaboration

Implementing Instruction

Organizing a Productive Environment

Assessing Learning & the Instructional Program

Orchestrating a Positive Environment

Positive Learning-Centered Environment
New Teacher Self-Assessment and Goal Setting

_____ Learn student names and information about each one early in the year

_____ Greet students at the door with a smile and a handshake

_____ Use student names in examples

_____ Make a strong effort to interact in a positive way with each student each day

_____ Develop a system for monitoring the nature and frequency of your interactions with students

_____ Create opportunities for students to learn about themselves and each other

_____ Be knowledgeable about the fads, fashions, music, hobbies, sports, and other recreational activities that are of interest to your students

_____ Display student work both in the classroom and in public areas; identify the standard of learning the work represents

_____ Teach students how to set and work toward learning goals

_____ Encourage students to ask for and get help from one another

_____ Encourage students to monitor their own academic progress

_____ Set up conditions where students can assess the effectiveness of their learning habits

_____ Teach students to self-assess the appropriateness and effectiveness of their social skills

_____ Model respect in words spoken, voice tone, eye contact, and in body language

_____ Use music, books, posters, and pictures from different cultures

_____ Practice equity and explain to students the difference between equity (get what you need when you need it) and equality (all get the same thing at the same time)

_____ Role-play situations with students to identify appropriate and inappropriate behavior

_____ Provide student choice of learning process, teach them to make good choices, and analyze why the choices were or were not the best for the learner

_____ Explain the reason why you are doing what you are doing or making the decision you are making

Planning Instruction

Professionalism & Collegial Collaboration

Implementing Instruction

Organizing a Productive Environment

Assessing Learning & the Instructional Program

Orchestrating a Positive Environment

Positive Learning-Centered Environment
New Teacher Self-Assessment and Goal Setting continued...

____ Change strategies to meet students' needs rather than expecting students to change to meet teacher needs (Centennial BOCES)

____ Take advantage of opportunities to use humor

____ Remind yourself that you are a role model

____ Develop a repertoire of ways to encourage your students

____ Reinforce students' attempts to solve problems and exert effort

____ Make it a practice to recognize effective effort

____ Resolve behavioral issues privately with minimum disruption of instruction

____ Avoid sarcasm and ridicule

____ Promote intrinsic motivation (I did it!) rather than extrinsic motivation (you did it so you get a sticker or piece of candy)

____ Show interest in students lives beyond the classroom by becoming involved in student activities

____ Monitor student attributions and use attribution retraining with those who make external attributions

____ Demonstrate respect for students as individuals with different personal and family backgrounds and a wide range of skills, talents, and interests

____ Use flexible room arrangements to match instructional objectives and desired student interaction

____ Identify room arrangements that work best in small group work, whole class discussion, and testing

____ Teach students to help you arrange/rearrange the student desks/tables quickly and safely

____ Arrange the room so that you can move around the room with ease

____ Reduce distance and barriers between you and your students

____ When working with a small group, position yourself so that you can monitor other students at work

Planning Instruction

Professionalism & Collegial Collaboration

Implementing Instruction

Organizing a Productive Environment

Assessing Learning & the Instructional Program

Orchestrating a Positive Environment

Productive Learning-Centered Environment
New Teacher Self-Assessment and Goal Setting

____ Be sure you have student attention before beginning instruction or giving directions

____ Use high-results attention moves such as Wait Time, the look, proximity, and circulation

____ Provide practice and processing time

____ Post the agenda and the learning outcomes on the board, overhead or chart in the same place each day

____ Explain the work to be done and how to do it

____ Before students start working, check to be sure they know what to do and how to do it

____ Repeat and stress complex directions and difficult points; write out steps to any process having three or more steps

____ Repeat or rephrase questions and explanations students do not understand or have students do so for each other

____ Use known or easy content to teach a new process, and use a known process to introduce or teach difficult new material

____ Assist students in developing organizational systems that work for them

____ Teach students how to use graphic organizers, mnemonics, and visualizations

____ Teach students note-taking and reading strategies

____ Provide opportunities for students to use a variety of learning strategies and to learn which works best for them so that they can become independent learners

____ Build in movement

____ Teach students to identify text structure and to use the appropriate graphic organizers to capture key information

____ Warn students of upcoming transitions

____ Match the pace of the instruction with the complexity of the concepts being studied and with the amount of unfamiliar vocabulary

____ Mass practice at the beginning of new learning and follow up with distributed practice throughout the learning

____ After practice of small chunks, move quickly to meaningful use of the information and skills

Planning Instruction

Professionalism & Collegial Collaboration

Implementing Instruction

Organizing a Productive Environment

Assessing Learning & the Instructional Program

Orchestrating a Positive Environment

Productive Learning-Centered Environment
New Teacher Self-Assessment and Goal Setting continued...

____ Write directions for classwork and homework on board, chart, or transparency

____ Use flexible grouping determined by such variables as readiness levels, interest, information processing styles, student choice, and, on occasion, random order

____ Stay focused on learning; do not let "off-the-mark" behavior or backtalk take you off track; notice and deal with it when it fits your agenda

____ Identify the causes of inattentive or disruptive behavior and match your response to the perceived cause

____ Wait to hold discussions about inattentive or disruptive behavior, or unmet expectations, until both of you are calm

____ Focus on future behavior rather than on past behavior

____ Include students in developing procedures for handling inappropriate behavior or unmet expectations

____ Use logical consequences directly related to the behavior

____ Use a clearly articulated range of consequences for unmet expectations based on the quality, intensity, and frequency of the action

____ Organize supplies, equipment, and papers so that they are easily accessible; eliminate clutter

Professionalism & Collegial Collaboration
New Teacher Self-Assessment and Goal Setting

_____ Use the district mission and vision statements, the district learning standards, and the criteria for professional performance as benchmarks for professional practice

_____ Demonstrate knowledge about and use of current state and federal laws regarding special services students

_____ Consult with and inform appropriate personnel about legal questions

_____ Keep your grade book updated and legible

_____ Maintain accurate attendance records

_____ Inventory school property, books and instructional materials and maintain accurate records

_____ Perform duties such as restroom supervision, lunch duty, hall duty, and bus duty as assigned

_____ Use clear, concise, and grammatically correct language in oral and written communication

_____ Submit reports correctly and on time

_____ Attend required meetings

_____ Be prompt to and attentive at staff, departmental, and team meetings

_____ Participate and contribute at staff, departmental, and team meetings

_____ Provide substitutes with thorough instructional plans and notes on classroom procedures

_____ Develop and make accessible emergency substitute plans

_____ Handle situations involving staff members in a professional manner

_____ Implement decisions made by groups in which teacher served or was represented

_____ Maintain Internet access safeguards appropriate to age level and as identified by the district

_____ Use discretion in handling confidential information and difficult situations

Planning Instruction

Professionalism & Collegial Collaboration

Implementing Instruction

Organizing a Productive Environment

Assessing Learning & the Instructional Program

Orchestrating a Positive Environment

Professionalism & Collegial Collaboration
New Teacher Self-Assessment and Goal Setting continued...

____ Ensure that supportable facts, rather than rumors or insinuations, are discussion points in conversations and conferences

____ Be available for conferences with parents

____ Seek out parents and make parents feel comfortable contacting you and interacting with you as a partner in their child's education

____ Teach parents about the instructional program and your approach to learning through newsletters and evening academic events that feature student work and expected standards

____ Collaborate with special education teachers/general education teachers to facilitate the learning of students with IEPs

____ Seek out and use professional expertise for assistance and guidance in supporting students with intellectual, emotional or physical challenges

____ Serve as a school representative when asked to do so

____ Serve as a catalyst for constructive change

____ Demonstrate responsibility in attendance and punctuality as required by school policy

____ Always be professionally groomed and attired

____ Express views and ideas to others in a professional manner that is respectful of the possibility and probability of different perspectives

____ Align professional development work with school and district goals

____ Adjust classroom practice as a result of professional learning completed independently, in collaboration with colleagues, and/or sponsored by the school or district

____ Work with colleagues across grade levels to align curriculum and decrease redundancy

____ Recognize that collegial sharing is essential to the learning process for both students and educators

____ Use all available resources accessible locally, at the state level, nationally, and technologically

____ Use communication skills that demonstrate an awareness of cultural, gender, and generational differences

____ Assess group dynamics and productivity and adjust own behavior to maximize the outcomes of the work

Planning Instruction

Professionalism & Collegial Collaboration

Implementing Instruction

Organizing a Productive Environment

Assessing Learning & the Instructional Program

Orchestrating a Positive Environment

Professional Growth Plan

New Teacher _____ Date _____

Mentor teacher _____

School _____ Grade/Subject _____

Identified Strengths:

Identified Areas for Professional Growth:

Goal related to Standard/Domain:	Date:
Actions:	Time line:
Evidence:	Date:

Goal related to Standard/Domain:	Date:
Actions:	Time line:
Evidence:	Date:

3 First Semester Professional Accomplishments That Help Me Recognize My Growth

- ●
- ●
- ●

2 Two Areas of Professional Growth on Which I Want to Work Second Semester

- ●
- ●

1 Way You as My Mentor Can Help Me Achieve My Professional Growth Goals

- ●

Professional Growth Plan
Reflection and Goal Setting

As you review your goals last quarter, what progress have you made?

What evidence or indicators demonstrate growth towards your goals?

What new goals do you have for yourself for the next quarter?
1.

2.

3.

Why are these good goals for you right now?

Action steps toward meeting new goals:

Professional Growth Plan
Reflection and Goal Setting

What support will you need to meet your new goals?

Up to this point, what mentoring support has been most valuable?

What mentoring support would be most useful during the upcoming quarter?

Home Run/Strike Log for Teachers

Use this log as a practical, speedy means of entering impressions of each teaching day's successful "home runs" and not so successful "strikes," which may need improvement. Reflect briefly and make a note in each column daily. It can be analyzed informally in terms of frequencies, trends, and patterns.

Date	Home Runs	Strikes

My Own Top 10 List of Tips to Remember in
Planning & Pacing

1. Begin with the End in Mind...and Keep IT in Mind!

2.

3.

4.

5.

6.

7.

8.

9.

10.

My Own Top 10 List of Formative and Summative
Assessment Ideas I Want to Remember

1.

2.

3.

4.

5.

6.

7.

8.

9.

10.

My Own Top 10 List of
Instructional Tips I Want to Remember

1.

2.

3.

4.

5.

6.

7.

8.

9.

10.

My Own Top 10 List of Systems for Organizing
Professional, District & School Documents

1.

2.

3.

4.

5.

6.

7.

8.

9.

10.

My Own Top 10 List of Systems for
Organizing Myself & My Teaching Materials

1.

2.

3.

4.

5.

6.

7.

8.

9.

10.

My Own Top 10 List of Systems for
Organizing My Learners & Their Materials

1.

2.

3.

4.

5.

6.

7.

8.

9.

10.

My Own Top 10 List of Strategies for Orchestrating
A Positive Learning-Centered Environment

1.

2.

3.

4.

5.

6.

7.

8.

9.

10.

My Own Top 10 List of Strategies for Organizing
A Productive Learning-Centered Environment

1.

2.

3.

4.

5.

6.

7.

8.

9.

10.

My Own Top 10 List of Strategies for
Working with Parents as Partners

1.

2.

3.

4.

5.

6.

7.

8.

9.

10.

My "TO DO" List
To Be Ready for the Opening of School

1.

2.

3.

4.

5.

6.

7.

8.

9.

10.

Induction/Mentoring Program
Reflection and Evaluation

Mentor _____

New Teacher _____

School _____

Please assist us in evaluating this year's induction and mentoring programs. We are asking both the new teachers and the mentors to complete this reflection and evaluation from their perspectives. Use these stems to identify what worked well and what did not work as well as it might have. We will use your responses to plan adaptations for next year's program. Thanks for your time and trouble.

1. Please describe the manner in which you were introduced to the induction and mentoring program and to your mentor.

2. Please describe the way in which you and your mentor set up communication systems and interactions with each other.

3. How did written mentor/new teacher agreements and/or goal setting influence your professional interactions throughout the year?

Induction/Mentoring Program
Reflection and Evaluation

4. Please describe how your mentor made you feel welcome in your new professional setting.

5. Please describe the ways your mentor provided guidance and assistance in obtaining resources and materials to support your work.

6. What are the ways your mentor helped you plan and pace instruction and design, implement, and reflect on lessons and units based on district criteria?

Induction/Mentoring Program
Reflection and Evaluation

7. Describe how you and your mentor analyzed student work and student achievement data and used that data to make instructional decisions.

8. Explain the assistance you needed in working with the students in this district and the ways in which your mentor assisted you with this skill area.

9. Describe your collegial interactions with teachers and administrators in your school and throughout the district.

Induction/Mentoring Program
Reflection and Evaluation

10. Describe how you used the professional development opportunities offered by the school and district to refine and enhance your professional knowledge and skills.

11. In what ways did your mentor and the district induction program assist you in working with parents as partners?

12. What recommendations do you have for the induction of new teachers in this school/school district in future years?

Tools for Mentors

Chapter X

Tools for Mentors

Self-Assessment of Mentoring Knowledge and Skills

Use this tool to provide an overview of the knowledge and skills mentors need in order to work as a well-rounded mentor.

Mentoring a New Teacher Three Column Chart

Use this tool to identify specific actions you want to take, the resources you have on hand, and those that you need to gather to support new teachers.

Mentoring Professional Growth Plan

- Use this form to establish your mentoring goals for the quarter or the year.
- Use this form to model goal setting and reflective practice by completing it and sharing your goals and action plans with the new teachers.
- See corresponding new teacher tool on page 262.

3-2-1 Goal Setting

- Use this tool to model reflection and goal setting.
- See corresponding new teacher tool on page 263.

My Mentoring "TO DO" Lists

- Use this five page tool to identify the selections you make from the suggestions listed in this book.
- See **Chapter V, Mentoring Calendar** for recommended actions for each month of the school year.

A Mentoring Culture

- Use this survey with your colleagues to assess where you are as a group in creating a culture which welcomes and supports new teachers.
- See the listings in the **Colleagues** section of each month in **Chapter V, Mentoring Calendar** and pages 55-56 for possible collegial interactions with new teachers.

Mentoring Log

- Use this log to track your interactions with new teachers.
- Be sure to check the "action to be taken" column and follow-through with promised actions and resources.

Induction/Mentoring Program Reflection and Evaluation

Use this four-page survey to provide each other and the district about how well the mentoring program worked this year.

Self-Assessment of Mentoring Knowledge & Skills

Score your knowledge and skills from 1 to 5 with 5 the highest

_____ Best practice in mentoring

_____ Proactive mentoring in the interest of teacher growth and student learning rather than giving own opinion on topic at hand

_____ Roles mentors play

_____ Responsibilities of mentors in my district

_____ Use of resources available to support mentors and novice teachers in my district and stage

_____ The needs of beginning teachers and experienced teachers new to the district, how they change over time, and which mentor interactions to use given the needs

_____ Plan of action for new teacher orientation week and an outline for regularly scheduled interactions with new teachers throughout the school year

_____ Observation of classroom practice, analysis of the teaching and learning observed, and giving constructive feedback to peers

_____ Looking collaboratively at student work and using that data to inform instructional decisions

_____ Standards-based instructional decision making and practices are aligned with the district criteria for teacher performance recognize them in action

_____ Knowledge and use of school/district policies and procedures including student assessment, curriculum guides and supplemental resources

_____ Literature and tools available to support standards-based education

_____ Communication skills for coaching, collaborating, and consulting

_____ Problem solving issues related to mentoring

_____ Analysis and reflection on my own practice

Analyze the results of the self-assessment and identify those areas you need to learn more about or in which you need to build skills. Establish a plan of action. Use this text, the listed print and web resources, and experienced mentors for assistance in implementing your plan.

Mentoring a New Teacher

Use this form to build a list of the information and materials you already have on hand to share with your new teacher and to create a list of information and materials you need to gather.

Materials and Information on Hand	Materials I Need to Gather	Information I Need to Find

Mentoring Professional Growth Plan

Mentor Teacher_____ Date_____

New Teacher_____

School_____ Grade/Subject _____

Identified Strengths:

Identified Areas for Professional Growth/Learning:

Goal:	Date:
Actions:	Time Line:
Evidence:	Date:

Goal:	Date:
Actions:	Time Line:
Evidence:	Date:

3. First Semester Professional Accomplishments That Help Me Recognize My Growth

-
-
-

2. Two Areas of Professional Growth on Which I Want to Work Second Semester

-
-

1. One Action I Plan to Take to Achieve My Professional Growth Goals

-

My Mentoring "TO DO" List
...Before School Opens

1.

2.

3.

4.

5.

6.

7.

8.

9.

10.

My Mentoring "TO DO" List

...First Quarter

1.

2.

3.

4.

5.

6.

7.

8.

9.

10.

My Mentoring "TO DO" List
...Second Quarter

1.

2.

3.

4.

5.

6.

7.

8.

9.

10.

My Mentoring "TO DO" List

...Third Quarter

1.

2.

3.

4.

5.

6.

7.

8.

9.

10.

My Mentoring "TO DO" List

...Fourth Quarter

1.

2.

3.

4.

5.

6.

7.

8.

9.

10.

A Mentoring Culture

Use this survey to analyze the mentoring culture at your school. It can help you determine to what degree your school prepares for, welcomes, befriends, supports, develops, and retains new teachers and to then plan next steps.

Reflective Questions	My View My Data	My Colleagues View Their Data
• How are new teachers perceived? Are they eagerly anticipated as new resources and a source of energy to the school?		
• Is there an existing, on-going committee or group that annually plans and coordinates activities and experiences to bring new staff on board?		
• Do you regularly question new staff regarding their "rookie" or "new kid on the block" experiences in your school in order to ascertain needs and interests to help you plan?		
• Does the staff at large feel interest in or responsibility for the success of new teachers, or is that to be taken care of only by mentors?		
• Are there known ways for a veteran teacher to express his or her interest in mentoring or being involved in the school's induction of new teachers?		
• In allocating professional development resources, is consideration given to the needs of new teachers and their mentors in meeting the induction requirements?		

Reflective Questions	My View My Data	My Colleagues View Their Data
• Are you and other administrators visible and vocal supporters of mentors and new teachers? Are you involved in activities designed to support their relationship and work together?		
• How do teachers feel about the mentoring role and responsibilities? Do they volunteer or accept your invitation to serve? Do they follow through on commitment?		
• Are grade-level, departmental, or team meetings structured and conducted to help a new teacher make good use of the time and learn the purpose and value of the meetings?		
• Are new teachers allowed to settle in, "learn the ropes," and focus on learning to teach, or do they have multiple committee assignments and extra duties?		
• When classes are scheduled, is consideration given to providing common planning time for mentors and new teachers?		
• To what degree do all staff members regularly observe each other teaching and engage in collegial, reflective conversation and instruction?		
• To what degree is continuous professional development to improve instruction modeled by senior staff?		

Mentoring Log

Teacher_____ **Mentor**_____

School _____

Grade Level/Subject_____

Date/Time	Focus & Format of the Interaction	Action to be Taken/Comments

Induction/Mentoring Program
Reflection and Evaluation

Mentor _____

New Teacher _____

School _____

Please assist us in evaluating this year's induction and mentoring programs. We are asking both the new teachers and the mentors to complete this reflection and evaluation from their perspectives. Use these stems to identify what worked well and what did not work as well as it might have. We will use your responses to plan adaptations for next year's program. Thanks for your time and trouble.

1. Please describe how and why you became a mentor and then how you met the new teacher(s) with whom you worked this year.

2. Please describe the way in which you and your new teacher(s) set up communication systems and interactions with each other.

3. How did written mentor/new teacher agreements and/or goal setting influence your professional interactions throughout the year?

Induction/Mentoring Program
Reflection and Evaluation

4. Please describe what you did to make the new teacher(s) with whom you worked feel welcome in a new professional setting.

5. Please describe the ways you provided guidance and assistance in obtaining resources and materials for the new teacher(s).

6. What are the ways you helped new teachers plan and pace instruction and design, implement, and reflect on lessons and units based on district criteria?

Induction/Mentoring Program
Reflection and Evaluation

7. Describe how you and the new teachers analyzed student work and student achievement data and used that data to make instructional decisions.

8. Explain the assistance you provided the new teachers working with the students in this district.

9. Describe how you facilitated collegial interactions between the new teachers and teachers and administrators in your school and throughout the district.

Induction/Mentoring Program
Reflection and Evaluation

10. Describe how your work as a mentor and the related professional development opportunities that helped you refine and enhance your professional knowledge and skills.

11. In what ways did you assist new teachers in working with parents as partners?

12. What recommendations do you have for the induction of new teachers in this school/school district in future years?

Tools for Peer Observations And Data Driven-Discussions

Tools for Peer Observation and Data-Driven Discussion

The tools in this section are designed to be used with **Chapter VI, Peer Observations** and **Chapter VII, Data-Driven Discussions.**

Planning Conference Log
- Use this log to record brief notes from planning conferences.
- Keep these logs in chronological order in your mentoring notebook for a record of issues discussed and use to identify trends and growth over time.

Areas of Focus for Standards-Based Observations I
Areas of Focus for Standards-Based Observations II
- Have new teachers use these two tools to identify areas of focus for peer observations.
- They can be used when the new teachers are going to observe you or another teacher or when you are going to observe them.
- It is important to narrow the focus of observations so that you can have data-driven discussions about what was observed.

Observation Data Gathering and Analysis
Classroom Observation Log
Data Log for Peer Observations and Learning Walks
These three tools provide three different formats for gathering data during classroom observations or learning walks and for recording comments or points to ponder.

Peer Observation Reflections
- This tool provides new teachers with a format for recording their reactions to teaching and learning episodes they observe. It does not have a place for data gathering.
- A collection of these reflections would provide a record over time of what was significant in the observations. Even if the new teachers do not use the ideas right away, they could revisit the reflections at a later date.

Tools for Peer Observation and Data-Driven Discussion

Mentor Observation Log

- This tool is designed to provide a brief record of mentor observations of new teachers.
- Although space is provided for four areas of focus, there may only be one or two in a given observation.

Notes for Data-Driven Discussions of Teaching and Learning I
Notes for Data-Driven Discussions of Teaching and Learning II

- These two tools provide formats for analyzing data gathered during observations.
- The first focuses on teacher behavior/action and the second focuses on student behavior/action.
- The listing of evidence for any generalizations made about teacher or student behavior/action provides the data for the data-driven discussions that follow the observation.

Planning for the Collaborative Conference

- This two page tool provides questions to answer in preparation for a collaborative conference.
- The questions follow the steps of the six-step problem-solving process.
- See pages 211-212 for further information on collaborative conferences and the six-step problem-solving process.

Item/Indicator Analysis

- Use this tool with new teachers to do item analysis of assessment results.
- See page 219 for ways to disaggregate the data.
- Assist the new teacher in making instructional decisions based on the data analysis.

Cause and Effect Analysis

- Use this tool to assist new teachers in comparing desired and actual student learning results.
- Use this tool to identify instructional changes to be made the next time the lesson or unit is taught.
- See page 218 for more information on cause and effect analysis.

Planning Conference Log

Mentor: _____ Date: _____ Time: _____

New Teacher: _____

Analysis of Current Data	New Areas of Focus	Data to be Gathered	Artifacts to be Collected	Mentor Support Needed

Areas of Focus for
Standards-Based Observations I

Use this form to plan observations of the novice teacher by the mentor and/or to provide focus for an observation by the novice teacher with or without the mentor. Have the novice teacher select two to three areas of focus.

_____ How are standards, or what a student must know and be able to do, communicated to students? How is the learning "framed" so that students know what to do and why?

_____ How does the teacher diagnostically determine what students already know related to a standard?

_____ How is students' prior knowledge used to facilitate new learning?

_____ How are new concepts or skills introduced?

_____ What strategies are used to support students in "making meaning" of information and concepts?

_____ How are questions, activities and assignments all shown to be linked to support students in achieving content standards?

_____ How are multiple ways to learn provided to students with different skills, knowledge levels, abilities and interests?

_____ How is student learning monitored as the lesson progresses?

_____ How does the teacher seek to clarify information, or clear up misunderstandings or misinformation that is detected?

_____ How is feedback on student work or learning provided?

_____ How is the lesson adjusted in progress as the teacher becomes aware of student responses to instruction?

_____ How is student learning formally assessed?

_____ How do students assess their own and others' work?

Areas of Focus for
Standards-Based Observations II

Use this form to plan observations of the novice teacher by the mentor and/or to provide focus for an observation by the novice teacher with or without the mentor. Have the novice teacher select two to three areas of focus.

_____ Match of lesson to standards
Specifically:

_____ Classroom routines and procedures
Specifically:

_____ Classroom arrangement of space, furniture, learning materials
Specifically:

_____ Management of student learning groups
Specifically:

_____ Dealing with student behavior issues
Specifically:

_____ Giving instructions for student work
Specifically:

_____ Questioning strategies
Specifically:

_____ Strategies for providing feedback on student work
Specifically:

_____ Strategies for working with special needs students in the regular classroom
Specifically:

_____ Transitions between instructional activities
Specifically:

_____ Literacy/numeracy strategies in the content area
Specifically:

_____ Uses of instructional technology
Specifically:

Observation Data Gathering & Analysis

Teacher_____ Date_____ Time_____

Grade/Subject _____

Standard(s) addressed_____

Number of Students_____ Other Information _____

Observation Data of Significance (Teacher, Student, Student Work, and Environment)	Comments/Questions (After Lesson)

New Teacher
Classroom Observation Log

Date _____ Teacher Observed _____ School _____

Observation Focus _____

Observations: What did you observe?

- Evidence of a standards-based classroom

- Student-centered learning

- Instructional methods

- Classroom organizational systems

- Classroom arrangement

What did you learn?

How can you apply to your own classroom?

Data Log for
Peer Observations and Learning Walks

Teacher's Name_____

Date _____

Subject/Grade _____

Focus of Observation/Learning Walk (Optional) _____

Standards/Indicators being addressed:

Students were:

Teacher was:

Evidence of rigor:

Evidence of positive and productive environment:

Points to Ponder:

Peer Observation Reflections

Teacher Observed _____ **Start Time** ____ **End Time** ____ **Subject** ____

Observer _____ **Date** ____ **Room** ____ **Grade** ____

This sheet reflects my thoughts about:

☐ Planning
☐ Rigor
☐ Literacy
☐ Presentation Modes
☐ Framing the Learning

☐ Real World Connections
☐ Active Student Learning
☐ Formative Assessment
☐ Collaborative Learning

Organizational Systems for:
☐ Instructional Materials
☐ The Classroom
☐ Students
☐ Student Learning

Ahas!	Questions that surfaced
Resources I liked	**Ideas to use in my classroom**

Mentor Observation Log

Mentor: _____ New Teacher: _____ Date: _____ Time: _____

Focus Areas	Data Gathered	Discussion Points	Reflection/Follow-Up
1.			
2.			
3.			
4.			

Notes for Data-Driven Discussions
of Teaching & Learning

Performance Indicator/Teacher Behavior noted:

Data:

Data:

Impact on Student Learning:

Performance Indicator/Teacher Behavior noted:

Data:

Data:

Impact on Student Learning:

Performance Indicator/Teacher Behavior noted:

Data:

Data:

Impact on Student Learning:

Performance Indicator/Teacher Behavior noted:

Data:

Data:

Impact on Student Learning:

Performance Indicator/Teacher Behavior noted:

Data:

Data:

Impact on Student Learning:

Performance Indicator/Teacher Behavior noted:

Data:

Data:

Impact on Student Learning:

Notes for Data-Driven Discussions of Teaching & Learning

Student Learning/Behavior Noted:

Performance Indicators/Teacher Behavior(s) that promoted student learning:

Student Learning/Behavior Noted:

Performance Indicators/Teacher Behavior(s) that promoted student learning:

Student Learning/Behavior Noted:

Performance Indicators/Teacher Behavior(s) that promoted student learning:

Student Learning/Behavior Noted:

Performance Indicators/Teacher Behavior(s) that promoted student learning:

Student Learning/Behavior Noted:

Performance Indicators/Teacher Behavior(s) that promoted student learning:

Student Learning/Behavior Noted:

Performance Indicators/Teacher Behavior(s) that promoted student learning:

Planning for
The Collaborative Conference

New Teacher_____ Mentor_____

Date _____ Time _____

Purpose of Conference _____

How will I create a congenial beginning?

How will I/we identify the problem, issue, or area of focus? What data will be used?

How will I check for understanding and/or agreement on the issues or area of focus?

What criteria will we use to weigh the alternatives?

What questions might I ask to facilitate the consideration of the alternatives?

Who will identify the acceptable action? The new teacher, the mentor, or the two collaboratively?

What data will be used to determine the success of the action?

When will a follow-up meeting be held to determine how the solution is working?

The Action Plan:

Item/Indicator Analysis

Student	Item/Indicator 1	Item/Indicator 2	Item/Indicator 3	Item/Indicator 4	Item/Indicator 5	Item/Indicator 6	Item/Indicator 7	Item/Indicator 8	Item/Indicator 9	Item/Indicator 10
Class Average										

Cause/Effect Analysis

Desired Effect - What were the **desired** group and/or individual assessment results?

Effect - What were the **actual** group and/or individual assessment results?

Cause: Methods

Methods used this time:	Potential changes for next time:

Cause: Materials

Materials used this time:	Potential changes for next time:

Cause: People

People involved this time:	Potential changes for next time:

Cause: Time

Time used this time:	Potential changes for next time:

Tools for Instructional Planning

Chapter XII

Tools for Instructional Planning

New teachers always ask when will they ever find the time to get ahead in the planning process. The reality is that they end up staying up late at night or just doing whatever comes next in the textbook or program. They go from day to day, end up harried and exhausted, and have to rush through important parts of the curriculum. They wonder how may days should they plan at a time, where they will find the materials they need, and how to chunk the year. These tools for instructional planning are designed to help mentors help the new teachers with these challenges and concerns.

SBE Planning Process

Use this tool with page 175 in *Why Didn't I Learn This in College?* and with the unit and lesson design tools in this chapter.

Key Concepts and Generalizations/Essential Understandings

- See page 130 in this book for a list of concepts which can be combined to create generalizations/essential understandings.
- Use this tool with pages 177-180 in *Why Didn't I Learn This in College?*

Task Analysis

Use this tool with page 185 in *Why Didn't I Learn This in College?* and pages 193-194 in *Instruction for All Students.*

See and Hear T-Chart

Use with all instructional strategies or student behaviors to help the new teachers know what they would look like in their own classrooms.

Assessment Planning Worksheet

Use this tool with pages 140-166 in *Why Didn't I Learn This in College?*

Assessing My Assessment as a Learning Tool

- Use this tool with new teachers to have them reflect on the impact of their assessment practices.
- Use it also to help them build their repertoires of ways to increase the impact of their assessment practices.
- See 311 in *Why Didn't I Learn This in College?* for an error analysis chart for students to use.

Tools for Instructional Planning

Worksheet for Creating a Rubric
- This tool provides a template for creating an analytical rubric. Use it with new teachers to help them build an understanding of how to construct rubrics.
- Use this tool with page 217, **Looking at Student Work: Writing Rubrics Using Student Work**, in this book.
- See pages 156-157 and 165-166 in *Why Didn't I Learn This in College?*

Making Connections
- Use this tool with new teachers to help them build their repertoires of active learning strategies that help students access prior knowledge and make real world connections.
- See pages 65-106 in *Why Didn't I Learn This in College?*

Active Learning Structures Log
- Have new teachers use this two-page tool to record their ideas about how to use active learning structures.
- See pages 65-106 in *Why Didn't I Learn This in College?* for explanations of the purposes and processes for over thirty active learning structures for new teachers to use.

Building Your Own RAFT
- Use this tool with page 101 in *Why Didn't I Learn This in College?* and with pages 129-133 in *Instruction for All Students.*
- See pages 175-186 in *Instruction for All Students* for an extensive list of roles, audiences, and products for students to create.

Homework Planning Sheet
- Assist new teachers in using this tool to design homework in all four categories.
- See pages 147-149 in *Why Didn't I Learn This in College* and pages 35-145 in *Instruction for All Students* for supporting information on homework.

Course Map
- Have new teachers use this graphic tool to map out the year through the lens of essential understandings and key concepts.
- Using this tool with new teachers will help them move beyond fact and/or chapter teaching and focus on concepts and generalizations that can provide unifying themes throughout the year.

Tools for Instructional Planning

Unit Planning Worksheet
Unit Plan A
Unit Plan B

These three tools are all standards-based design tools. Different formats are provided to better match the planning style of the new teachers.

Unit Design Brainstorming Map

- This tool provides a format for brainstorming interdisciplinary connections for key concepts and skills.
- New elementary teachers can use this tool to identify ways to spiral concepts and skills throughout the day.

Standards-Based Planning/Analysis Matrix

- Use this tool with new teachers to analyze basal texts, packaged programs, and units previously designed and used by teammates for alignment with district learning standards.
- Once areas not included in the basal texts and packaged programs are identified, help the new teachers identify alternative resources for addressing learning standards.

Top Ten Questions to Ask Myself as I Design Lessons

- This six page tool is a detailed lesson plan format presented in question form. It is designed to help new teachers think through all the questions one needs to ask when planning a lesson.
- Each of the ten questions are cross-referenced to pages in *Why Didn't I Learn This in College?* and *Instruction for All Students.*

Lesson Planning Worksheet
Lesson Planning Guide

These one and two page planning tools can be used with new teachers when they are designing many lessons and want to sketch out some general ideas for the lesson.

Tools for Instructional Planning

Getting Started with Differentiation

- This two page tool is a nonthreatening approach to use in coaching new teachers in differentiating instruction.
- See pages 39-42 in *Why Didn't I Learn This in College?* for ideas the new teachers can use to better meet the needs of struggling learners.
- Mentors of experienced teachers new to the district can use pages 189-215 in *Instruction for All Students* for further work with differentiation.

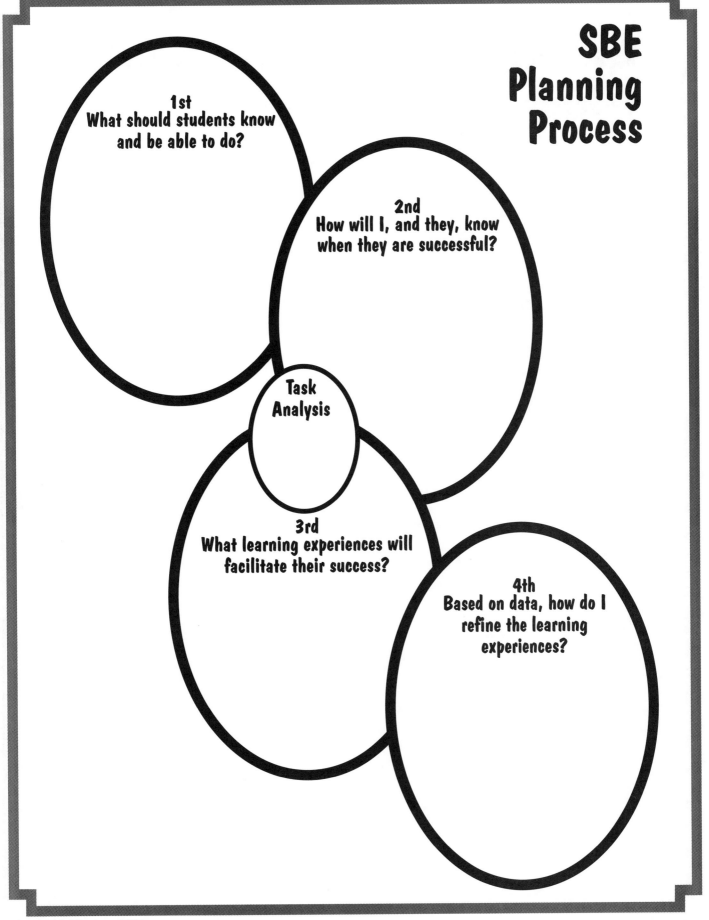

SBE Planning Process

1st
What should students know and be able to do?

2nd
How will I, and they, know when they are successful?

Task Analysis

3rd
What learning experiences will facilitate their success?

4th
Based on data, how do I refine the learning experiences?

Key Concepts and Generalizations/Essential Understandings in the Study of _____

1.

2.

3.

4.

5.

6.

7.

8.

9.

10.

Task Analysis

Knowledge   **Skills**

Knowledge   **Skills**

If _____
was happening in the classroom, we would

See	Hear

From Formative to Summative
Planning Assessment Worksheet

Unit Focus: **Date:**

How will I use the following assessment strategies in this unit?

Preassessments:

Checks for Understanding:

Observations/Anecdotal Records:

Student Questions/Comments (In-class and in Journals):

Teacher Questions & Prompts (In-class):

Assignments, including Homework (Student Work Samples):

Peer Assessment:

Self-Assessment:

Quizzes:

Tests:

Performance Tasks (Short-Term and Long-Term):

What form(s) will the assessment criteria take?

_____Analytical Rubric

_____Holistic Rubric

_____Performance Assessment Task List

_____Checklist

Assessing My Assessment as a Learning Tool

"I'm buried in papers, all the weekend long
Figuring out what they got right and what they got wrong
All these hours of work to get data in the grade book
Seems like students ought to give it more than a two-second look!"

How do I/How might I ensure that students are learning and growing from the grading, critiquing, correcting that I do?

How do I/How might I present data about performance to students so that they can and are expected to react to that data?

How do I/How might I provide opportunities for student reflection and growth as a result of the data I provide through my assessment of their work?

How do I/How might I use test, performance task and other assessment data to plan future instruction?

Worksheet for Creating a Rubric
Standards to be Addressed:

Essential Understandings:

Description of the Task:

	Does not Meet Criteria	Meets Criteria	Exceeds Criteria
Skill/Component: • • •			
Skill/Component: • • •			
Skill/Component: • • •			

Making Connections

How might I find out what students already know about what we are about to read/study?

How might I help them access what they know and have experience with both inside and outside the classroom that is related to what we are about to read/study?

To Past Experiences

To Future Experiences

How might I help them not only build on prior experiences, but reframe their thinking when appropriate?

What are the "beyond the classroom" applications/implications of what we are about to read/study? How might I incorporate them into the learning experience?

Between Learning Experiences in the Present

Active Learning Structures	How I Might Use This Strategy	Why It Might Be Useful Here!

Active Learning Structures	How I Might Use This Strategy	Why It Might Be Useful Here!

Building Your Own
RAFT

Role _____
Audience _____
Form (product) _____
Time _____

Role _____
Audience _____
Form (product) _____
Time _____

Role _____
Audience _____
Form (product) _____
Time _____

Homework Planning Sheet

As you plan a unit of study, use the homework categories below to thoughtfully design homework that will help your students move toward mastery of the standards on which the unit is based and will also give you good formative assessment data.

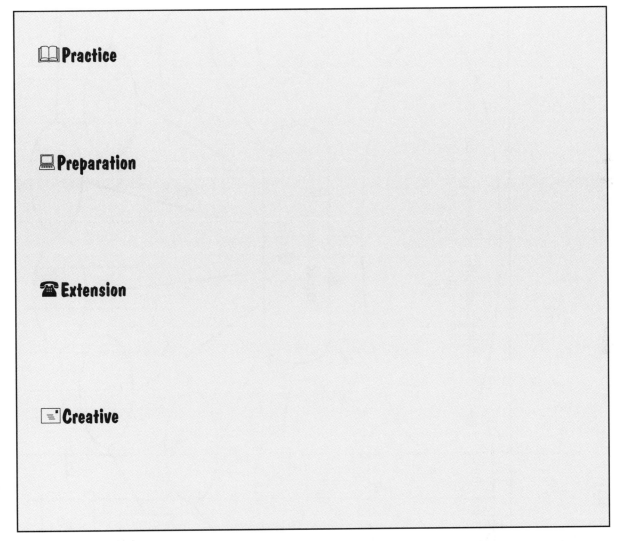

📖 **Practice**

💻 **Preparation**

☎ **Extension**

🖃 **Creative**

What language could you use to communicate the homework assignments in a way that students know what to do, know why they are doing it, and know when they are successful?

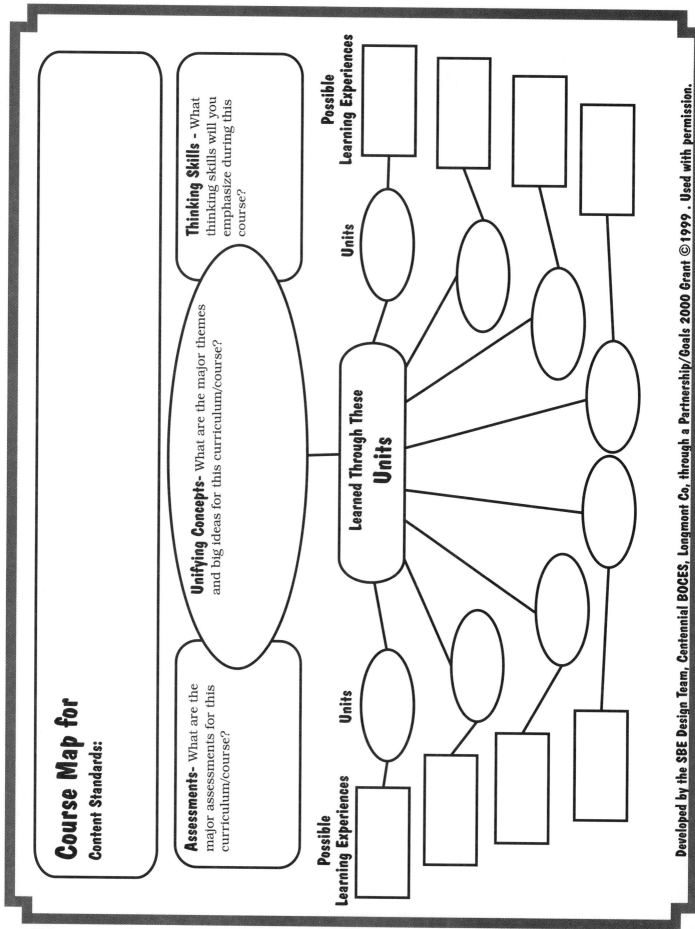

Course Map for

Content Standards:

Unifying Concepts- What are the major themes and big ideas for this curriculum/course?

Thinking Skills - What thinking skills will you emphasize during this course?

Assessments- What are the major assessments for this curriculum/course?

Learned Through These Units

Units

Possible Learning Experiences

Units

Possible Learning Experiences

Developed by the SBE Design Team, Centennial BOCES, Longmont Co, through a Partnership/Goals 2000 Grant ©1999 . Used with permission.

Unit Planning Worksheet

Title:

Time Frame:

Standards: What will students know and be able to do as a result of this unit? What are the essential understandings, key concepts, big ideas?

Assessments: Performance tasks, projects, quizzes, tests, observations, work samples, etc. How will I and they know when they are successful?

Task Analysis: What knowledge and skills are needed for success? Which students will need extra help and which students will need enrichment? How will I scaffold instruction?

Instruction: What learning experiences will help all students learn targeted understandings?

Unit Plan A

Unit of Study:

Standards:

Essential Questions/Key Ideas/Concepts:

Assessment Strategies
   Preassessment:

   Formative:

   Summative: (What criteria?)

Possible Learning Experiences/Assignments

Materials and Resources Needed

Unit Plan B

Unit Title:	Grade/Subject:

Standards to be Addressed:	Key Concepts and Generalizations/ Essential Questions:
Summative Assessment:	Task Analysis of Knowledge, Skills, and Levels of Understanding Required:

Map of the Unit: Sequence of Events/Lessons	Time Allocation:

Materials and Resources:	Technology Resources:
Vocabulary:	**Differentiation Strategies:**
Instructional Strategies:	
	Formative Assessment Strategies:

Unit Design
Brainstorming Map

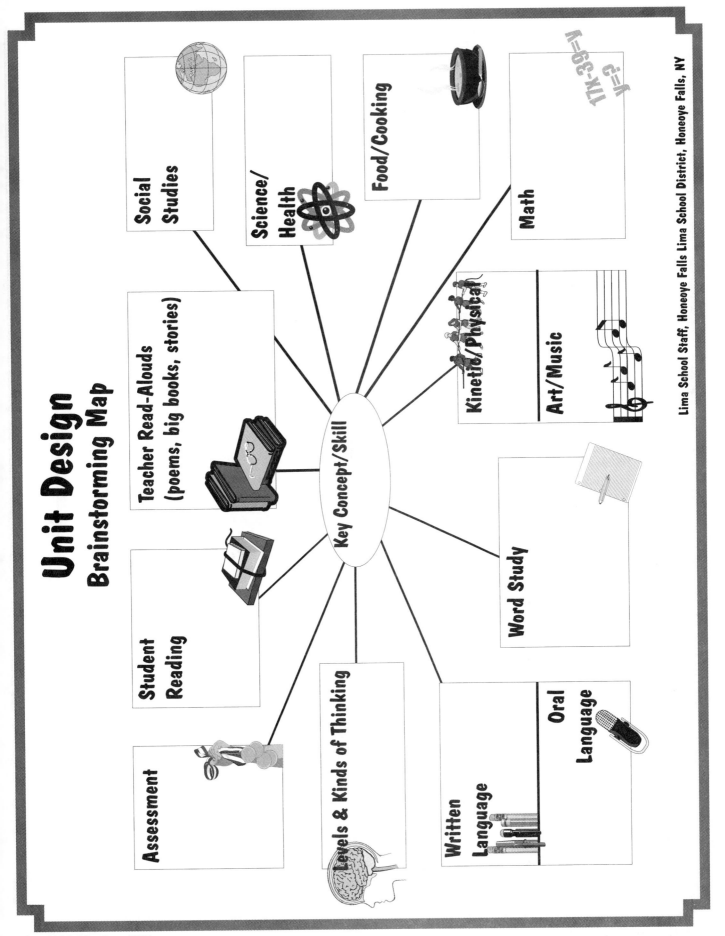

Social Studies

Science/Health

Food/Cooking

Math

$y = \frac{c}{?}$
17x-39=y

Teacher Read-Alouds (poems, big books, stories)

Kinetic/Physical

Art/Music

Key Concept/Skill

Student Reading

Word Study

Assessment

Levels & Kinds of Thinking

Written Language

Oral Language

Lima School Staff, Honeoye Falls Lima School District, Honeoye Falls, NY

Standards-Based Instruction Planning/Analysis Matrix

Standard	Assignment #1	Assignment #2	Assignment #3	Assignment #4	Traditional Assessment	Performance Assessment
Indicator #1						
Indicator #2						
Indicator #3						
Indicator #4						
Indicator #5						
Indicator #6						
Indicator #7						
Indicator #8						

Use this matrix to analyze current units or to plan future units. Cross reference each component of the unit with subsets of the standards to ensure a high correlation. Make necessary adjustments before, during, and after instruction.

TOP TEN QUESTIONS
to ask myself as I design lessons

1st Step

1. What should **students know and be able to do** with what they know as a result of this lesson? How are these objectives related to national, state, and/or district **standards**? How are these objectives related to the **big ideas/key concepts** of the course?

2nd Step

2. How will **students demonstrate what they know and what they can do** with what they know? What multiple forms of assessment including **self-assessment** can I use? What will be the **assessment criteria** and what form will it take? (See pages 140 through 166 in *Why Didn't I Learn This in College?* or pages 159 through 167 in *Instruction for All Students*.)

TOP TEN QUESTIONS
to ask myself as I design lessons

3rd Step: Questions 3 - 10 address the 3rd Step.

3. How will I find out what **students already know (preassessment),** and how will I help them access what they know and have experienced both inside and outside the classroom? How will **I help them** not only **build on prior experiences,** but **deal with misconceptions** and **reframe their thinking** when appropriate?
(See pages 66 through 106 and 141 in *Why didn't I Learn This in College?* or pages 79 through 107 in *Instruction for All Students*.)

4. How will new knowledge, concepts, skills be introduced? Given the diversity of my students and my **task analysis**, what are **my best options for sources and presentation modes** of new material?
(See pages 109 through 134 in *Why didn't I Learn This in College?* or pages 51 through 71 and 193 through 194 in *Instruction for All Students*.)

TOP TEN QUESTIONS
to ask myself as I design lessons

5. How will **I facilitate student processing (meaning making)** of new information or processes? What are the key questions, activities, and assignments (in class or homework)?
(See pages 52 through 60, pages 68 through 106, and pages 147 through 149 in *Why didn't I Learn This in College?* or pages 79 through 107 and 115 through 145 in *Instruction for All Students*.)

6. How will **I check for student understanding** during the lesson?
(See pages 142 through 146 in *Why Didn't I Learn This in College?* or pages 108 through 111 in *Instruction for All Students*.)

TOP TEN QUESTIONS
to ask myself as I design lessons

7. What do I need to do to **differentiate instruction** so the learning experiences are productive for all students?
(See pages 189 through 215 in *Instruction for All Students*.)

8. How will I **"Frame the Learning"** so that **students know the objectives**, the **rationale** for the objectives and activities, the directions and procedures, as well as the **assessment criteria** at the beginning of the learning process?
(See pages 48 through 52 and pages 179 through 180 in *Why Didn't I Learn This in College?* or pages 52 and 115 in *Instruction for All Students*.)

TOP TEN QUESTIONS
to ask myself as I design lessons

9. How will I build in opportunities for students to make **real world connections** and to learn and use the **varied and complex thinking skills** they need to succeed in the classroom and the world beyond?
(See pages 54 through 60 in *Why Didn't I Learn This in College?* or pages 129 through 134, 175 through 187, and 219 through 247 in *Instruction for All Students*.)

10. What adjustments need to be made in the **learning environment** so that we can work and learn efficiently in a positive and productive classroom setting? How is **data** being used to make these decisions?
(See pages 9 through 42 and pages 224 through 250 in *Why didn't I Learn This in College?* or pages 251 through 267 in *Instruction for All Students*.)

TOP TEN QUESTIONS
to ask myself as I design lessons

Materials to be Gathered or Prepared

Time Line/Sequence for Lesson

350

Lesson Planning Worksheet

Unit:

Date(s):

Standard and/or indicators addressed:
1.

2.

3.

Standards in kid-friendly language:
1.

2.

3.

Concepts, generalizations, or essential questions:
1.

2.

3.

Ways to assess students' level of learning during and at the end of the lesson:
Formative:
1.

2.

3

Summative:
1.

2.

Lesson Planning Worksheet continued...

Ways to access prior knowledge and help students make real life connections:

1.

2.

Learning Experiences:

1.

2.

3.

4.

5.

6.

Materials and resources needed:

1.

2.

3.

Ways to scaffold instruction:

1.

2.

3.

Ways to have students summarize:

1.

2.

Lesson Planning Guide

State or District Standards Being Addressed:

Essential Understandings:

Summative Assessment(s):

Instructional Strategies:

Assignments/Learning Tasks/Formative Assessments:

Planning Questions

1. What new learning will occur in this lesson?

2. How will students use/apply their knowledge in meaningful ways?

3. How will the information in this lesson connect to students' prior knowledge?

4. How will the learning connect with students' lives beyond the classroom?

5. How will student thinking be extended?

6. What resources/materials are needed in order to provide multiple pathways to learning?

7. How will students know the learning outcomes and the assessment criteria?

8. How can students engage in self-assessment and self-adjustment?

Adapted from Kathleen Walts, West Irondequoit Central School District, Rochester, NY

Getting Started with Differentiation

Differentiation of instruction does not mean that you individualize instruction or provide something "different" from the normal lesson for a few struggling or advanced students. It means that you think proactively, from the beginning, and that the "normal" lesson includes more than one avenue for success. It means that you think about the diversity of your learners when you are planning and don't ever again fall into the trap of thinking that "One size fits all."

1. What do you expect your students to know and be able to do when they study _____?

2. What assessment opportunities might you give students to demonstrate what they have learned about the above concept?

3. Given the task analysis, what is the information and the learning processes with which all students should work? List a few instructional strategies and practice and/or processing activities that would promote learning those items.

Getting Started with Differentiation continued...

4. What might you do to extend and expand the thinking of students ready to and/or interested in going beyond what you've planned? Include both inside and outside of class possibilities.

5. What do you know about your struggling learners that you need to address up front? What about your ESL students? Your special education students? List specific examples of instruction strategies, adaptations, and support systems that would be helpful to several of them.

6. What might you do to reteach or help students who are having difficulties in understanding this concept? Include both inside and outside of class possibilities.

Print and
Web Resources

Chapter XIII

Web Sites for New Teachers

Tips for New Teachers

www.hannahmeans.bizland.com - New teacher guide book

www.adprima.com/ideamenu.htm - Ideas for new teachers

www.ed.gov/teachers/become/about/survivalguide/index.html

www.teachersfirst.com/new-tch.shtml - New teacher resources, tips

www.education-world.com/a_admin/admin139.shtml - Links to online mentoring, networking, and professional development

General/Lesson Plans

www.school.discovery.com/schrockguide/edlearn.html - Kathy Schrock's Guide for Teachers (discovery channel)

www.proteacher.com - Teaching practices, child development, etc.

www.austega.com/education/articles/effectivepraise.htm - Effective praise

www.sitesforteachers.com/index.html - Sites for teachers

www.teacherplanet.com/calendar/01-JAN.html - 150 Theme-based resource pages

www.712educators.about.com/cs/activelistening/a/activelistening.htm - Active listening

www.mrsalphabet.com/links.html - Kindergarten alphabet worksheets and games

www.education-world.com/research - On-line reference tools, maps, dictionaries, etc.

www.educationworld.com/a_lesson/lesson131.shtml - First day of school icebreakers 2000 (vol. 4)

www.encarta.msn.com - Lesson plans and information resources

www.coreknowledge.org - Lesson plans

www.logo.com/index.html - Fun and creative educational software

www.microsoft.com/education - Microsoft tutorials, lesson plans, etc. Comprehensive website that uses age, theme, product and learning areas to create tailored lesson plans and ideas

Web Sites for New Teachers

www.teachnet.org - Lesson plans, online discussions, idea exchange, etc.

www.wested.org - Educational texts

www.thegateway.org - Lesson plans

www.theeducatorsnetwork.com/lessons/index.htm - Lesson plans

www.brainpop.com Lessons and quizzes with high visual appeal

www.enchantedlearning.com Elementary teaching tools including dual language picture dictionaries

www.learnnc.org - The North Carolina Teachers' Network - Lesson plans and classroom technology

Science

www.gooseholler.com/main/soft/testpg.html - Science quizzes

www.sierraclub.org/education - Sierra Club educational materials on ecology and conservation

www.2nsta.org/sciencesites/ - National Science Teachers Association's list of recommended science web sites

Language Arts Sites

www.paragraphpunch.com - Guides paragraph writing. Helpful in teaching structure, grammar and proofreading. Interactive and comprehensive.

www.sdcoe.k12.ca.us/score/cyberguide.html - Cyberguides for the study of the most frequently read literature. A comprehensive site containing the California Language Arts standards and supplemental units with complex literary themes.

www.graphic.org/goindex.html - Graphic organizers

www.k-6educators.about.com/es/literaturebooks/idex.htm - Elementary school educator's sample summer reading list

www.expage.com/4writing - Writing skills, "Make Writing Fun"

History/Civics

www.archives.gov/digital_classroom/teaching_with_documents.html- National Archives and Records Administration (NARA) teaching with documents lesson plans

Web Sites for New Teachers

www.besthistorysites.net/USHistory.shtml - A list of the top five U.S. history web sites

www.vcdh.virginia.edu/teaching/vclassroom/vclasscontents.html - 7-12 lesson plans and paper topics of American History

www.kids.gov/k_history.htm - Links to the CIA Homepage for Kids, Library of Congress, government web sites in Spanish, and many more

Math

www.forum.swarthmore.edu/teachers - Math focused lesson plans

www.coolmath4kids.com - Math games including lemonade stand, math jigsaw puzzles, and brain benders.

www.aplusmath.com - Math flash cards, worksheets, and homework helper

www.aaamath.com - Practice sheets for basic math skills K-12

www.cuisenaire.com - Hands-on math and science products, K-12

www.enc.org - Eisenhower National Clearinghouse for math and science, lessons, software, etc.

www.illuminations.nctm.org - Standards-based lesson plans for math K-12

Classroom Management

www.geom.umn.edu/%7edwiggins/plan.htm - High school classroom management plan

www.newideas.net - Helpful hints for teachers with ADD and ADHD kids

www.education-world.com/a_curr/curr261.shtml - Ten teacher-tested tips for classroom management

www.education.indiana.edu/cas/tt/v1i2/what.html - A test to help determine your classroom management profile

www.inspiringteachers.com/tips/management/index.html - Classroom management strategies

Associations, Foundations, etc.

www.nea.org - National Education Association

Web Sites for New Teachers

www.aft.org - American Federation of Teachers

www.ed.gov - US Department of Education

www.ascd.org - The Association for Supervision and Curriculum Development (ASCD)

www.glef.org - The George Lucas Educational Foundation

www.nbpts.org - National Board for Teaching Standards

www.nsdc.org - National Staff Development Council

www.pdkintl.org - Phi Delta Kappa International

www.schoolcounselor.org - American School Counselor Association

www.nctm.org - National Council of Teachers of Mathematics

Miscellaneous

www.freetranslations.com - Free translations. Type in text, select language and translation appears. Translation may not be 100% accurate but it is close.

www.portaportal.com - Bookmarks your selected website for access from multiple computers

Induction and Mentoring Web Sites

Alabama
www.alsde.edu/html/sections/section_detail.asp?section=75&footer=sections

Alaska
www.educ.state.ak.us/Educators.html

Arizona
www.ade.state.az.us/resourcecenter/teacher_resources.asp

Arkansas
www.arkedu.state.ar.us/teachers/#Mentoring

California
www.btsa.ca.gov/

Connecticut
www.state.ct.us/sde/dtl/t-a/best/begininngteachingguide/bt_guide.pdf

Delaware
www.doe.state.de.us/NewTchrMentor/newtchrmentor.htm

Florida
www.teachinflorida.com/logon/logondefault.asp?fromPage=Telementoring

Georgia
www.doe.k12.ga.us/support/recognition/mentor.asp

Idaho
www.sde.state.id.us/Dept/teachers.asp

Illinois
www.isbe.net/recertification/i_inductmentorprg.htm

Iowa
www.state.ia.us/educate/ecese/tqt/tc/resources.html

Kansas
www.ksde.org/cert/Mentoring.htm

Louisiana
www.doe.state.la.us/lde/pd/623.html

Maine
www.maine.gov/education/aarbec/

Massachusetts
www.doe.mass.edu/eq/mentor/r_mentor.html

Michigan
www.michigan.gov/mde/0,1607,7-140-5235_6947-32580--,00.html

Induction and Mentoring Web Sites

Minnesota
www.education.state.mn.us/html/080612.htm

Mississippi
www.mde.k12.ms.us/mtc/

Missouri
www.dese.mo.gov/divteachqual/teachrecruit/TTPMentoring.html

Montana
www.opi.state.mt.us/Supt/NewsStories/0441E7EF1C.nclk

Nebraska
www.nde.state.ne.us/EEC/Mentor%20Teacher/TextHP.html

New Hampshire
www.ed.state.nh.us/TQE/TQE.htm

New Jersey
www.state.nj.us/njded/profdev/mentoring/newsletter/

New Mexico
www.teachnm.org/prof_dev_opportunities/beg_teacher_mentoring.htm

New York
www.highered.nysed.gov/tcert/resteachers/teacherinduction/teacherinduction.htm

North Carolina
www.ncpublicschools.org/mentoring_novice_teachers/mentoren.htm

Ohio
www.ode.state.oh.us/TeachingProfession/Teacher/Professional_Development/

Oregon
www.ous.edu/aca/otrm/mentoring.htm

South Carolina
www.myscschools.com/reports/adept.htm

Texas
www.tea.state.tx.us/awards/toy/network.html

Virginia
www.pen.k12.va.us/VDOE/newvdoe/legislat.PDF

Washington
www.k12.wa.us/profdev/tap/faq.aspx

Wisconsin
www.dpi.state.wi.us/dlsis/tel/pdf/tiehndbk.pdf

Active Learning Strategies from *Why Didn't I Learn This in College?*
If You Want...

Students to work in pairs
Think-Pair-Share - 98
Learning Links - 88
Learning Buddies - 246
Reciprocal Teaching - 133
Discussion Partners - 53

Students to work in small groups
Teammates Consult - 97
Reciprocal Teaching - 133
Graffiti - 79
Numbered Heads Together - 90
Sort Cards - 93-95
Consensus Conclusions - 76

To gather preassessment data
Anticipation Reaction Guide - 68
Signal Cards - 144-145
Sort Cards - 93-95
Frame of Reference - 78
Line-Ups - 89
Think-Pair-Share - 98
Stir the Class - 96
Journals - 81-82
Three Column Charts - 100
Graffiti - 79

Students to access prior knowledge
Anticipation Reaction Guide - 68
Corners - 77
Stir the Class - 96
Frame of Reference - 78
Line-Ups - 89
Think-Pair-Share - 98
Three Column Charts - 100
Journals - 81-82
Word Splash - 123, 125
Graffiti - 79
Learning Links - 88

To surface misconceptions and naive understandings
Anticipation Reaction Guide - 68
Journals - 81-82
Three Column Charts - 100
Frame of Reference - 78
Line-Ups - 89
Think-Pair-Share - 98

Active Learning Strategies from *Why Didn't I Learn This in College?*
If You Want...

Students to set purpose for reading, listening or viewing
Learning Links - 88
Walking Tour - 105
Three Column Charts - 100
Corners - 77
Line-ups - 89
Word Splash - 123, 125

Journals - 81-82
Anticipation Reaction Guide - 68

Students summarize their learning
3-2-1 - 99
Ticket to Leave- 104
Journals - 81-82
Interactive Notebooks - 83
Reciprocal Teaching - 133
ABC to XYZ - 106

Discussions over Time and Place - 101
Biopoems - 71
Learning Links - 88
Scavenger Hunt - 91
Consensus Conclusions - 76
Connection Collections - 72-74

To check for understanding
Signal Cards - 144-145
Ticket to Leave - 104
Journals - 81-82
Sort Cards - 93-95
Scavenger Hunt - 91
Line-Ups - 89

3-2-1 - 99
It's All in The Cards - 85-86
Slates - 146
Numbered Heads Together - 90

To have students "handle" their learning
It's All in the Cards - 85-86
   Tic-Tac-Toe
   Mix and Match
   I Have the Question, Who Has the Answer?
Connection Collections 72-74
Sort Cards - 93-95

Inside-Outside Circles - 87

To build in movement
Scavenger Hunt - 91
Stir the Class - 96
Graffiti - 79
Consensogram - 75
Line-Ups - 89
Simulations - 101

Walking Tour - 105
Learning Buddies - 246
Corners - 77
Inside-Outside Circles - 87

Active Learning Strategies from *Instruction for All Students*
If You Want...

Students to work in pairs
Think-Pair-Share - 104
Learning Buddies - 89-92
Discussion Partners - 59

Students to work in small groups
Graffiti - 82
Numbered Heads Together - 95
Sort Cards - 84 & 110
Collaborative Controversy - 68
Literature Circles - 67
Walking Tour 106-107

Five-Card Draw - 87
Jigsaw - 240-241

To gather preassessment data
Anticipation Reaction Guide - 102
Signal Cards - 109
Sort Cards - 84 & 110
Frame of Reference - 81
Line-Ups - 93-94
Think-Pair-Share - 104

Exclusion Brainstorming - 100
Three-Column Charts - 105
Graffiti - 82
Stir the Class - 98
All Hands on Deck - 86

Students to access prior knowledge
Anticipation Reaction Guide - 102
Corners - 80
Stir the Class - 98
Frame of Reference - 81
Line-Ups - 93-94
Think-Pair-Share - 104

Graffiti - 82
Personal Opinion Guide - 103
Exclusion Brainstorming - 100
Three-Column Charts - 105

To surface misconceptions and naive understandings
Anticipation Reaction Guide - 102
Personal Opinion Guides - 103
Three-Column Charts - 105
Frame of Reference - 81
Line-Ups - 93-94
Think-Pair-Share - 104

Facts and Folklore -101

Active Learning Strategies from *Instruction for All Students*
If You Want...

Students to set purpose for reading, listening or viewing
Walking Tour - 106-107
Three-Column Charts - 105
Corners - 80
Line-ups - 93-94
Personal Opinion Guide - 103
Anticipation Reaction Guide - 102

Students to summarize their learning
3-2-1
Interactive Notebooks - 227
Three-Column charts - 105
Scavenger Hunt - 96 - 97
Most Important Idea I Heard Today...

To check for understanding
Signal Cards - 109   I Have the Question...? - 85
Line-Ups - 93-94   Numbered Heads Together - 95
Slates - 111
Sort Cards - 84 & 110
Scavenger Hunt - 96-97

To have students "handle" their learning
Inside-Outside Circles - 83
Tic Tac Toe - 88
MI Kinesthetic Strategies - 120 & 123
Sort Cards - 84 & 110
Five-Card Draw - 87
All Hands on Deck - 86

To build in movement
Scavenger Hunt - 96-97   Walking Tour - 106-107
Stir the Class - 98   Learning Buddies - 89-92
Graffiti - 82   Corners - 80
Inside-Outside Circles - 83
Line-Ups - 93-94
Simulations - 56

Resources and References

Aubizarreta, John. "Teaching Portfolios and The Beginning Teacher." **Phi Delta Kappan**. December 1994, pp. 323-326.

Beginning Teacher Assistance Program. Richmond, VA: Virginia Department of Education, 1986.

Blanchard, Ken and Paul Hersey. Management of Organizational Behavior. Englewood Cliffs, NJ: Prentice Hall, 1996 (first edition, 1969.)

Blase, Jo and Joseph Blase. **Handbook of Instructional Leadership: How Really Good Principals Promote Teaching and Learning**. Thousand Oaks, CA: Corwin Press, 1998.

Bolton, Robert. **People Skills**. New York, NY: Simon and Schuster, 1979.

Boyer, Lynn and Phoebe Gillespie. "Keeping the Committed: The Importance of Induction and Support Programs for New Special Educators." **Teaching Exceptional Children.** The Council for Exceptional Children. Sept/Oct 2000, pp. 10-14.

Brennan, Sharon, William Thames, and Richard Roberts. "In Kentucky: Mentoring with a Mission." **Educational Leadership**, May 1999, pp. 49-52.

Buckner, Kermit. "No Teacher is An Island." **Journal of Staff Development**, Winter 2001, pp. 63-67.

Burke, Kay. **What to Do with The Kid Who...** Arlington Heights, IL: Skylight Professional Development, 2000.

Calkins, Lucy McCormick. **The Art of Teaching Reading**. New York, NY: Longman, 2001.

Camp, William and Heath-Camp Betty. **Induction Detractors of Beginning Vocational Teachers With and Without Teacher Education**. Paper presented at the annual meeting of the American Vocational Education Research Association, Orlando, FL, 1989.

Cook, Walter, Carroll Leeds, and Robert Callis. **Minnesota Teacher Attitude Inventory.** New York: The Psychological Corporation, 1951.

Costa, Arthur and Robert Garmston. **Cognitive Coaching: A Foundation for Renaissance Schools.** Norwood, MA: Christopher Gordon, 1994.

Creating a Teacher Mentoring Program. Washington, DC. The NEA Foundation for the Improvement of Education, 1999.

Resources and References

Curwin, Richard and Mendler Allen. **Discipline with Dignity.** Alexandria, VA: ASCD, 1998.

Daniels, Harvey. **Literature Circles: Voice and Choice in the Student-Centered Classroom**. York, Maine: Stenhouse Publishers, 2002.

DePaul, Amy. **Survival Guide for New Teachers.** U. S. Department of Education. Available at: www.edgov/teachers/become/about/survivalguide/pdf

Dodd, Anne. "Engaging Students: What I Learned Along the Way." **Educational Leadership**, September 1995, pp. 656-67.

DuFour, Rick and Richard Eaker. **Professional Learning Communities at Work.** Bloomington, IN: National Education Service, 1998.

Educators in Connecticut's Pomeraug Regional School District 15. **Performance-Based Learning and Assessment**. Alexandria, VA: ASCD, 1996.

Feiman-Nemser, Sharon. "What New Teachers Need to Learn." **Educational Leadership**, May 2003, pp. 25-29.

Glasser, William. **Control Theory in the Classroom**. New York, NY: Harper & Row, 1986.

Gless, Janet and Ellen Moir. "When Veteran Meets Novice." **Journal of Staff Development**, Winter 2001, pp. 61-65.

Glickman, Carl, Stephen Gordon, and Jovita Ross-Gordon. **Supervision and Instructional Leadership: A Developmental Approach**. Boston, MA: Allen and Bacon, 2004

Gordon, Stephen and Susan Maxey. **How to Help Beginning Teachers Succeed**. Alexandria, VA: ASCD, 2000.

Gordon, Thomas. **T.E.T. Teacher Effectiveness Training**. New York, NY: David McKay Company, Inc, 1974.

Guide to The BEST Program for Beginning Teachers 2004-2005. Connecticut State Department of Education Bureau of Educator Preparation, Certification, Support and Assessment.

Haack, Paul and Michael Smith. "Mentoring New Music Teachers." **Music Educators Journal**, November 2000, pp. 23-27.

Resources and References

Handbook for New Teachers 2004-2005. St. Vrain Valley School District Re-1J, Longmont, CO.

Harvey, Stephanie and Anne Goudvis. **Strategies That Work**. Portland, ME: Stenhouse Publishers, 2000.

Heller, Daniel. **Teachers Wanted: Attracting and Retaining Good Teachers**. Alexandria, VA: ASCD. 2004.

Howe, Neil And William Strauss. **Millennials Rising: The Next Generation**. New York, NY: Vintage, 2000.

Hunter, Madeline. "Six Types of Supervisory Conferences." **Educational Leadership**. 37(5), 1980, pp. 408-412.

Hurst, Beth and Ginny Reding. **Teachers Mentoring Teachers**. Bloomington, IN: Phi Delta Kappa, 2002.

Ingersoll, Richard. **Teacher Turnover, Teacher Shortages, and the Organization of Schools**. Center for the Study of Teaching and Policy: University of Washington. January 2001. Available at depts.washington.edu/ctpmail/study15.html

Joerger, Richard and Christine Bremer. **Teaching Induction Programs: A Strategy for Improving the Professional Experiences of Beginning Career and Technical Educators**. Columbus, OH: National Dissemination Center for Career and Technical Education, 2001. Available at: www.nccte.org/publications/secure/index.asp

Johnson, Susan Moore, Sara Birkeland, Susan Kardos, David Kauffman, Edward Liu, and Heather Peske. "Retaining the Next Generation of Teachers: The Importance of School-Based Support." **Harvard Education Letter Research Online**. July August 2001, pp. 1-4. Available at www.edletter.org

Joyce, Bruce and Beverly Showers. "The Coaching of Teaching." **Educational Leadership**, October 1982, pp. 4-9.

Joyce, Bruce and Marsha Weil. **Models of Teaching**. Boston MA: Allyn and Bacon, 1996.

Kagan, Spencer. **Cooperative Learning**. San Clemente, CA: Kagan Cooperative Learning, 1994.

Resources and References

Keene, Ellin Oliver and Susan Zimmermann. **Mosaic of Thought**. Portsmouth, NH: Heinemann, 1997.

Kohn, Alfie. **Beyond Discipline: From Compliance to Community**. Alexandria, VA: ASCD, 1996.

Kardos, Susan. **New Teachers' Experiences of Mentoring, Classroom Observations, and Teacher Meetings: Toward an Understanding of Professional Culture**. Paper presented at American Educational Research Association, 2002.

Lancaster, Lynne and David Stillman. **When Generations Collide**. New York, NY: HarperBusiness, 2002.

Lifelong Learning: Beginning Teachers Grow Together through a Colleague Teacher Program. Unpublished document from the Office of Staff Development and Training, Fairfax County Public Schools, VA, 1988.

Lipton, Laura and Bruce Wellman. **Mentoring Matters: A Practical Guide to Learning-Focused Relationships**. Sherman, CT: MiraVia, 2001.

Marzano, Robert J., Deborah Pickering, and Jane Pollack. **Classroom Instruction That Works: Research-based Strategies for Increasing Student Achievement**. Alexandria, VA: ASCD, 2001.

Moir, Ellen. "Phases of First Year Teaching - Attitudes Toward Teaching." Santa Cruz, CA: New Teacher Center: University of California, 1992. Available at www.newteachercenter.org/article2.php

Moran, Sheila. "Schools and the Beginning Teacher." **Phi Delta Kappan**, November 1990, pp. 210-213.

No Dream Denied: A Pledge to America's Children. Washington, DC: National Commission on Teaching and America's Future, 2003.

Retention of Special Education Professionals: A Practical Guide of Strategies and Activities for Educators and Administrators. The National Clearinghouse for Professions in Special Education, The Council for Exceptional Children. 1998. Available at www.specialedcareers.org

Rowley, James. "The Good Mentor." **Educational Leadership**, May 1999, pp. 20-22.

Resources and References

Rutherford, Paula and Ann Michnowicz. "BTAP: Beginning Teacher Assistance Program." **The Red Apple**. Fairfax County Public Schools, October 1988. pp. 17-19.

Rutherford, Paula, **Why Didn't I Learn This in College?** Alexandria, VA: Just ASK Publications, 2002.

_____ **Instruction for All Students**. Alexandria, VA: Just ASK Publications, 2002.

_____ **Leading the Learning**. Alexandria, VA: Just ASK Publications, 2003.

Ryan, Kevin. **The Induction of New Teachers**. Bloomington, IN: Phi Delta Kappa, 1986.

Saphier, Jon and Mary Ann Haley. **Activators**. Carlisle, MA: Research for Better Teaching, 1993.

_____ **Summarizers**. Carlisle, MA: Research for Better Teaching, 1993.

Saphier, Jon and Robert Gower. **The Skillful Teacher**. Carlisle, MA: Research for Better Teaching, 1997.

Stansbury, Kendyll and Joy Zimmerman. **Lifelines to the Classroom: Designing Support for Beginning Teachers**. San Francisco, CA: West Ed, 2000.

Tapping the Potential: Retaining and Developing High-Quality New Teachers Alliance for Excellent Education. Available at: www.all4ed.org

Teague, Tori, Editor. **Standards-Based Classroom Operator's Manual**, 3rd Edition. Longmont, CO: Centennial BOCES, 2002.

The Mentor's Attache. St. Vrain Valley School district Re-1J, Longmont, CO: multiple issues. 1999-2004.

Tomlinson, Carol Ann. **The Differentiated Classroom: Responding to the Needs of All Learners**. Alexandria, VA: ASCD, 1999.

Torres-Guzman, Maria. Mentoring the Bilingual Teacher. **National Clearinghouse for Bilingual Education** (NCBE) Resource Collection Series, No. 7, November 1996.

Villani, Susan. **Mentoring Programs for New Teachers.** Thousand Oaks, CA: Corwin Press, Inc. 2002.

Resources and References

"Wanted Teachers." NAESP Communicator. October 2001.

Wiggins, Grant and Jay McTighe. **Understanding by Design**. Alexandria, VA: ASCD, 1998.

Wiggins, Grant. **"Feedback - How Learning Occurs."** A Presentation at the 1997 AAHE Conference on Assessment and Quality, Pennington, NJ, 1997.

Wildman, Terry, Jerome Niles, Susan Magliaro, and Ruth Anne McLaughlin. "Teaching and Learning to Teach; The Two Roles of Beginning Teachers." **The Elementary School Journal**. March 4, 1989, pp. 471-493.

Wildman, Terry. **Supplement to the Beginning Teacher's Handbook**. Blacksburg, VA: Virginia Polytechnic Institute and State University, 1986.

Wong, Leonard. **Generations Apart: Xers and Boomers in the Officers Corps**. Strategic Studies Institute, U. S. Army War College, 2000.

Zemke, Rom, Claire Raines, and Bob, Flipczak. **Generations at Work: Managing the Clash of Veterans, Boomers, Xers, and Nexters in Your Workplace**. New York, NY: American Management Association, 1999.

Index

D

H

I

M

©Just ASK Publications, ASK Inc.